INSIDE

THE VATICAN

INSIDE

THE VATICAN

Pope John XXIII on the papal throne wearing the triple tiara—
Attualità Giordani, Rome

INSIDE
THE VATICAN

By
Corrado Pallenberg

HAWTHORN BOOKS Inc.
NEW YORK

FIRST EDITION   *May, 1960*

To my wife Peggy

Foreword

EVEN IF ONE is not a Catholic one cannot but admit that the Church of Rome is a great fact, one of the greatest which humanity has known since the beginning of history.

First of all, Catholicism is the religion which groups together more of the faithful than any other denomination, that is, nearly half-a-billion people.[1] The three great religions of the East—Hinduism, Confucianism and Buddhism—have about 750,000,000 believers combined, while the Moslems number 320,000,000. Furthermore, one should remember that Catholics constitute the backbone of the great Christian family to which

---

[1] The reader will hardly fail to notice, as he peruses this book, a certain reluctance on my part to give an exact figure concerning the number of Catholics existing in the world, and a constant tendency to keep rather vague in this connection by resorting to such expressions as "over 400,000,000," "nearly half-a-billion" and so on. A truly exact figure of the number of faithful who follow the dictates of the Church of Rome is absolutely impossible. First of all, the basis on which estimates are formed vary from country to country. While, for example, in the United States or in England the census of the faithful is carried out by the local clergy with the greatest care, in the countries where the vast majority of the population are Catholics, as in Italy, France and Spain, all the inhabitants are reckoned en bloc as belonging to the Church. If this is pretty near the truth in the case of Spain, it certainly cannot apply to France, nor to Italy, where a third of the electorate votes for parties of materialistic inspiration. In South America the situation is still more confused. Another point is that one must note whether among the Catholics all those baptized must be counted or, rather, all those who have taken their first Communion and who continue to practice the faith. The tendency of the Catholic Church is to consider as Catholics active within the Church, all who have been baptized, hence her figures (one often hears talk in the Vatican of 480,000,000) err on the side of optimism, while, naturally, those from Protestant sources often reduce the total, in view of the tendency which exists to diminish the importance of the Roman Church. Among all the statistics and estimates that have come to my notice I consider the report prepared by the American Institute of Management one of the most reliable. This is both for the care with which the investigation was conducted (it lasted from 1948 to 1955 and documents and reports in thirty different languages were consulted) and for the impartiality of the research team, who did not set out upon their task with any object of religious controversy or proselytizing. I therefore believe I am offering the reader something useful and interesting by giving the following table (which refers to the year 1955) published by the Institute.

9

also belong over 200,000,000 Protestants and nearly 200,000,000 Eastern Orthodox, mostly living behind the Iron Curtain.

The Roman Catholic Church possesses other characteristics which distinguish her from other religions and place her in a unique position. Let me outline them briefly. United, disciplined and organized, the Catholic Church is the richest and the most aggressive church—from the point of view of proselytizing and for nourishing the deep-rooted belief of being the only true Church, which compels her to combat all other religions. Unlike any other religion, for many centuries she exercised—and still does today on a minute scale—temporal power. She also has an extraordinary unity and continuity of command, which no other dynasty in the world can boast. From Peter, the Prince of the Apostles, to Angelo Giuseppe Roncalli, the present Pope, 263 pontiffs (not counting the antipopes) have succeeded each other on the throne of Peter in an uninterrupted line for nineteen centuries.

One can therefore confidently state that no other religion has influenced so deeply and for so long the way of living, of behaving and of thinking of so great a part of humanity. Today 5,000,000 persons work, in one capacity or another, for the Catholic Church, 20,000,000 boys and girls are being educated in Catholic schools and 13,000,000 adults and children receive assistance from Catholic charitable organizations.

At present the Church of Rome is still playing a leading role on the international scene, having inserted herself in dramatic fashion into the vast struggle between West and East, between democracy and communism, between freedom and dictatorship, into that struggle which will perhaps decide the personal destiny of all alive today and almost certainly that of our children. Atheistic and materialistic communism is by its very nature

Catholic churches	416,466
Parishes	177,027
Priests of the dioceses	257,763
Seminarists	65,328
Regular priests	119,445
Priests ordained only recently	8,011
Male religious	210,248
Nuns	950,865
Male Catholic schools	85,296
Pupils of these schools	10,317,797
Female Catholic schools	75,275
Pupils of these schools	9,511,317
Charitable organizations	31,110
Persons assisted	13,854,533
Total number of Catholics	451,593,832
Total world population	2,170,442,562

While on this subject let me recall that the *Encyclopaedia Britannica* estimated the number of Catholics in 1954 as 469,630,000. This is a figure that comes pretty close to the 480,000,000 mentioned in the Vatican (the difference could easily be explained by the increase of population between 1954 and 1958); I do not know however on what the *Encyclopaedia Britannica* based its estimate. To complete the picture, let me add the figures of the same encyclopaedia for the other religions of the world.

Eastern Orthodox	128,520,000
Protestants	201,756,066
Mohammedans	321,931,336
Jews	11,627,450
Shintoists	30,000,000
Taoists	50,053,000
Confucians	300,290,500
Hindus	309,949,000
Buddhists	150,310,000
Primitive religions	121,150,000
Other religions	348,336,448

the enemy of supernatural beliefs; having found in the Catholic Church an exceptionally tough and determined adversary, the Kremlin has submitted her to particularly violent and cruel persecutions. On the other hand, the Holy See has become the standard-bearer and the champion of faith in general, a beacon, a resistance center to which millions of men of other religions and many lay forces that are opposed to communism turn with sympathy and respect. This leadership of the Catholic Church has asserted itself to such a degree that several Moslem countries have established diplomatic relations with the Holy See, while at one time even the formation of an alliance between Moslems and Catholics to present a united front against communist atheism was contemplated. After the Suez crisis the plan was put into cold storage, but it cannot be ruled out that one day the Arab countries, when their acute nationalism has subsided or has been satisfied, will realize that communism constitutes a danger for them too and will again seek the support and solidarity of the believers in Christ.

The Catholic Church is a subject so vast, so complex and so important, that to handle it well and exhaustively one should possess the learning of a Gregorovius or a Mommsen, the synthesis capacity of a Gibbon, the poetic drive of a Kipling, the polemical ardor of a Mauriac, plus a deep theological, philosophical, historical and political grounding. I have therefore set myself a much more limited, modest and attainable task: I propose to relate in a simple way, as in a chat among friends, some of the things I have come to learn about the Vatican and about the men who in recent years have been running it; what was the importance and significance of Pacelli's pontificate, what the present Pope, John XXIII, has already done and what he is likely to do; how the ancient and venerable organization is working; and what the main problems are which the Church of Rome is facing. This book is the result of twelve years of journalistic work carried on in Rome for American, Italian and English newspapers and magazines, during which time the Vatican represented the main object of my interests.

I shall not attempt to write history nor shall I allow myself to be dragged into controversy or discussions of a theological or political nature. I shall not try to reach conclusions. I shall merely record facts, data, curious episodes, things that are not too well known, and small secrets that I hope will interest you. In view of these self-set limits I have confined myself to the period from Pius XII to John XXIII.

At the outset, the reader-author relationship should be made quite clear. I am not a Catholic. I was baptized forty-seven years ago in a Lutheran church in Rome. I have, however, never been a practicing member of this Church and cannot therefore describe myself as a real Protestant, or, to be absolutely honest, as a true believer. However, I don't have toward the

Catholic Church any of the prejudices and animosities which have inspired the pens of a Peyrefitte or a Blanshard, nor have I the enthusiasm, the tendency to approve of everything without question, the apologetic tone, which inspire most Catholic writers. I hope I have succeeded in placing myself in a position of relative impartiality toward the Vatican—absolute impartiality does not and cannot exist—and I also hope that the reader will show indulgence toward this attempt to probe into the complex and mysterious world that lies behind the heavy Bronze Door.

—CORRADO PALLENBERG

Contents

Contents

Illustrations

15

Cardinal Tardini, Vatican Secretary of State, greeting Japanese Prime Minister Kishi

Pope John XXIII talking to Francis Cardinal Spellman of New York

The makeup row in the linotype room of *L'Osservatore Romano*

Prince Rainier and Princess Grace of Monaco in a private audience

The meeting of President Eisenhower and Pope John XXIII

The Bernini columns and canopy over the papal altar

Ground levels under St. Peter's

The late Monsignor Ludwig Kaas who helped uncover the tomb of St. Peter

Artist's reconstruction of the shrine over St. Peter's tomb

Remains of human bones found near St. Peter's tomb

This second group of illustrations appears between pages 202 and 211.

INSIDE

THE VATICAN

1

Pope Pius XII

OF PIUS XII it could be said that he was three times Roman: he
was the Pope, he was born in Rome and he was descended from an
old Vatican family. The Pacellis came from Onano, a village near
Viterbo, and they were already connected with the Church several
centuries before they moved to Rome. Going back into the family
history many of its members are found to have been priests. The
turning point for the Pacelli family fortunes was the year 1819 when
Cardinal Caterini summoned to Rome his young nephew Marcantonio
Pacelli and persuaded him to study Canon Law.

Young Marcantonio did not disappoint the hopes his Cardinal
uncle had placed in him. His studies went well; he made a quick
and brilliant career as a solicitor at the Vatican tribunal, the *Sacra
Rota*. In November 1848 the Roman populace, which, under the influence of liberal ideas, had been showing signs of unrest for some
time, rose and compelled Pius IX (1846-1878) to flee from the
capital. The Pope found refuge inside the sea fortress of Gaeta, half-
way between Rome and Naples, and took with him his solicitor,
Marcantonio Pacelli, as his political adviser. Pius IX came back in
April 1850 under the protection of French bayonets, and Marcantonio
became a member of a censorship committee. One year later he was
appointed Secretary of the Interior or Home Minister for the whole
of the papal dominions. He held this key post until the Piedmontese

troops occupied Rome and put an end to the temporal power of the Church in 1870, a significant date in church history to which repeated references will be made.

The Pope shut himself inside the Vatican as a voluntary prisoner, the "Black" aristocracy (whose titles derived from the Church) kept the front doors of their palaces half-closed in sign of mourning, and the Vatican officials refused to collaborate with the "usurpers." The Italian Government offered Marcantonio Pacelli a job as state councillor, but he disdainfully refused.

In 1861 Marcantonio founded the *Osservatore Romano*, a paper which, for its authority, sedateness, ponderousness and lack of typographical errors has frequently been compared with the London *Times*. In those days there was an official Vatican newspaper called *Il Giornale di Roma*, but Marcantonio thought this was too formal and stuffy and that Catholic readers should have something lighter and more entertaining. If you take a look at the *Osservatore Romano* you can imagine how stodgy the old *Giornale di Roma* must have been. In any case, the *Giornale di Roma* ceased publication shortly afterward and the *Osservatore* became what it still is today—the semiofficial mouthpiece of the Holy See. It was probably also because of this family connection that Eugenio Pacelli, in his day, took a very lively interest in the *Osservatore Romano* and often used to ring up its editor, Count Giuseppe dalla Torre, with advice and criticism.

The Pacellis have always been a long-lived family. Marcantonio reached the age of 102, while his brother Felice lived to be 103; his life thus touched three centuries, for he was born in 1799, went right through the nineteenth century and died in 1902.

Marcantonio had ten children, the second of whom, Filippo, the father of Pius XII, entered what had become the family profession and became a solicitor at the *Sacra Rota*. He had a great interest in politics and twice sat in the Capitol as town councillor. Filippo married Virginia Graziosi, a sweet, pretty girl of the Roman bourgeoisie, who was extremely pious and gave her children a religious education from their earliest years. Filippo and Virginia had four children—Giuseppina, Francesco, Eugenio and Elisabetta.

Giuseppina, of whom the Pope was particularly fond, married Ettore Mengarini, director of the Child Jesus Hospital in Rome. Her health was poor and she was partly paralyzed; she spent many years of her life in a wheel chair. She left her house only to go to the polls and vote and, once a year, on the afternoon of Christmas Day, to pay a visit to her illustrious brother in the Vatican. Although Eugenio and Giuseppina saw each other so rarely, they kept in daily touch by telephone. About 11 o'clock every morning the Pope telephoned to his sister, asked her how she was and listened to any news there was to tell about their numerous relations. Giuseppina's death was a great blow to Pius XII who, after he learned the sad news, passed the whole night praying, in tears.

The other sister, Elisabetta, married Luigi Rossignani, whose brother, Mgr. Pio Rossignani, was for some time secretary to Cardinal Eugenio Pacelli while he was Secretary of State. As soon as he was elected Pope, Pius XII engaged another secretary, probably to avoid any charge of nepotism.

The brother of Pius XII, Francesco, likewise followed the family profession and became dean of the lawyers of the Holy Rota. As personal representative of the Pontiff, he took part, showing great diplomatic ability, in the negotiations for the Concordat between the Vatican and the Italian Government creating the Vatican City State in 1929. In recognition of his labors the Vatican conferred upon him the hereditary title of Marquis, while the Italian Government, on the proposal of Mussolini, made him a prince, also a hereditary title. He died in 1934.

His three sons, Princes Carlo, Marcantonio and Giulio Pacelli, are all solicitors at the Holy Rota. Of the three, Carlo seemed to be the favorite of the late Pope, who often received him in private audience. These three nephews of the late Pope hold a number of posts in the Vatican. Carlo is councilor general of the pontifical commission for the Vatican City State, legal adviser to the Administration of the Holy See Property, advocate of the Sacred Consistory, member of three Vatican permanent commissions, and legal adviser to three Congregations. Giulio is a colonel in the Pope's Noble Guard, works in the legal section of the Congregation for the Propagation of the Faith, and is Costa Rica's diplomatic representative to the Holy See, with the rank of ambassador. Marcantonio, too, is a colonel of the Noble Guard. The three nephews of Pius XII are all extremely wealthy, particularly Carlo, and they appear as presidents, vice-presidents or directors on the boards of a number of banks, insurance, public utility and other industrial and commercial concerns.

Eugenio was born on March 2, 1876 in the Palazzo Pediconi. But don't let the word "palazzo" mislead you. The house in which he was born has nothing of the magnificence associated with famous Roman palaces. It's an unpretentious, old-fashioned, four-story affair tucked away in the short, narrow Via degli Orsini, just across the Tiber as you come from St. Peter's. The Pacellis, who were not as wealthy then as they are now, rented an apartment on the third floor. The district today is no longer fashionable and the Palazzo Pediconi looks a bit dilapidated. Walking through its high front door, and before you reach the sunny courtyard, you can see in the passage a modest, gold-lettered tablet that says: "In this house was born March 2, 1876 Eugenio Pacelli elected Pope Pius XII March 2, 1939."

The baby was baptized by his great-uncle, Don Giuseppe Pacelli, in the nearby tiny church of San Celso e Giuliano and christened Eugenio Maria Giuseppe Giovanni. Later, when the parish of San Celso e Giuliano was suppressed, the baptismal font was removed to the Church of San Pancrazio, run by the Discalced (barefoot) Carmelites. A tablet set up by the Carmelites records that the holy water with which the Pope was baptized was taken from this font.

Already as a little boy Eugenio, who felt very strongly the influence of the family background and particularly of his pious mother, was attracted to religion. To the usual question, "And what are you going to be when you grow up?" Eugenio invariably replied, "A priest."

He liked pretending he was celebrating Mass and he made himself a small altar in his bedroom. To adorn his altar he got his mother to give him candle stumps and some tinfoil. He also found a piece of faded damask which he used as a stole when playing at Mass. As soon as he was able he became an acolyte to a cousin-priest, Don Vincenzo Cirilli. An uncle, probably the one who had baptized him, once told him about the missionaries and how they sometimes died in faraway lands, pierced through by the arrows of the savages or nailed to crosses. Little Eugenio is reported to have said, "I want to become a martyr too . . . but without nails." This episode was told by the Pacelli family to the American journalist, John McKnight, who has written an interesting and well-documented book on the Papacy.[1]

The only person who at first did not encourage this precocious tendency to the vocation was Eugenio's father. Filippo Pacelli was quite determined that this son should embrace the legal profession, and after passing through the preparatory schools the boy was first sent to a State school, the "Ennio Quirino Visconti," where he pursued his secondary studies. But Eugenio was disinclined to become a lawyer and was enrolled at the Faculty of Letters of Rome University. A year later, seeing that the determination of his son to become a priest was unshakable, the father gave way and allowed him to enter the Capranica College, the famous and aristocratic seminary of Rome. After studying theology for five years, Eugenio was ordained a priest on April 2, 1899. A short account of the ceremony appeared in the *Osservatore Romano*, which predicted an "enviable career" for the young priest.

What he wanted to do above all was to devote himself to the saving

[1] John P. McKnight, *The Papacy*, Rinehart, N.Y., 1952.

of souls. But destiny had something different in store for him. For two years only, from 1899 to 1901, was he able to remain in direct touch with the faithful, teaching the Catechism to the children, hearing confessions and preaching occasionally in the Chiesa Nuova, a few steps from his home. Overwork and excessive study (he had begun a course of Canon Law at the St. Appollinare Institute) had exhausted him physically and he was several times compelled to interrupt his apostolate and go away into the country at Onano to recover.

Pacelli's dream to have a parish of his own, even if only a small one in some desolate village high up in the mountains, was shattered once and for all by Cardinal Vincenzo Vannutelli. The Cardinal, who was an old friend of the Pacelli family, had noticed the brilliant qualities of the young priest and had recommended him to the State Secretariat (the Vatican State Department or Foreign Ministry). When he was offered a post in this important Vatican office, Pacelli accepted it, but with considerable regret. Thus, in 1901, he began that diplomatic career which he was to follow up to the day when he was elected Pope.

The State Secretary at the time was Cardinal Mariano Rampolla, whose name became known throughout the world because of the veto exercised against him in the Conclave of 1903 by the Emperor of Austria, Francis Joseph. The Conclave elected the meek and saintly Cardinal Giuseppe Sarto, who took the name of Pius X (1903-1914), and Rampolla was replaced as State Secretary by the clever and scheming Cardinal, Merry del Val, a personality worthy of the best Renaissance tradition. Merry del Val's under-secretary was Mgr. Giacomo della Chiesa, who was to succeed Pius X in 1914 with the name of Benedict XV (1914-1922). The head of the Congregation of Extraordinary Ecclesiastical Affairs, the main section of the State Secretariat, was Mgr. Pietro Gasparri, destined to become Cardinal and to act as State Secretary under two Popes. So it was that from the very beginning young Pacelli found himself in touch with outstanding personalities. He could not have wished for better mentors.

Eugenio Pacelli did not stay long at the bottom of the ladder. After three years he was appointed *minutante*, which meant that he had a certain amount of responsibility preparing the first drafts of official documents. When he was only 29 Pius X made him a Monsignore. In the meantime Gasparri, with the help of Pacelli, had embarked on a monumental task—the codification of Canon Law.

This work entailed collecting and collating all the decrees, bulls, constitutions, edicts, ordinances and regulations issued by Popes, sovereigns and Church councils since the days of the early Christians and condensing the rules they contained into a single code. Five thousand priests all over the world collaborated in this huge task which was carried on for years in secrecy. It was completed in 1914 but not published until 1917. In recognition of his valuable services, Pacelli was, in 1911, first appointed Under-Secretary for Extraordinary Ecclesiastical Affairs and by 1914 he had risen to be Secretary. During this period he was offered the chair of Roman Law at the Catholic University of Washington, D.C., but declined it at the wish of Pius X, who was very keen on seeing the codification work completed.

His diplomatic career brought with it Pacelli's first missions abroad that were to impress so vividly on the future Pope the universal character of the Church. In 1896 he had taken part in an astronomers' congress in Paris as secretary to the Philippine Father, Giuseppe Lais. In 1904 he was once again in Paris, and also made a trip to Belgium. In 1911 he was a member, as a counselor, of the special mission led by Cardinal Pignatelli di Belmonte that was sent by the Holy See to the coronation of George V of England.

It was in 1917 that Pacelli appeared on the international stage in his first important role. After the death of Pius X, his successor, Benedict XV, nominated Gasparri to succeed Merry del Val as State Secretary, and Pacelli was called upon to assist the new Secretary in preparing that plan for "peace without victory" by which the Pontiff attempted to stop the bloodshed of World War I. In May of that year Pacelli was appointed Papal Nuncio to Bavaria. His mission was to try to convince the Kaiser to accept the peace plan. After presenting his credentials to King Ludwig III of Bavaria, Pacelli went to Berlin and had some preliminary talks with the German Chancellor, Theobald von Bethmann-Hollweg. At first, things appeared to be progressing pretty favorably, so that the Kaiser received the Vatican envoy at his general headquarters in Kreuznach. Pacelli handed to Wilhelm II a letter of Benedict XV imploring him to accept the Vatican peace plan. The German Emperor was greatly impressed by the personality of the young nuncio, about whom he made the following entry in his diary: "Pacelli is a likable, distinguished man, of high intelligence and exquisite manners, a typical example of an eminent prelate of the Catholic Church."

Unfortunately the Russian revolution and the breakup of the Czarist army gave the Kaiser renewed hopes that victory was within his reach and the Vatican peace plan was forgotten. After conducting fresh but unavailing negotiations in Berlin with the new Chancellor, Michaelis, Pacelli retired to the Nunciature in Munich to await the end of the war.

In 1918 he fell ill and on the advice of the bishop, Faulhaber, went for a short holiday above Rorschach, in the Swiss mountains, and stayed at the "Stella Maris" Institute of the nuns of Menzingen. It was here that he met the nun, Sister Pasqualina, who was to become so closely associated later with him. The meeting proved to be important, for Sister Pasqualina was soon called to the Munich Nunciature and from that time on remained constantly at Pacelli's side until his death forty years later. An indefatigable and invaluable head of his household, she relieved the Pope of every domestic worry and guided his daily life with the accuracy of a chronometer.

From his Munich post Pacelli watched the defeat of the Central Empires and was nearly struck down by the wave of Social-Communism that swept postwar Germany. In April 1919 an armed gang of Spartacists invaded the Munich Nunciature. Pacelli, wearing his bishop's robes, went to meet the invaders. The Spartacists aimed their rifles at him and for a second the life of the future Pope hung by a thread. Only his great calm and presence of mind saved him. With a quiet smile Pacelli said, "It's never wise to kill a diplomat." The Spartacists looked at each other, lowered their rifles and left without a word, taking with them, however, the Nuncio's car.

In 1920, while still in charge of the Munich Nunciature, Pacelli was appointed Nuncio to Berlin also. He remained in Munich, however, until he had succeeded in concluding a Concordat with Bavaria, which was ratified in 1925. Only then did he move to Berlin, where he had numerous and cordial contacts with Marshal Hindenburg and the statesman Stresemann. There he began negotiations for another Concordat with Prussia, which was ultimately signed in 1929. Thereupon he took a well-deserved holiday at Rorschach where, returning one day from a climb in the mountains, he found a telegram awaiting him from Rome telling him that Achille Ratti, now Pope Pius XI (1922-1939), Benedict's successor, had made him a Cardinal.

When Pacelli returned to Rome to receive the Red Hat, he found his friends in the Vatican elated by the two Concordats that had just been concluded with Prussia and Italy. The first was the work of the new Cardinal Pacelli and the second had been achieved thanks to the skillful mediation of his brother, the Holy Rota solicitor, Francesco Pacelli. Soon afterwards the State Secretary, Gasparri, announced that he would like to retire and Pius XI appointed Pacelli in his place.

The new State Secretary immediately distinguished himself as a faithful and reliable executor of the Pope's orders and gained the full confidence of Pius XI. Unlike so many of his predecessors, he did not attempt to carry out a policy of his own, to become a "grey eminence," pulling strings in the shadow of the throne. Now and then, however, he used his influence to restrain the impulsive and irritable Achille Ratti.

During the ten years that he was State Secretary, Cardinal Pacelli concluded Concordats with Baden, Austria (signed by Dollfuss and Schuschnigg) and the Third Reich. In this period, too, he made many trips abroad. In 1934 he took part as the Pope's legate in the Eucharistic Congress in Buenos Aires and was accorded royal honors by the Argentine President, Augustin Juste. Before returning to Rome he visited Rio de Janeiro and Montevideo. In 1935, still as pontifical legate, he visited the Lourdes sanctuary in France. In 1936 he paid an unofficial visit to the United States in the company of the Vatican architect Enrico Galeazzi, traveling nearly always by plane and stopping in New York, Boston, Philadelphia, Baltimore, Washington, Chicago, San Francisco, Los Angeles, Cincinnati and other cities. The American press nicknamed him "the Flying Cardinal." His friend Francis Spellman, then Auxiliary Bishop of Boston, now Archbishop of New York and a Cardinal (the two had known each other in Rome when they were both working as minor officials in the State Secretariat) took him to see President Franklin D. Roosevelt at Hyde Park. The meeting was long and cordial and it established the basis for a friendship which was to blossom and become fruitful during the Second World War. In 1937 he went to Lisieux to inaugurate the basilica of St. Thérèse and on the way back stopped in Paris to preach in Notre Dame Cathedral. In 1938 he represented the Pope at the Eucharistic Congress in Budapest and was the guest at the royal palace of Admiral Horthy, who in his honor organized a procession of thousands of torch-lit boats floating down the Danube.

While Pacelli was State Secretary relations between the Holy See and the Fascist regime had their ups and downs, but as a whole they remained fairly good. There was a rather serious clash in 1931 when the Fascists launched an attack on Catholic Action and the *Osservatore Romano* was being seized from news dealers and burnt in the streets by the Blackshirts. The Pope reacted violently with the famous encyclical letter *Non Abbiamo Bisogno,* but in the end the Holy See had to give in and the ecclesiastical authorities had to restrict the activities of Catholic Action. There was another critical moment in 1938 when Mussolini, to ape Hitler, started persecuting the Jews. In particular, the prohibition by the Government of mixed marriages between non-Jews and Jews was an infringement of the rights of the Church in the field of marriage as laid down by the Concordat.

On the other hand the Italian Catholic clergy was, on the whole, very pro-Fascist and their support proved very useful to Mussolini.

The Church also backed Mussolini's conquest of Abyssinia and his intervention in the Spanish Civil War. Pius XI himself in one of his speeches had described Mussolini as "the man whom Providence made us meet." Fascist propaganda exploited the phrase labeling Mussolini "the Man of Providence." As has been said, Pacelli, as State Secretary, was a faithful executor of orders, at least outwardly; and it is difficult to judge to what extent it was he who was responsible for the pro-Fascist policy of the Holy See.

When Pius XI died early in 1939, the long flirtation between the Vatican and Fascism was drawing to a close, while relations between the Vatican and Nazi Germany had already reached the stage of open hostility. The war in Spain was dragging to an end and the clouds of a larger conflict were gathering over the world. It was a period of extreme tension, which required a "political" Pope who could also be considered by all countries as neutral. Only an Italian Pope could satisfy this neutrality condition since a long tradition had already accustomed the world to Popes as simultaneously champions of peace and natives of Italy. As for a politically-minded Pope, nobody could satisfy the requirement better than Pacelli. His election was therefore almost certain, and the old Vatican saying that "he who enters the Conclave a Pope, comes out of it a Cardinal," was for once disproved.

Rarely had a Cardinal shown such reluctance to be elected. To anyone who predicted that he would be successful, Pacelli would reply, "Too good of you," and add immediately that no State Secretary had ever been elected Pope. He even got to the point, before entering the Conclave, of having his suitcases packed and reserving railway accommodations for Switzerland, as he intended to take a short holiday at Rorschach after the Conclave.

As a matter of fact, a small group of Italian Cardinals, who would have preferred not to have a "political" Pope but one with greater experience in episcopal work (Pius XI had been a scholar and a diplomat just like Pacelli) were backing Cardinal Elia della Costa, Archbishop of Florence. The Fascists in their hearts were for Cardinal Schuster, Archbishop of Milan; but the Fascist press, knowing that he was too compromised with the Fascist regime, preferred to support the candidature of Della Costa. The press hoped that the saintly Archbishop of Florence would keep aloof from politics and be less difficult to influence than the experienced and determined Pacelli. The praise of the Fascist press probably did Della Costa more harm than good; Pacelli was left with no serious opponents.

The Conclave in which Pacelli was elected Pope was one about which the utmost secrecy was preserved. All Conclaves are secret, at least in theory, but in the past the pledge of secrecy has not been taken too seriously and it has usually been possible to reconstruct exactly what had happened. In this case very little has ever leaked out. However, it appears that from the very beginning Pacelli had on his side all the non-Italian Cardinals and at least ten of the Italians. The voting, according to one account, went as follows: thirty-five voted for Pacelli on the first ballot and forty on the second, out of a total of sixty-one Cardinals. Although already elected, it is said that he asked for a third ballot and received the whole of the votes cast, minus his own. However this may be, beside being one of the most secret, it was also one of the shortest Conclaves in the history of the Church, lasting barely twenty-four hours. While the Cardinals knelt to kiss his hand and foot, Eugenio Pacelli was heard to murmur several times, *Miserere mei, Deus* (Have mercy upon me, O God).

Soon after Pius XII had ascended Peter's throne, world affairs started going from bad to worse. Italy occupied Albania, and the Pope, although rejecting a British request for an open condemnation, in his Easter homily, deplored the violation of solemn treaties and the fact that the attack had been launched on Good Friday.

In March 1939 the Pope received a visit from the German Foreign Minister, von Ribbentrop. The former champagne salesman erroneously thought he could succeed in inducing him to side with Germany. It may never be known just what exactly was said between the two, but the fact is von Ribbentrop came away from the conversation very upset and pale with anger.

In August of the same year the new Pope started a peace campaign with a dramatic radio broadcast in which he said, "With peace, nothing is lost. With war, everything can be lost." Only a month later Hitler, who was to find out in time how true the papal warning was, attacked Poland. Once the war had begun, Pius XII did everything he could to keep it circumscribed. He started to assist prisoners, refugees and victims of political and racial persecutions. As the conflict spread, the relief work of the Vatican grew to an impressive extent. Intervention in favor of the Jews was especially powerful. At his death numerous Jewish communities renewed their expressions of gratitude to Eugenio Pacelli.

Italy had declared her "non-belligerency," which meant that, at least for the time being, she was sitting on the fence and not marching with her Nazi ally. Pius XII tried very hard to keep Italy out of the war. He had had enough of both Nazis and Fascists and of their deification of the State. In his heart he had sided with the Western democracies, but, hoping to be able to keep Italy out and one day to act as mediator (an attempt in which he had earlier failed in the First World War), he kept up the appearance of impartial neutrality.

In December 1939 he received King Victor Emmanuel III and a few days later reciprocated the State visit, driving from the Vatican to the Quirinal in an impressive procession.

In February 1940 Roosevelt sent Myron Taylor to Rome as his personal representative to the Pope. Officially the Holy See and the United States had no diplomatic relations but, practically speaking, the collaboration thus established and continued throughout the war, was firmer than if they had had any. In April of the same year Pacelli wrote a letter to Mussolini imploring him to remain neutral. Probably by arrangement with Myron Taylor the letter was timed to reach the Duce on the same day as a similar one by President Roosevelt. The Pope also kept in close touch with Count Galeazzo Ciano, Mussolini's son-in-law, who then led the neutralist wing of the Fascist Party. Because of his attitude Ciano had been removed from the Foreign Ministry and, at his own request, had been appointed Ambassador to the Holy See. But all attempts were in vain. On June 10, 1940 Italy entered the war and the diplomats of the Allied powers accredited to the Holy See took refuge inside the walls of the already overpopulated Vatican City.

For more than two years the roar of the guns silenced the voice of diplomacy. As the war spread to the rest of the world, there was nothing left for the Pope to do but to renew his desperate appeals for the carnage to stop. Again and again he pleaded for "peace with justice" and became more and more outspoken in condemning the racial myth and brutal aggressions, and increasingly eloquent in defense of the freedom of the individual and of the small nations. During this period the Holy See entered into its first diplomatic relations with Japan, Chiang Kai-shek's China and Finland.

In July 1943 about one hundred American bombers attacked the Rome marshaling yards, almost destroying the ancient basilica of San Lorenzo and killing many civilians. Pius XII, who was also the Bishop of Rome, left the Vatican and went to comfort his stricken flock among the still-smoking ruins. Back in his study he wrote a strong letter of protest to President Roosevelt, vividly describing the terrible scenes he had just witnessed.

The bombing of San Lorenzo precipitated the internal crisis which was already brewing in Italy. On July 25, 1943 King Victor Emmanuel summoned Mussolini to his summer residence and after a dramatic talk had him placed under arrest. Marshal Badoglio was placed at the head of a caretaker government. On August 13 another wave of Allied bombers again hit Rome. Again Pius hurried to the bombed quarter and this time the blood of one of the injured soiled his white soutane. The next day, as a result of negotiations between the Vatican and Marshal Badoglio, Rome was declared an open city. An enormous cheering crowd invaded St. Peter's Square to express their gratitude to Pius XII, jocularly described by the caustic Romans as "our only and best Ack-Ack."

Then came the Armistice, the German occupation, and the civil war. The Vatican and other Holy See buildings protected by extra-territorial rights opened their doors to give sanctuary to Jews, anti-Fascists and escaped Allied war prisoners, while the Pontifical Relief Committee multiplied its efforts to save the Romans from starvation. After nine tough months, punctuated by scares, sharp conflicts with the German High Command, apocalyptic threats by Hitler to invade the Vatican and remove the Pope to Germany, Rome was at last liberated. Again the populace hastened to St. Peter's Square to thank the Pontiff who had done so much for the safety of the city.

Pius XII sighed with relief. To Major General E. N. Harmon who had apologized for the clatter American tanks made in passing near the Vatican, Pacelli replied, "Any time you liberate Rome, you can make all the noise you want," which is one of the very few witty remarks attributed to Pius XII. Officially, however, the Vatican maintained an attitude of rigid neutrality. The day after the Allied troops entered Rome the *Osservatore Romano* did come out with an eight-column headline spread all over the front page but . . . it was all about a religious ceremony. The news of the liberation of Rome was tucked away on the last page, condensed into a few lines. I shall never forget the face of an American Catholic G.I. who had bought the *Osservatore* because he wanted to send it home as a souvenir. But I don't think that the editor of the Vatican paper, Count dalla Torre, intended to snub the conquerors of Rome. It was just his tactful way of reminding his readers that wars are won or lost, empires crumble, regimes rise and fall, but the Church goes on forever because her power is spiritual and not material. And while Allied war prisoners and Jews left the Vatican by one door, stray German soldiers entered it by another to avoid being captured.

In August 1944 the Secretary of State, Cardinal Luigi Maglione, died and the Pope himself took over his duties, with the valuable collaboration of the two deputies, Mgr. Giovan Battista Montini and Mgr. Domenico Tardini. Henceforth until his death Pius XII acted as his own Secretary of State and found this system so satisfactory that he never chose an official for that post.

It was only after the war ended and Hitler and Mussolini had both disappeared from the scene that the Pope delivered, in his allocution of Christmas Eve, 1945, a clear and sharp condemnation of totalitarianism. And this brings up a question that has been much debated, especially in the Anglo-Saxon countries: Was Pacelli a Fascist or a democrat? Put in these terms, the question makes little sense. The yardstick with which for two thousand years the Church has measured the vicissitudes of history is not the same as that used by politicians, just as the aims it has pursued are different from theirs. The supreme object of the Church is the salvation of as many souls as possible for a life beyond this earth. A dictator who sets up a police regime (yesterday Mussolini, today Franco and Salazar) but who at the same time protects the clergy, introduces obligatory religious teaching in the schools, safeguards the sanctity of matrimony and combats Malthusianism, is far more useful to this end than the mildest, most honest and most admirable democratic prime minister who allows the people freedom to divorce, to give their children whatever education they prefer and to resort to birth control.

In any case, both during and after the war, Pacelli was far closer, both ideologically and from the point of view of his personal sympathies, to the Western democracies than all the preceding Popes had been. The deadly danger of communism acted as a bond and produced the paradoxical phenomenon whereby the most effective allies of the Vatican must today be sought among the fundamentally Protestant countries. The Communist menace has also led to a rapprochement between the Church and the Islamic world. Pacelli was the first Pontiff to receive the credentials of an ambassador representing an Islamic state, namely Egypt. The developments and consequences of such an establishment of cordial relations cannot yet be evaluated.

As regards the international policy of the Holy See, for the entire postwar period of the reign of Pius XII this has turned on a tenacious struggle between the Vatican and the Kremlin, between the smallest and the largest State in the world, between a power that bases everything on the spirit and another power that bases everything on materialism. During this struggle Pacelli on six occasions used the weapon, once so terrible—but today somewhat blunted, of excommunication. Among those excommunicated were all those responsible for the trials of Cardinals Stepinac and Mindszenty, the persecutors of the Archbishop of Beran, the organizers of a schismatic "Catholic Action" in Czechoslovakia, and those who took part in the pro-Communist movements of the clergy in Poland, Hungary and the China of Mao Tse-tung. Finally, by a radical decision all those who voluntarily became members of the Communist party have been excommunicated.

In the more strictly religious sphere the name of Pacelli will remain linked with various important events and initiatives, taking place after the war: the Holy Year, the Marian Year, the proclamation of the dogma of the bodily Assumption of Mary into Heaven, important liturgical reforms, among them afternoon and evening Masses, a return to ancient customs in the Easter ceremonies and the official announcement of the discovery of the tomb of St. Peter below the altar of the Confession in St. Peter's basilica. His fundamental reforms in various spheres—ecclesiastical studies, the training of priests and the organization of the religious and lay orders—will be dealt with in a separate chapter in which I shall also attempt to appraise his long and laborious pontificate.

After a lifetime spent in the service of the Church, during which, up to the very last, he never spared himself, Eugenio Pacelli died at Castel Gandolfo from a stroke and lung complications on October 9, 1958 at 3:52 A.M., according to the official announcement, and at 3:57 A.M., according to the watch of the Pontiff's own physician, Riccardo Galeazzi Lisi.

2

Pacelli the Man

LATER I shall try to show what the role of Pius XII was on the international scene, and also to appraise the impact he had on the Catholic Church. But before that let me give you an idea of the kind of man Pacelli was.

Physically he looked the part perfectly. He was tall, thin, erect, had long, incredibly beautiful hands, bright, almost feverish eyes, a strong, aquiline nose and thin lips. One look at him told you that in this human being it was definitely the spirit that dominated the flesh. But what struck you most about the Pope, if you had the chance of watching him at close quarters, was his complexion. The skin, tightly drawn over strong features, almost ash-gray, resembled old parchment, yet at the same time it had a surprisingly transparent effect, as if reflecting from the inside a cold, white flame.

During religious functions he looked impassive, almost expressionless and his movements were slow, beautifully rehearsed, hieratic. When he mixed with the common people during general audiences his attitude was fatherly and benign, and particularly kindly toward children. During private audiences he had a knack of putting people at their ease and making them talk. At the end of the conversation, however, the visitor realized that it was he who had done all the talking, something which, especially in the case of journalists, was not too good. With his collaborators, on the other hand, from the

33

Cardinals to the humblest secretary, he always went straight to the point. His manner was brusque, and very often impatient and authoritarian.

His voice was clear, strong, somewhat high-pitched and nasal, its tone sonorous and emphatic, but it lacked warmth and very often when he meant to be moving he succeeded only in sounding offended and querulous.

Pope Pius XII had a fantastic memory, an incredible capacity for absorbing and retaining facts, data and figures, for remembering circumstances and faces. Here is a first-hand example: When my son was seven years old he went with the Anglo-American school of Rome to a papal audience. Pius XII picked him out for a little chat and asked him where he came from. "England," replied my son, who was born in London and had just been spending a holiday with his English grandparents. "And what part of England?" inquired the Pope. "Kent," replied my son. Three years later the boy went with another class from a different school, this time Italian, to another papal audience. Pius XII recognized him immediately and told him in English, "I know you. You are the boy from Kent." Things like this happened all the time and must be considered truly amazing when you consider that he received hundreds, sometimes thousands every day.

The Pope's memory was mainly visual. When he learned a speech by heart (he did not like to read his speeches) he would look at the typewritten page several times and the text remained, as it were, photographed on his brain. Thus, when he was delivering his addresses and looked as if he were improvising, actually he was "seeing" the text and reading it aloud. Once, while he was making a public speech which was also being broadcast, one of the monsignori in attendance had to move a microphone closer as it was too far from the Pope for proper transmission. The ceremony over, the monsignore apologized, "I'm sorry, your Holiness, that I had to disturb you by shifting the microphone, but your voice wasn't coming out clear." To which Pacelli replied, "I didn't even notice it. I was looking at the page." Then, noticing that the priest looked somewhat surprised, Pius added, "I mean the page I had in my mind."

The Pope was a remarkable linguist. Besides Latin, of course, he spoke English, French, German, Spanish and Portuguese fluently. Because of his long stay in Germany and also because his closest collaborators were Germans, German was the foreign language he preferred. He spoke it without the slightest effort and often used colloquial expressions. His knowledge of English, French, Spanish and Portuguese was perfect as regards grammar, but his accent was not too good and his style rather scholarly and stilted. After having practiced for a short time he could, and sometimes did, deliver very short speeches in Danish, Dutch, Swedish and other languages. Shortly before his death he had begun to study Russian, probably with the intention of broadcasting to the Russian people or in the hope that Russian tourists might come to Rome more often and might attend his audiences. He loved dictionaries and grammars and had a stupendous collection of them.

Together with an amazing memory went an incredible capacity for work. An account of a normal day in Pacelli's life will show graphically how hard he used to work. He got up about 6:30 and said a short prayer in front of an open window overlooking St. Peter's Square. Until a few years before his death he used to go to a small, well-equipped gymnasium in which he did some exercises, used a rowing machine and rode on a mechanical horse. Then he took a cold shower, shaved with an electric razor, dressed and celebrated Mass in the private chapel next to his bedroom. His old butler, Giovanni Stefanori or his chauffeur–valet, Mario Stoppa served the Mass, which was attended by Mother Pasqualina Lehnert and the three other German nuns who looked after the Pontiff's household. Mother Pasqualina, indeed, acted indirectly as a barometer of the Pope's health. When she turned up in St. Peter's at one of the early Masses, this meant that Pacelli was not well and had been unable to celebrate his usual Mass.

After Mass the Pope took breakfast: a cup of light coffee, a little bread and occasionally fruit. Gretchen, his favorite sparrow, was let out of the cage and hopped first on to the Pope's shoulder or arm and then on to the table to peck at the breadcrumbs. While having breakfast the Pope read the papers or skimmed through documents connected with the morning's audiences. At ten minutes to ten he was always sitting at his desk in the red-and-gold study one floor below his apartment and at ten o'clock sharp the first visitor was let in. Until shortly before his death this was invariably Mgr. Montini, then the State Pro-Secretary and later to be Cardinal Archbishop of Milan, who brought him the latest news and placed before him the papers with which he would later have to deal. Afterward the next visitor was the other Pro-Secretary, Mgr. Tardini, or one of the higher officials of the State Secretariat, Mgr. Angelo Dell'Acqua or Mgr. Carlo Grano.

Other visitors followed in quick succession: Cardinals, heads of religious orders, bishops from all parts of the world paying their visit *ad limina,* diplomats accredited to the Holy See, prominent persons who happened to be passing through Rome, and so on. This went on till about noon when the Pope began granting the special or general audiences. At the special audiences the visitors were collected into small groups (usually from five to ten) in a sequence of rooms in the Vatican, and the Pope moved quickly from one group to the other, exchanging a few words with at least one of the persons of each group. The general audiences were held in the large Hall of the Benedictions or in St. Peter's itself, or in the courtyard of the papal summer residence at Castel Gandolfo. The Pope used to walk through the cheering crowds, then go back to his throne and address the various groups of pilgrims, often in their own languages.

Lunch was usually taken at half past one and was a very frugal affair. His normal diet consisted of a vegetable soup, spaghetti or rice, then a thin slice of veal or some roast chicken, with salad, and then fruit, which often took the form of baked apples. For drink he had a *quartino* (a quarter of a liter, corresponding to a large glass) of white Frascati wine diluted with water. He ended the meal with a tiny cup of black coffee. After lunch he used to lie down for a half-hour siesta, after which he began work again in his apartment.

At four o'clock he went down by elevator to the street floor, where he found a car waiting with the faithful Mario Stoppa at the wheel. The car was an imposing black, old-fashioned Cadillac, with special body and gold handles, a gift he received from American Catholics during the first years of his pontificate. It was made in such a way that the Pope did not have to stoop to get into it. It had a single back seat in which the Pope sat. Stoppa would drive him about a quarter of a mile to the Vatican gardens, and there the Pope would walk up and down for an hour, his eyes glued to documents and reports. Once, in 1947, he was so absorbed in his reading that he made a misstep, fell and sprained an ankle. He used to take his walk in the garden even in the snow, and when it rained he walked under a shelter that was erected especially for him and that covered a path about 100 yards long. Stoppa used to follow him, walking a few steps behind and carrying a brief case containing other papers the Pope might want to consult.

During the pontificate of Pacelli, the Vatican gardens were taboo, and to visit them a special pass had to be obtained that specified the day and hour of the visit. While the Pope took his walk even the gardeners had to disappear from sight. Pius hated the idea of squashing under his feet, even inadvertently, ants or other insects. The gardeners therefore kept the paths clear by spraying them with insecticide. But this the Pope probably did not know.

By five o'clock the Pope had returned to his apartment, and after reciting the rosary he read part of the breviary and then sat down at his table to work once again. If necessary he asked some of the State Secretariat officials to come up and confer with him. At eight o'clock he took dinner. This was even lighter than his luncheon and often consisted of two soft-boiled eggs and some vegetables. After dinner he said prayers, listened to the radio or watched the television for a quarter of an hour or so, and then went back to work. It was at night that Pius XII used to prepare his speeches and encyclical letters. He would make a first draft in ink in a small, precise, extremely clear hand and then copy it on his portable typewriter. He was very difficult to please and after correcting the typewritten page he would again copy it on the machine. If he did not write he read—practically anything you can think of except fiction: newspapers and magazines, books on history, science, philosophy, archeology, theology or law. It was by this extensive reading that Pacelli acquired the amazing wealth of knowledge with which he surprised his visitors by showing himself well informed in so many fields of learning. His work done, the Pope returned to the chapel to pray, recited the rest of the breviary and between one and two in the morning retired to bed.

Probably no other man in the world met so many people every day as did Pius XII, since it was he who instituted general audiences on a scale unknown to his predecessors. Despite all this, Pacelli was fundamentally a very lonely man.

Italians often use the expression, *fare una vita da Papa* (to live like a Pope) to indicate a pleasant, leisurely life. They are evidently referring to the Popes of the Renaissance, to those brilliant, sensuous, temporal sovereigns who took a delight in the fine arts, good food and delicious wines and who were sometimes not insensible to feminine charms. In modern times, however, to be a Pope is a rather grim affair; the high office imposes a burden that only an exceptional man can accept and bear. The austerity introduced in the Vatican by the Counter Reformation, the self-imposed imprisonment that followed the loss of Rome in 1870, the dogma of the Pope's infallibility (too widely interpreted in the popular belief but no less binding) have all conspired to isolate the Pope from the rest of mankind. His loneliness is spiritual rather than physical, but this does not make it any the less complete.

During the nineteen years of his pontificate, Eugenio Pacelli took his meals alone, met his family only once a year, while the people who could be called his friends might be counted on the fingers of one hand. Christmas Day, which was the only day in the year that Pacelli did not work, was reserved for his annual meeting with his family. The private manner in which the Popes pass Christmas also dates back to 1870. As a protest against the occupation of Rome,

Pius IX had abolished all the great religious ceremonies that used to take place at Christmas, and the practice has been maintained even after the pacification between Church and State brought about by the Concordat of 1929.

The family reunion used to take place at 4 o'clock in the afternoon when all the Pacellis, the Mengarinis, the Rossignanis, with their children, grandchildren and in-laws—more than thirty persons all told—trooped into the Pope's study. Pius always took the children to see the beautiful seventeenth century German crib he had bought in Munich when he was Nuncio there and of which he was extremely fond. Every Christmas he spent a couple of hours arranging the figures to compose the Nativity scene. Having been born in an old-fashioned Roman family, the Pope preferred the traditional crib to the more Nordic Christmas tree. But, so as not to displease his housekeeper, Mother Pasqualina, he did allow a small Christmas tree to be set up in a corner. After distributing presents to the children, Pacelli used to return to his study and chat for a couple of hours with the family, while the Bavarian nuns served tea to the grown-ups and cups of chocolate to the children. After this all-too-short family interlude, Pacelli returned to his austere solitude.

There was, however, one exception to Pacelli's detachment from his family—his nephew, Prince Don Carlo. The Prince could freely enter the Pope's apartment and now and then Pius XII invited him to come along after dinner for a little chat. But not even Carlo ever had a meal with the Pope, and their relations, although very cordial, were always kept on a formal footing. Other friends of the Pope were Cardinal Francis Spellman, Archbishop of New York, and Enrico Galeazzi, one of the higher-ups in the financial administration of the Vatican City, as will be seen later. These two are mentioned together because their friendship with the Pope went back to youthful days, when Pacelli was an official of the State Secretariat, Spellman, thirteen years his junior, a modest member of the same office, and Galeazzi then an up-and-coming Vatican architect. The friendship thus formed grew stronger as time went on. Spellman was the only Cardinal who, as soon as he reached Rome, was immediately received by the Pope, the only one who was sometimes invited to take tea with him, and the only one who was able to take the liberty of making the Pope a present such as an electric razor. None of the other Cardinals were intimate enough with Pacelli to do anything of the sort.

Another good friend of Pacelli's was the blunt Secretary of the Congregation of St. Peter, the late Mgr. Ludwig Kaas. He had been the leader of the German Catholic Party, *Centrum,* and after the advent of Hitler, when Kaas was already getting on in years, he became a priest and came to Rome. He knew Pacelli from the days when the latter had been Nuncio in Germany, and the old friendship was resumed in the Vatican. Mgr. Kaas often saw Pius XII, who liked the sincerity and lack of flattery shown by the German former politician. Kaas was very outspoken, and if he considered that Pacelli had made some mistake—not in questions of faith, of course—he told him so very plainly.

Finally, a certain friendship also grew up between Pacelli and his personal physician, Professor Riccardo Galeazzi Lisi, half-brother of the architect Galeazzi, who bore the resounding title of *Archiatra Pontificio*. The *Archiatra* used to follow the Pope like a shadow in all official ceremonies and often used to call on him when it was not a matter of giving his professional services.

Immediately after the death of Pacelli, Galeazzi Lisi gave an article and allegedly also some photographs of the dead Pope to the French magazine, *Paris Match,* and another article to a Milan magazine. A few days later (and, as a matter of fact, through me) he gave to the press the rather moving, but perhaps rather crude, text of a diary he had kept during Pacelli's last four days. Thereupon there was an uproar in the Vatican and he had to resign all his positions. The Italian Medical Council considered his deportment unethical and struck him from its register. Galeazzi Lisi appealed to the State Council which quashed the decision of the Medical Council on procedural grounds. The whole matter is now before the Court of Cassation. I, having been directly involved in the affair, am able to state that Galeazzi Lisi refused to accept any money for the publication of the diary. What the situation is so far as the other two articles are concerned, I am not in a position to state.

But the affair of this diary was only an episode in an extraordinary atmosphere of sensationalism that was a feature of Pacelli's death. The photographs of the dying Pope, the premature announcement of his death, the documentary film shot by a motion picture company and the invasion of the dead Pontiff's bedroom by television lights, reflectors and cameras a few minutes after his death are all factors which taken together form a picture that is anything but edifying.

The blame for all this must be laid partly on the modern systems of news gathering, partly on the unscrupulousness of those who took the photographs and kept the diaries as well as of those who wildly competed for them at fantastic figures and then published them. But a part was the result of the confusion that reigned at Castel Gandolfo, due to the fact that many of the traditional posts in the pontifical Court had long been left vacant and that the Court itself had

for years no longer functioned in accordance with the ancient cere-
monials and the rigid rules that were the result of centuries of experience. The new Pope, within a few hours of his election, took
steps to fill these posts and re-establish traditional ceremony.

Another person with whom Pacelli remained upon a friendly footing was the Swiss physician Paul Niehans. As a young man Niehans
had studied theology and had become a Protestant minister. At a
certain point however he abandoned his mission to devote himself
to medicine and had invented the so-called "cellular therapy" which,
among its other virtues, is said to possess the power of rejuvenating
the patient. Niehans' method consists in injecting into the patient
living cells of freshly slaughtered animals. Speed is an essential factor
in this process as not more than fifty minutes may elapse between
the moment when the animal is killed and the injection is given.
Niehans himself goes to the slaughter-house and chooses a pregnant
ewe or young cow that is in perfect health. Just as soon as the sheep
has been slaughtered he performs a Caesarean operation and extracts
the fetus. A car is waiting for him which rushes him to his laboratory.
There he dissects the fetus, sorting out the liver, the spleen, the
kidneys, the colon, the forepart of the brain, the thyroid and other
endocrine glands. As the sexual organs are not yet developed in the
fetus, he takes small sections of these from young but fully grown
animals. Then, still racing against time, he chops up very finely and
delicately the bits he needs, so as to damage the cells as little as
possible. The resulting pulp is then diluted in a physiological solution and injected under the skin of the patient. The lists of diseases
Niehans claims to be able to cure is really impressive. Among them
are those connected with growth and development (dwarfism, gi-
gantism and mongolism) and various degenerate diseases of the organs
such as cirrhosis, nephritis, diseases of the heart and the blood stream,
those caused by glandular failures and, particularly, sexual defi-
ciencies. He also states that he has cured a few cases of cancer. The
cure normally consists of one injection only, to be repeated, if necessary, after a certain number of years. Pacelli, according to Niehans
himself, had three injections. Most physicians are rather skeptical
about the Niehans method and many believe that the injections can
result in a dangerous shock condition.

But it was not only because of this danger that many in the Vatican
were opposed to Niehans and his cure. There was also the moral
aspect of the case. As we have seen, Niehans also used, especially in
the cure of senility, the cells of male sexual organs. It wasn't like
transplanting monkey glands as the famous Voronoff used to do—a
practice that was condemned by the Church—but it was something

similar. The fact remains that the Pope took a great liking to the former Protestant preacher, continued to take the cure until 1955, when it was firmly forbidden by Drs. Gasbarrini and Paolucci di Valmaggiore who had been called in for consultation. Even afterward the Pope always received Dr. Niehans privately as a friend whenever the Swiss physician came to Rome. Pius XII showed his gratitude to Niehans by appointing him a member of the Pontifical Academy to the place left vacant by the death of Fleming, the discoverer of penicillin.

The twelve years Pacelli spent in Germany left a deep mark on his mentality and habits. Being himself rather meticulous by nature, he had acquired a great admiration for German precision, dependability, thoroughness and capacity for hard work. A rather cold and uncommunicative person, he did not feel at ease in the Vatican world 95 per cent of which consisted of easygoing, jovial Italians who enjoyed good food, amusing talk and a bit of gossip. He therefore lived aloof and remote, in a small German island. A German was his private secretary, a short, thin, bespectacled Jesuit, Father Leiber, and German too was another Jesuit, Father Hentrich, who did research work for him in the Vatican Library and helped him to draft his learned speeches on all subjects under the sun. Another German was the Pope's confessor, the Jesuit Father Augustin Bea, who has been made a Cardinal by John XXIII.

Soon after the death of Pius XII in the papal villa at Castel Gandolfo, a short, aged woman, in nun's garb, unobtrusively left the huge, rather gloomy building where the Pope, as was his custom in recent years, had spent the hot summer months. Her face was tired and sad, her gait slow and heavy. She was Mother Pasqualina Lehnert, the nun who had become an almost legendary figure in the Vatican. For forty years, for most of the time as his housekeeper, she had faithfully watched over the late Pontiff's daily life, with a devotion approaching fanaticism after this frail, sensitive man had assumed the heavy burden of head of the Roman Catholic Church.

But that which had become her chosen mission in life—a position without precedent in the history of the pontificate—was now ended. This extraordinary chapter of her life had closed. She had become again just a Bavarian nun.

Symbolic, perhaps, of the great change that had suddenly fallen upon her was the simplicity of her departure. Declining to use her customary Vatican car, a small black English one, she stepped into a hired automobile onto which was loaded a single large suitcase containing her more precious possessions. Faithful to the last, she carried a cage of sparrows and canaries, the birds of which the dead Pope had been particularly fond. Not for her were the solemnity and grandeur of the long funeral procession that was about to accompany her revered master to his last resting place in the Basilica of St. Peter. Her heart was too full of grief to take any part in it.

Mother Pasqualina has irreverently been nicknamed *la Papessa* (the Popess). To some extent she was the only person in the world who could give orders to the Pope; in fact, Pacelli himself authorized her to do so. He had set himself a very strict daily routine and Mother Pasqualina's job was to see that he kept to it. She reminded him when it was time to eat, or to go for his walk, or to take his medicine. And she was ruthless in her duty, as the late John Foster Dulles, United States Secretary of State, once discovered. He was in audience with the Pope, and as they both had much to say to each other he overstayed the allotted time. Suddenly a short, plump, elderly nun walked briskly into the Pope's study without knocking, gave a little nod with her head and said in German, *"Heiliger Vater, Sie müssen essen!"* (Holy Father, you must eat). Pacelli replied, *"Ganz recht, Mutter Pasqualina, ich lasse die Suppe nicht kalt werden."* (You are quite right, Mother Pasqualina, I shan't let the soup get cold). Dulles had understood what was said, and was waiting for the nun to leave before taking his departure. But Pasqualina just stood there and showed no intention of leaving. Thereupon the Pope got up, smiling, and explained to Secretary Dulles, "There is no power on earth that could make our good Mother Pasqualina move when the soup is on the table."

This little woman who ruled the Pope's domestic life so completely was born at Ebersberg in Bavaria, on October 29, 1894. Her father was a farmer who also acted as village postman. At the age of fifteen she decided to become a nun and join the humblest order, that of the Franciscans. She was first a novice in the *Kreszentia-Heim* at Al-tötting and then, after having taken the vows and changed her name from Josefine to Pasqualina, she went to the mother-house of the Teaching Sisters of the Holy Cross at Menzingen, near Zurich. There the sisters were taught to cook, serve at table, wash, iron, mend clothes, and do other domestic chores, before being sent to work as servants in religious establishments all over the world. Pasqualina learned very quickly and at the age of twenty was already supervising other young nuns. Later she was sent to the Stella Maris Abbey at Rorschach, in the mountains of Switzerland, where Roman Catholic priests in ill health went to recuperate.

It was there as has already been told that she first met Don Eugenio Pacelli, then an official of the State Secretariat. She immediately felt a motherly, protective affection for the thin, pale, Roman priest who seemed so helpless in all practical matters and, with German thoroughness, she decided to take him under her wing and see that he got over his chest trouble. His Swiss holiday, under Pasqualina's stern and sensible management, worked wonders for Don Pacelli.

In 1917, when Mgr. Pacelli had been appointed Apostolic Nuncio to Munich, the staff of the Nunciature there included an old layman and two German woman servants. One day the Nuncio overheard a quarrel between the two women, one of whom shouted at the other a word that he, in spite of his perfect knowledge of German, could not understand and failed to find in a dictionary. A few days later, during a conversation with the German Cardinal Faulhaber, he asked the meaning of the word. It proved to be a vulgar insult and the old Cardinal, after explaining diplomatically to the Nuncio that the word was a "term of endearment," asked him where he had heard it. On learning of the episode between the servants, he asked Pacelli, "But why do you keep those women? Why not get some of the good nuns of the Holy Cross?" It was then that Pacelli recalled the little, brisk, rosy-cheeked Bavarian nun who had been so efficient and so kind to him, and eventually it was arranged that she should come and keep house for him. Since that time, for more than forty years, Pasqualina looked after the Pope with intense dedication and unflagging energy. To sanction this privilege in the first place a special authorization from Pope Benedict XV had been necessary.

Among the unusual situations in which Mother Pasqualina found herself was that of being the only woman in history to remain as housekeeper of a Cardinal within the rigorously supervised boundaries of a Conclave, where invariably only the Cardinals and their male assistants are allowed to live isolated from the world during the period until the new Pope is elected. This happened in 1939, after the death of Pius XI. At that time no definite arrangements had been made for lodging the Cardinals. They were however aware that Cardinal Pacelli was accustomed to, and would suffer were he deprived of his own particular way of living, which was the more necessary to him since he had just relinquished his duties as Secretary of State to assume the onerous task of *Camerlengo*, the supreme authority in the Vatican until the new Pope is elected. Agreement was unanimous that Cardinal Pacelli should be allowed the exclusive use of his ordinary apartment during the Conclave. Moreover, a special authorization of the Congregation of Cardinals permitted Mother Pasqualina to remain there also so that Pacelli should lack nothing of his customary diet or of the medicines necessary to his well-being.

One cannot help wondering whether Pacelli would have attained, and been able to bear the burden of, the Papacy had he not met

Josefine Lehnert early in his career in the Swiss mountain resort of Rorschach. For not only did she keep him in relative health but she relieved him completely of all practical matters, thus allowing him to concentrate wholly on his lofty task and thoughts. After all these years the Pope and his housekeeper understood each other so well that very few words had to be exchanged between them. Pacelli detested noise and futile chatter and Pasqualina glided about him in felt slippers like a silent, benevolent ghost, anticipating all his needs and wishes. She looked after his clothes, which were always immaculate and dazzlingly white (but it was the old butler, Giovanni Stefanori, who helped the Pope to get dressed), she disinfected with alcohol his much-kissed hand and ring as soon as he returned from the audiences, she kept his personal papers in order, his desk supplied with writing paper, his fountain pen filled, and she changed the Pope's cuffs, which he often soiled with ink while writing. Pius XII probably no longer even noticed her presence, as everything was done so quietly, swiftly and without any fuss.

Mother Pasqualina knows more about the late Pope than anybody else in the world, and this is not just because she was with him for so long. At one point Pius XII suffered from arthritis in his right hand and was unable to do any writing. He took to dictating to Pasqualina not only official papers but also the daily entries in his private diary. This became a regular practice, at least as far as the diary was concerned, and so Pasqualina was able to share the Pope's innermost thoughts. His trust in her was complete, and with good reason—for she never once, not even inadvertently, betrayed his confidence. Because of her exceptional and delicate position Pasqualina became absolutely inaccessible to most people. No journalist has ever been able to talk to her and few managed even to catch a glimpse of her. Many who actually lived in the Vatican never saw her. Very few pictures are available of Pasqualina before the death of Pius XII forced her into the limelight; one is a very old passport photo and the others were taken with a long-range lens during a religious ceremony and are far from clear.

Although Pasqualina may not have been seen often, her presence was very definitely felt in the Vatican. She ruled the papal household with an iron hand. Short-tempered, despotic, frightfully outspoken, she often clashed with the butler, Stefanori. The other three German nuns, all from the same order of the Holy Cross of Menzingen, were terrified of her. But she could also be very kind in her gruff sort of way. It is told that one night she saw a young member of the Noble Guard, on duty outside the papal apartment, who had fallen asleep leaning on his sword. Pasqualina woke him up and a few minutes later brought him a cup of strong coffee. "Drink it quickly," she is said to have whispered, "the Pope must not catch you asleep."

This mystery woman of the Vatican seldom left the papal apartment, and then mainly on charitable errands. She used to ride in a small automobile, with drawn blinds, and being always in a hurry she kept telling the driver *"Più presto! Più presto!"* (Faster! Faster!) Now and then some old, impoverished members of the Roman aristocracy, who were too proud to ask for help, would receive an unexpected visit from Mother Pasqualina who, on behalf of the Pope, tactfully persuaded them to accept financial assistance. All the private charities of the Pope were handled by Pasqualina, who also attended to his bookkeeping.

No one was allowed to cross the threshold of the Pope's private apartment without first going to Pasqualina—not even his closest relatives. It is related that Elisabetta Pacelli, sister of Pius XII, complained bitterly about this during the first illness of the Pope in 1954. Mother Pasqualina was equal to the occasion. In answer to Elisabetta's protests Pasqualina went personally to her house by car and after accompanying her to the Pope's apartment, later escorted her back in the same way, thereby putting the visit in the category of a personal concession!

One episode is characteristic of the way she felt about the Pope. When X-ray photographs were taken of him in 1955, Dr. Galeazzi Lisi, his personal physician, had the apparatus installed in the private apartment. Pius was supposed to lie naked to the waist on a foam rubber mattress, and Pasqualina had placed a beautiful white silk sheet on it. The X-ray specialist asked her to remove it since the silk might have affected the clarity of the plate. She did so but not without having protested loudly that it was an indignity to make the Pope lie on a rubber mattress. Just before the Pope was led to the X-ray room the specialist, to make sure, glanced under the mattress. There, neatly folded so as not to show, he found the silk sheet, which Pasqualina had surreptitiously slipped under it.

Besides being an extremely capable woman in practical matters such as cooking and general household management, Pasqualina is undeniably gifted with high intelligence. When to these qualities are added her strong will, firm character, and a deep streak of stubbornness, it is not surprising that she exercised an influence in papal circles that went far beyond that of an ordinary housekeeper. From all accounts Pasqualina often busied herself with matters that did not directly concern her regular duties and that sometimes even extended to the sphere of ecclesiastical affairs. The arranging of papal audiences is quoted as a case in point, and here Pasqualina was occasionally adamant. For her, the well-being of Pius XII was paramount, and she would insist that audiences, so important a feature of daily routine in the Vatican, be held or postponed according to the state of the Pope's health.

Again, Pasqualina to whose ears came information from many sources and under whose watchful eyes inevitably fell—as a daily visitor to the Pope's study—documents of the highest importance, often drew the attention of His Holiness to matters that the meticulous diplomatic procedure of the Vatican, or the maneuvers of interested parties, might have either delayed or pigeonholed altogether. In fact, various initiatives taken by Pius XII were attributed to her intervention, among them even the nomination of a Cardinal—the Canadian Mgr. Leger. Whether her influence ever reached to so high a level will probably never become known for certain, but that she had, as the saying goes, the Pope's ear has never been doubted. Thus persons, both ecclesiastic and lay, who felt they had a grievance that could be removed by His Holiness, would find in Pasqualina the only sure channel for pleading their cause with the Pope once she was convinced of the justice of their case. It is, therefore, not surprising that in diplomatic circles connected with the Vatican, this once humble little nun was given the nickname of *virgo potens* (powerful virgin).

There is an old saying in Curia circles that the authority of persons in the Vatican can be measured by the ease or difficulty they have in being able to confer with the Pope. This privilege, which especially during the latter years of the reign of Pius XII was greatly restricted, was available to Mother Pasqualina as often as she wished to take advantage of it; she enjoyed wide influence, and was respectfully greeted by the highest personages inside and outside the Vatican.

Eugenio Pacelli, the Roman Pope, venerated by Catholics all over the world, the Angelic Shepherd as his biographers have described him, was not liked inside the Vatican. This may seem a paradoxical statement, but it was a fact. There were many reasons, even if not all were justified and rational, for this feeling of coldness on the part of those who were closest to him and should have been fondest of him. First of all there is the fact that he had surrounded himself with Germans. By so doing he broke a centuries-old tradition that the Vatican should be in the hands of Italians and thus aroused the hostility of many high Italian prelates, dignitaries and officials. Then there was the further fact that the only people who seemed to have a certain influence on him—with the exception of Cardinal Spellman and Mgr. Kaas (and he had become a priest only very late in life)—were all laymen, like his nephew Carlo Pacelli, the architect Galeazzi, Dr. Galeazzi Lisi, his personal physician, and, at least for a certain time,

Professor Gedda, President of Catholic Action. This, of course, didn't go down too well with the Cardinals who, by their very rank and duties, felt they were entitled to be the Pope's closest friends and advisers.

Again, Pacelli had the habit of preparing his projects in great secrecy and of springing the most important decisions on others with out any warning. So it was that the Cardinals, the heads of religious orders and other personalities of the Catholic Church were taken by surprise and placed before a *fait accompli* which only too often con- flicted with their own initiatives, and they could hardly fail to resent such a state of affairs. Those responsible for ecclesiastical policy and affairs therefore lived in a continuous state of anxiety, fearing from one moment to another the announcement of papal decisions that would fall upon them like a bolt from the blue.

He had, besides, a mystical, almost medieval conception of the greatness of the papacy and treated the highest officials, including the Cardinals, with great formal courtesy but without any human warmth. Being such a hard, efficient and precise worker himself he could not stand slackness, delays or mistakes. And when he found someone in the wrong, he let him have a piece of his mind without any mincing of words. Usually the papal reprimands caught the culprits by sur- prise. The telephone would ring and a clear, icy voice would say, "*Qui parla Pacelli*" (Pacelli speaking). Without any preamble he would proceed to tell the offender in great detail just where and how he had gone wrong. He would then hang up without giving the victim a chance to explain or justify himself. All that those who had incurred his wrath could do was to ask for an audience, which was not always granted, or to express their apologies or reasons in writing.

Eugenio Pacelli shattered many traditions and precedents. He was the first Pope to have been to North America, to have flown in a plane, to have used a typewriter and the telephone (his predecessor Pius XI had had one installed in his study but never once lifted the receiver) and also the first to appear on television, the first to put on make-up to act in an Anglo-Italian documentary film about the Vati- can, the first to receive bicycle champions and football players (and discuss with them how the game should be played), the first to admit officially, in opposition to the letter of the Bible, that man could have appeared on the earth fifty million years ago . . . and one could go on for some time quoting the Pope's "firsts." On the strength of all this Pacelli would appear to have been an extremely modern Pope. And he was, in the sense that he realized the importance of modern tech- niques (and made good use of them, especially the great vehicles for informing and educating the masses, such as the cinema, radio, television and the press) and that, unlike so many of the Popes before him, he never looked with mistrust at scientific progress.

But to him these were just material means to achieve spiritual aims. For Pacelli was fundamentally a medieval character set down into the modern world. His burning devotion, his ascetic life, his declared preference for the philosophy of St. Thomas Aquinas, his courage and strong will, his authoritarian character and his mysticism, even his physical appearance, all reminded you of the great saintly Popes of the Middle Ages.

As regards his mysticism, Pius XII had a number of visions, some of which were officially confirmed. In 1950, for three consecutive days, on October 30, 31 and November 1, while he was taking a walk in the Vatican garden, he saw a repetition of the Fatima miracle.

Fatima is a village in Portugal where the Virgin Mary is said to have appeared to three children, Francisco, aged eight, Jacinta, seven, and Lucia, nine, on May 13, 1917. The three were children of a shepherd; when they saw the vision they were out in the fields looking after their sheep. After the first apparition the Madonna appeared to them four more times, at intervals of one month, and each time she spoke to them. According to what the children said, the Virgin Mary predicted five events: (1) the premature death of two of the children; (2) the end of the First World War; (3) the appearance of a mysterious light which was to precede the outbreak of a Second World War; (4) minor conflicts after the Second World War; and (5) the conversion of Russia.

Two of the children, Francisco and Jacinta, died a few years later of Spanish 'flu. The third, Lucia de Santes, became a nun in the closed order of the Carmelite convent at Coimbra. The fifth prophecy text is only approximately known. It says, in part, "An impious propaganda will spread terror throughout the world, causing wars and the persecution of the Church; many good people will suffer martyrdom; the Holy Father will have much to suffer. If my pleas are heeded Russia will be converted and we shall have peace; otherwise many serious errors will spread in the world; many nations will be destroyed and in the end my Immaculate Heart will triumph and humanity will have a period of peace."

The rest of the last prophecy is still a secret kept in a sealed envelope locked in the safe of the Bishop of Coimbra, to be opened only in 1960. Pius XII, however, knew the rest of the prophecy as Sister Lucia de Santes herself told it to him.

At the time the three Portuguese children had their visions, an enormous crowd assembled in the Fatima plain hoping to see and hear the Madonna too. This didn't happen, as the privilege of seeing and hearing the Madonna seemed reserved to the three children only. But, instead, many of those present saw another portentous event— the sun rotating in the sky with a fireworks effect, then dipping down almost touching the horizon and swinging up to its place again. And this is what the Pope saw in 1950 while walking in the Vatican garden. On that occasion he also saw the Virgin Mary but it has never been disclosed whether he heard her speak too. This vision was officially revealed for the first time in 1950 by Cardinal Federico Tedeschini.

The second papal vision took place during his serious illness of 1954. One day his condition became so alarming that the Pope's Sacrist, the Dutch Mgr. C. Van Lierde, was called to give him extreme unction. But the Pope sent him away. The night before, or rather toward dawn, Christ had appeared by his bed and told him that his time had not yet come. This vision was described by the Pope himself to a group of Jesuits of the "For a Better World" move- ment, and they in turn made it public by giving the story to the Milan magazine *Oggi*. I had also heard about it the day before *Oggi* appeared and, after having satisfied myself about its authenticity, sent it to the London *Daily Express* which printed it on the same day as *Oggi*. When the story came out in Milan and in London there was a bit of a rumpus. The Vatican press office was bombarded by requests for a confirmation but as they knew nothing about it, as so often happens where the Pope is concerned, they first issued an imprudent denial and then barricaded themselves behind the usual "No comment." *Oggi*, however, incensed by the denial, protested to the State Secretariat and threatened to reveal the source of their information and to prove that the Pope himself had read, corrected and approved the article before it was printed. Finally, the Vatican Press Office was compelled to issue an official confirmation of the story.

The Romans, who have always treated the Catholic Church with great familiarity and often with irreverence, immediately made up a number of jokes about this vision. One of these related that an American news agency had been pestering several Vatican mon- signori (and this was true), wanting to know how Christ had looked and what he was wearing when he appeared to the Pope. Finally, one of the monsignori was said to have lost his patience and to have answered, "He was wearing tails, white tie and decorations. That's the way you dress when you have a private audience with the Pope." The other joke was to the effect that Mother Pasqualina had knocked at the Pope's bedroom door early one morning and asked, "Holy Father, can I bring you the coffee?" "Yes," a powerful voice is supposed to have boomed from inside, "and make it for two."

But it cannot be denied that Pius XII was strongly influenced by his mysticism. He firmly believed in the Fatima prophecies and also in those of the Bavarian wonder-girl, Theresa Neumann, whom he met in Munich and who predicted to him that he would become a Pope and that he would die shortly after his second Consistory. Actually Pacelli did hold only two Consistories at which Cardinals were created.

A prophecy easy for us to make is that Pius XII will be made a saint. His stature as a Pope, his ascetic life, his complete dedication to the lofty task to which he was called, the way he worked and gave the last ounce of himself, his visions and also a number of miracles attributed to him are all factors which will help toward the causes of beatification and canonization that will certainly be introduced in a not-too-distant future.

The miracles attributed to Pius XII have all been carefully recorded with testimonials and medical certificates in a special dossier kept at the Vatican State Secretariat. They are all faith healings of people received by him in audience, the outstanding case being that of a boy from Turin who is said to have recovered his sight without the doctors being able to give a scientific explanation of the phenomenon.

3

The Reformer

POPES USUALLY don't reign long. In general they ascend Peter's throne when they have already attained a ripe age and the strain and worries of their post undermine their health. Pacelli was an exception in this respect also. He reigned for nineteen years, seven months and seven days which, even though not approaching the thirty-two years of Pius IX, the twenty-five of Leo XIII (1878-1903) and the twenty-four of Pius VI (1775-1799), is still one of the longest pontificates.

But apart from the duration of his reign, it can be said that he will have a notable place in the history of the Church. And this not only because he lived and reigned in such momentous times (Fascism, Nazism, the Second World War, the spread of communism over a great part of the world, the nationalist awakening of the colonial peoples, the atomic age) but also because of the sweeping reforms he carried out within the Catholic Church. Let me therefore try to draw up, even if only in summary fashion, a balance sheet of Pius XII's pontificate.

The most striking of his reforms was the internationalization of the Sacred College. Before Pius XII this most important organ of the Catholic Church had been an actual Italian monopoly. The preponderant Italian influence had started fading as long as a century ago, but it was a slow, very gradual process until Pacelli appeared on the scene and quickly began to change things. Here are some figures that speak for themselves:

	Italian Cardinals	Non-Italian Cardinals
1853	54	16
1859	49	18
1889	43	27
1906	34	24
1939	35	29
1946	28	42
1958	17	34

The critical turning-point was the Consistory in 1946, on the eve of which there were twenty-three Italian Cardinals and fifteen of other nationalities. Pius XII distributed thirty-two new Red Hats at one time (never before had so many Cardinals been nominated in a single Consistory) to bring the Sacred College back to its standard figure of seventy. After this Consistory the positions were reversed; the Italians totaled twenty-eight and those from other countries forty-two.

On the occasion of the 1946 Consistory, an Italian Cardinal, worried by this new situation, remarked to the Pope that the traditional Italian majority had been shattered and wondered what the consequences might be. "Well," replied Pacelli with a smile, "it means that I could have a foreign successor." This has not yet happened, but never before as on the eve of the last Conclave did it seem even possible that a non-Italian, say the Armenian Agagianian or the French Tisserant, might ascend Peter's throne.

To illustrate the make-up of the Conclaves that elected Pacelli and Roncalli, respectively, here are the Cardinals grouped as to their nationalities.

1939 (Pacelli's election)		1958 (Roncalli's election)	
Italy	35	Italy	17
France	6	France	6
Spain	3	Spain	3
Belgium	1	Belgium	1
Portugal	1	Portugal	2
Brazil	1	Brazil	3
Argentina	1	Argentina	2
Chile	—	Chile	1

		1939 (Pacelli's election) / 1958 (Roncalli's election)	

1939 (Pacelli's election)		1958 (Roncalli's election)	
Cuba	—	Cuba	1
Colombia	—	Colombia	1
Ecuador	—	Ecuador	1
Germany	3	Germany	2
United States	3	United States	2
Canada	1	Canada	2
Australia	—	Australia	1
Ireland	1	Ireland	1
India	—	India	1
Armenia	—	Armenia	1
Syria	1	Syria	1
Hungary	1	Hungary	1
China	1	China	1
Jugoslavia	—	Jugoslavia	1
Poland	1	Poland	1
Austria	—	Austria	—
Czechoslovakia	1	Czechoslovakia	—
England	1	England	—

Beside the decline in the proportion of Italian Cardinals—which would have been still more evident if Mindszenty and Stepinac had been able to come to Rome—what is noteworthy is the great increase in the number of Latin American Cardinals as well as the admission of Cardinals of new nationalities such as the Chinese, the Indian, the Australian and the Armenian.

To find in the history of the Papacy a non-Italian pontiff we must go back more than four centuries, that is, to the Dutch Adrian VI (1522) (Hadrian Florensz) who died in 1523. Since then thirty-three Conclaves have elected Italian Popes only.

The decline in the number and percentage of Italian Cardinals under Pacelli appears even more pronounced, if after the Sacred College, the make-up of the Cardinals *di Curia*, one examines those who reside in Rome and who hold the key posts in the Church administration. In 1939, at the beginning of Pacelli's pontificate, there were twenty-seven Curia Cardinals, all of them Italian except the French Cardinal Eugene Tisserant. At Pacelli's death the Curia Cardinals had fallen to thirteen including Tisserant and Agagianian. In this connection mention may be made of the premature death of the American Cardinal Samuel Stritch, nominated by Pius XII as Pro-Prefect of *Propaganda Fide*, who would have brought the non-Italians in Curia up to three, and also of the fact that over half of the Italians were either so old or in such poor health that they could not carry out their duties with the necessary efficiency.

From Pacelli's point of view his action was more than logical. Being accustomed to doing everything possible by himself, after he had concentrated in his own hands and in the State Secretariat tasks and functions previously entrusted to other offices of the Curia (with the result that the Curia was deprived of almost all authority), he was not overly concerned with the fact that the number of his assistants was so greatly reduced. What he was far more anxious to do was to enlarge the horizons of the Church by conferring the dignity of the cardinalate on bishops of as many nationalities as possible. It is known that at the time of his death he was planning to nominate Cardinals for Africa, Mexico, Oceania and the Philippines.*

The activities that took up most of the time and labors of the late Pope were undoubtedly his audiences and his addresses. He was in the habit of saying that "whoever comes to Rome has the right to see the Pope," and he frequently postponed appointments with bishops and even Cardinals in order not to disappoint some group of pilgrims, even if they were of quite modest station. He used to receive actors and actresses, singers, dancers, automobile racing drivers, bicycle champions, football and baseball teams, fashion creators, midwives, butchers, streetcar conductors, astronomers, nuclear physicists and many others. To all he tried to teach something, and occasionally he would even issue warnings.

One habit of Pius XII was to read up on the specialized studies and even delve into the professional secrets of those whom he was to address. His object was to give his audience the impression that he was following their work very closely and that he had a thorough knowledge of their problems so that afterward the moral precepts that he imparted would appear more convincing. This exhausting work of research and assimilation placed upon Pacelli a strain that he was able to bear only because of his exceptional physical resistance and his prodigious memory.

Sitting in his study from five o'clock in the afternoon till midnight and later, Pacelli read manuals on football, studied the organization of the hotel and tourist industry, the most modern methods of extracting oil and coal, the procedures for killing animals in large slaughterhouses, the special regulations governing the work of railroadmen, the workings of printing houses, newspapers and the great news-

---

* On March 3, 1960, Pope John XXIII designated seven new Cardinals which included the first Negro Cardinal (Laurian Rugambwa), the first Japanese Cardinal (Peter Tatsuo Doi), and the first Filipino Cardinal (Rufino J. Santos).

gathering agencies, the techniques of film-making, astronomy, nuclear physics, obstetrics and thousands of other subjects.

Very often, of course, the game was not really worth the candle. It was certainly superfluous, for example, to explain to dentists how artificial teeth are made or how the most modern dental drills are used, to reveal to oil experts the mysteries of seismographic, magnetic and gravimetric prospecting and so on while the great administrative problems of the Church remained unsolved or shelved.

Yet it must be recognized that among these thousands of addresses there were some that were truly fundamental in pinpointing the attention of the Church on some of the most important and timely problems of the modern world. There were addresses delivered to judges, soldiers, civil servants, in which the Pope dealt with problems of conscience in which civil duties conflict with religious duties. Others to nurses and midwives, with particular reference to painless childbirth, birth control, the Ogino-Knaus method, and to the dramatic dilemma whether, in case of a difficult delivery, the life of the mother or of the unborn child should be saved. Still others to doctors referring to mercy killing, the limits of medical intervention to relieve the sufferings of the dying, to anesthetists (the legitimacy and limits in the use of drugs that relieve pain, the use of narcotics, tranquilizers, etc.) and to nuclear scientists and astronomers, including theories on the origin of the world, the period when our planet Earth came into existence, and attempts to reconcile modern science with Biblical tradition).

It must also be recognized that the audiences and addresses of Pius XII and the impressive success of the 1950 Holy Year (which drew to Rome four million pilgrims from every part of the world) enormously widened the sphere of influence of the Church and made the tall, white and hieratical figure of the late Pope almost as well known among Protestants as it was among Catholics.

My experience of more than a decade as Rome correspondent for American and English newspapers and periodicals has made me realize that the American and British press followed the doings of the Vatican, while Pacelli was Pope, with even greater interest than that shown in the subject by the Italian press.

But there is something more. Pacelli made of the Vatican a political center which, in Europe, is second only to London. For example, in the struggle between Russia and America, between the Communist world and the free world, the Vatican has taken a place of prime importance, and the prestige of the Pope, the influence of his opinion and of his counsel have not been so high for several centuries past. In addition, always in face of the threat of atheist materialism, a rapprochement of really noteworthy extent has come about during Pacelli's pontificate between Rome and the various Protestant sects, and most of the credit for this must be given to him. While an immediate and unconditional return of the Protestants to the authority of Rome is not immediately in prospect, it is certain that a kind of great Christian federation in which the Pope would have the position, if not of head, undoubtedly of *primus inter pares* is beginning to appear possible.

There are in the world, as has already been mentioned, about 500,000,000 Catholics, over 200,000,000 Protestants (divided into about 300 sects), and about 200,000,000 Eastern Christians (these latter for the moment cut off from the rest of Christianity since the majority of them live behind the Iron Curtain). Altogether they represent nearly 900,000,000 persons who live and work, even if not all of them do so according to the dictates of Christ, at least in an environment that is permeated and conditioned by Christian philosophy.

To reunite this portion of humanity in a single faith and to achieve Christian unity is the great vision of the ecumenical movement that was quietly born at Cincinnati in 1910 and that, with the conferences of Stockholm and Lisbon, took greater hold upon men's minds after the First World War. This project, inspired by the Protestants, of achieving a sort of world federation of Christian confessions, from the very start met with a big and apparently unsurmountable obstacle —the negative attitude of the Catholic Church. In the encyclical *Mortalium Animos* of 1928 the Pope made it clear that, according to the Holy See, the only way in which Christian unity might be achieved was through a return of the dissidents and schismatics to the fold of the Church of Rome.

Apart from this fundamental question of principle, there were obstacles of what may be called a disciplinary character that prevented or rendered difficult Catholic participation at such a meeting. In fact, paragraph 3 of Canon 1325 of the Code of Canon Law lays down, "Catholics should avoid taking part in discussions or meetings, especially if public, with non-Catholics without permission from the Holy See or, in urgent cases, from the local bishop."

During the Second World War, however, so many church buildings, both Protestant and Catholic, were destroyed by bombing that the "urgent cases" grew and grew and collaboration between Catholic and non-Catholic priests reached a point where they were celebrating rites in the same church edifice, though at separate hours. The observance of Canon 1325 had gradually become more and more slack and in June 1948 the Holy Office felt that a check was necessary.

The Holy Office warned, "It having come to our knowledge, that contrary to the prescriptions of the Holy Canons and without the permission of the Holy See, mixed meetings of Catholics and non-Catholics have been held in various places at which were discussed questions of faith, everyone is reminded that both laymen and secular or regular ecclesiastics are forbidden to participate in these meetings without the above mentioned permission. . . . Everyone is again reminded that any form whatsoever of communion in sacred things is wholly forbidden."

The warning came as a cold douche to the renewed hopes of the ecumenical movement. The official organ of the Ecumenical Council of Geneva commented, "Among the immediate consequences of this statement the following seem to be the most evident: interruption of the activity of the unofficial conferences and study groups which have become habitual between Catholics and members of other Christian confessions in several countries; Roman Catholics will be unable to participate as official observers at the meetings of the ecumenical movement; finally, a ban on interconfessional meetings except those explicitly permitted by the Vatican and which accordingly will be given a more or less official character."

But in Protestant circles there were people who appreciated the fundamental motives that had led the Holy See to adopt such an uncompromising attitude. The Waldensian journal of Rome, *La Luce,* wrote, "If they were to think and act differently in the ecumenical sphere the upper hierarchs of the Church of Rome would have to disavow not only the *Mortalium Animos,* which is the end of a stage, but all the preceding dogmatic-disciplinary legislation that from the Council of Trent onwards has accompanied the unrelenting claim to Rome's supremacy. This would be tantamount to ignoring the official interpretation of *Tu es Petrus* and, in the last analysis, to striking a mortal blow at the very existence of the pontiff and the Holy See."

Nevertheless, a few months after the stiffening of the Holy Office's attitude, there was a radical change in the tactics of the Catholic Church in respect to the ecumenical movement and, at the same time, a solemn reaffirmation of intransigence as regards questions of principle. The Holy Office itself issued a long and detailed series of instructions which, in substance, can be summarized in this way: First of all there was no longer any need to obtain previous authorization for participation in "mixed meetings of Catholics and non-Catholics at which problems of faith and morals should not be dealt with but which should discuss the way by which, uniting their common forces, the participants could defend the fundamental principles of natural right or of the Christian religion against the enemies of God, today united together, or else should examine the re-establishment of the social order or other questions of the kind."

As regards meetings of a theological character, it was no longer necessary for Catholics who wished to participate in them to obtain authority from the Holy See, as the bishops had been granted very wide discretional powers in this sphere. Again, the bishops were also empowered to appoint in every diocese priests whose express task was to follow closely the ecumenical movement, to watch Catholic publications on this subject, to supply the non-Catholics literature, information and advice on the Catholic religion and to place at the disposal of those already converted everything necessary both for their further instruction and to enable them to develop a more active religious life.

In short, there had been a change from an attitude of reserve and aloofness to one of keen interest in the ecumenical movement. On the other hand, as regards the principles of the Catholic Church, the Holy Office could not have made itself clearer in rejecting all possibility of compromise, "In discussions of a theological character the aim is to avoid that Catholic teaching (no matter whether of dogma or of truths connected with dogma) should, because of a spirit that today is termed 'irenical,' be so adapted to, or made to conform with the doctrines of the dissidents that the purity of Catholic doctrine should suffer. One must certainly not remain silent on or cloak with ambiguous words what Catholic truth teaches about the Constitution of the Church, about the primacy of jurisdiction of the Roman Pontiff, and about the sole, true union that is effected by the return of the dissidents to the sole, true Church of Christ."

Nothing, then, had changed, and nothing could change, in Catholic doctrine or in its attitude in face of the problem of Christian unity. The idea had been to attempt an experiment to see if the ecumenical movement could be exploited from the point of view of proselytism. Why, Pius XII must have thought, remain aloof from a movement that offers us an incomparable opportunity of explaining to the non-Catholics what the Church of Rome really is? Why not take advantage of it to make individual conversions and prepare the ground for eventual future collective conversions?

It is therefore to Pacelli that the chief credit must go if the Catholic Church has been able to take part in this promising dialogue between Christians of all kinds. To his credit must also be ascribed the fact that the Church of Rome has shown herself ready to compromise on secondary questions in the sphere of traditions, local practices, liturgy and rites as well as the organization of the clergy itself, a case in

point being the renewal by several Eastern communities of their ad-
hesion to Rome. Indeed, as to the 200,000,000 Christians of the East,
it is thought in the Vatican that the existing slight theological diver-
gencies could easily be composed and that a large number of them
could perhaps return to the bosom of the mother Church were it not
for the obstacle of the Iron Curtain.

And yet it was Pacelli himself who, after accomplishing so much
for a rapprochement with the Protestants in general and with the
Anglican Church in particular, struck a serious blow at the hopes of
being able to build a great Christian federation by proclaiming the
dogma of the bodily Assumption of the Virgin Mary into Heaven.
A kind of preliminary announcement of this dogma had been made
in his encyclical *Deiparae Virginis Mariae* of 1946. But when it was
solemnly proclaimed in the Bull *Munificentissimus Deus* of November 1, 1950, almost everyone was taken by surprise. Pacelli, the able
diplomat, the subtle politician, the most erudite jurist and codifier,
the man who had half-opened the door to the participation of
Catholics in the ecumenical movement, who had thereby seemed so
practical and accommodating, and who had made such substantial
concessions to modern science, suddenly showed himself as an uncompromising mystic who asked of his spiritual subjects a great act
of faith.

To judge whether Pacelli did the right thing or the wrong, whether
the dogma was advisable or not, is not my function. This intransigence, this rigidity, this absolute certainty of its own infallibility,
though it may at times seem a weakness or a defect, certainly constitutes the very essence of the Church of Rome, the motive for her
existence, the secret of her survival and of her success, tested by two
thousand years of history. By proclaiming the Dogma of the Assumption, Pacelli followed along the lines of the mystical tradition of the
great Popes of the Middle Ages.

The fact remains that during his reign Pius XII saw a great development of the Church's missionary work in various countries, above
all in Africa. He saw an improvement of the situation in Mexico,
where the laws against the Catholic Church are now a dead letter.
He saw the countries of Asia that have become independent, such as
India and Indonesia, and several Moslem countries, such as Egypt
and Iran, send their diplomatic representatives for the first time to
the Holy See. He saw great political parties of Catholic inspiration
grow and take root in Italy, Germany, France, Holland and Belgium,
the right-wing dictatorships of Franco and Salazar make the Catholic
Church one of the foundations of their power and, above all, he was
a witness to Catholic expansion in the United States. The number

of conversions, the higher birth rate of Catholics as compared with Protestants, the improved economic and social conditions of the typically Catholic communities in the United States such as the Italian and the Irish, all enabled Cardinal Spellman to prophesy: "If the rate of conversions to the Catholic Church is maintained, within a century the United States will be a Catholic nation."

These are the highlights of Pacelli's pontificate but there are also the shadows, among them the losses that the Church has suffered, under the wave of communism, in the countries beyond the Iron Curtain and in red China, and the very difficult situation in South America. These subjects will be dealt with in a separate chapter. I have also dealt separately with the reform work carried out by Pius XII in the sphere of the religious orders, and especially in the secular institutes—this new militia of Christ that is one of the principal and more significant characteristics of modern Catholicism.

4

The Conclave

IN ANCIENT TIMES the election of a Pope often went on for long periods. It was in 1216 that the pilgrims, tired of waiting, locked the Cardinals in so as to hasten the election of Savelli, a Roman who took the name of Honorius III (1216-1227).

However, it is not until the election of Gregory X (1271-1276) that there are references to the official beginnings of the Conclave (a name which comes from the Latin *cum clave* [with a key] and indicates the strict secrecy in which the election of Popes is carried out). Gregory's predecessor, the Frenchman Clement IV (1265-1268), had died in Viterbo, and it was there, as was customary in those days, that the Cardinals met to elect the new Pope. The opposing factions were almost equally strong, and no one was prepared to give way.

At that time the locking-in rule was not yet in force, and the Cardinals interspersed their rare sessions with a good deal of private talks, banquets, and even hunting parties on Monte Cimino. Things dragged on in this way for over two years, and with no sovereign power to enforce the law the atmosphere became bitter and explosive. One morning, when the whole Sacred College was at Mass, Guy de Montfort, Charles of Anjou's vicar in Tuscany, seized the occasion to end an old family vendetta with Prince Henry of Cornwall. While all those present were bowing at the elevation of the Host, he sidled up to his victim and drove a dagger into his heart. This horrible and sacrilegious crime, and the disorder that followed, so frightened the Cardinals that they locked themselves in the papal palace and dared not poke their noses outside, even to go hunting.

As for the population of Viterbo, they were angered by the long delay. They surrounded the palace, creating a food shortage within. But involuntary community life, instead of calming things down, only embittered the feud still further. The Cardinals tightened their belts but still could not decide to elect a Pope. One day the people of Viterbo, on the advice of the Franciscan Saint Bonaventura, took an even more drastic step—they removed the roof of the palace. The Cardinals threatened the populace with the wrath of God, but the people took no notice. The princes of the Church were forced to resign themselves and proceeded, with great wit, to head their diplomatic correspondence *Viterbii in palatio discoperto* (From the roofless palace of Viterbo). The captain of the city, Ranieri Gatti, finally put them on a diet of bread and water.

Although it was the end of August and the weather was still warm, a series of violent cloudbursts began. These, on top of their unwelcome fast, began to wear down the stubborn fiber of the Cardinals. On September 1, after two years, nine months and two days without a Pope, the longest period in the history of the Church, Tebaldi Visconti of Piacenza was elected, taking the name of Gregory X.

Remembering the discomforts he had been forced to put up with, and realizing the harm which the long vacancy had done to the Church, Gregory X confirmed and justified the emergency measures taken by the people of Viterbo, and even erected them into a system by instituting the Conclave. His laws were published in 1274. Beside being concise and colorful, they are still valid, with the exception of a few details. For this reason they are given here in full.

FIRST LAW: When the Pontiff dies the Cardinals will wait only ten days for those who are absent, after which, having spent nine days celebrating the funeral rites in the city where the Pontiff and the Curia were in residence, they will all lock themselves in the palace where the Pope lived, each with a single lay or clerical servant, unless there is a real necessity for two, in which case two may be permitted, the choice resting on the discretion of each Cardinal.

SECOND LAW: In the very building in which the Pontiff lived they will form a Conclave in which all will live in common, without dividing walls, curtains or other fabric between them, with only one private room. This Conclave will be completely locked in so that no one can get either in or out.

THIRD LAW: No one will have access to the Cardinals locked in Conclave, and no one will talk in secret with them, nor will they be permitted to see anyone except those who with the permission of all present may be summoned for the purposes of the election. No one may send deputations or letters to the Cardinals or any of those in the Conclave, under pain of excommunication.

FOURTH LAW: A few windows will, however, be left open in the Conclave, so that food may be passed in to the Cardinals, but no one whatsoever may pass through these windows.

FIFTH LAW: Three days after the Cardinals have entered the Conclave, if no new Pontiff has been elected, the priests and others responsible for the supervision of the Conclave must prevent more than one dish being prepared for the Cardinals' meals, either at lunch or dinner, for the next five days. When these five days have elapsed they will allow nothing but bread and water until the election has been concluded.

SIXTH LAW: The Cardinals will in the meantime take nothing from the apostolic chamber or from its income. During the period when the See is vacant this will be in the custody of whoever is given the Commission, who will be a person of faith and integrity. With the death of the Pope all ecclesiastical and legal offices of the Court will be suspended, except those of the Grand Penitentiary and the Chamberlain, who will continue to discharge their offices during the period of vacancy.

SEVENTH LAW: The Cardinals meanwhile must deal with nothing in the Conclave but the election of the new Pontiff, unless they are forced to defend the territory of the Church against imminent danger.

EIGHTH LAW: If some Cardinal does not enter the Conclave, or enters and then leaves again because of illness, the election will go on without him. But if he recovers he will be admitted to the Conclave, as will those Cardinals who come after the first have gone in, for no one outside the Conclave can vote in the election. Besides this, no one may prevent Cardinals who have been censured or excommunicated from entering the Conclave. A new Pope may not be nominated if he has not at least two-thirds of the votes cast by the electors. Not only the Cardinals, including those absent from the Conclave, but anyone else who has no just impediment is eligible for election to the Pontificate in the above manner.

NINTH LAW: If the Pope dies outside the city where he and the *Curia* resided, the Cardinals will meet in Conclave in the city in whose territory he has died; but if this city is prohibited or rebellious they will meet in the nearest city.

TENTH LAW: The governors and officials of the city where the Conclave takes place will see that the prescribed laws are observed.

ELEVENTH LAW: As soon as the death of the Pope is known,

these governors etc., will swear an oath in the presence of the clergy, or the people, called together for that purpose, that they will observe these laws.

TWELFTH LAW: If they do not observe them they are to be excommunicated, held in perpetual infamy; they will lose their lands and the city will be proscribed and deprived of vescoval dignity.

THIRTEENTH LAW: In the matter of the election the Cardinals must entirely disregard their own affairs and must have regard only to the common welfare of the Church.

FOURTEENTH LAW: None of the Sacred Electors, under pain of excommunication, can speak to, make promises to or canvass the other Cardinals in any way with a view to converting them to their view of the election; indeed, all pacts, agreements and obligations sealed with oaths are of no value, and whoever breaks them deserves praise, not the accusation of perjury.

FIFTEENTH LAW: In all cities and places of importance, solemn obsequies will be celebrated as soon as the Pope's death is announced, and every day that the See is vacant prayers will be offered to God for the speedy, harmonious and efficacious election of the new Pontiff, and this the Prelates of the churches will see to, by imposing an increased number of fasts.

These severe laws of Gregory X, and particularly the one which lays down that the Cardinals should be put on bread and water after the eighth day, were not always respected, and the Conclaves continued to drag on for long periods. There was, for example, the one at Carpentras, which ended more than two years later, on August 7, 1316. Shortly before the end, one of those locked in, exasperated by the two years of confinement, willfully set fire to the palace and obliged the Cardinals to escape through the narrow opening used for passing in food.

Among the most dramatic Conclaves was one, again at Viterbo, that lasted six months and ended on February 22 with the election of Martin IV (1281-1285). The people of Viterbo violated the rule of strict confinement to kidnap the two Orsini Cardinals, and the Cardinal Archbishop of Canterbury died in Conclave.

The last Conclave to elect a non-Italian Pope took place in Rome and lasted from December 27, 1521 to January 9, 1522. As already mentioned it resulted in the election of a Dutchman, Adrian Florensz, who was also the last Pope to retain his own name, calling himself Adrian VI. The Roman rabble, furious that a foreigner should have been elected, waited for the Cardinals to emerge and then stoned them.

At the very moment that the pontifical physician officially announces "The Holy Father is dead," a dictator, the Cardinal Chamberlain, is automatically born in the Vatican. Besides the rueful privilege of making all arrangements concerning the Pope's death, he has absolute power over everyone until the election of the new Pope. At the death of Pacelli there was no Cardinal Chamberlain, for this office and many others, including that of Secretary of State, had not been filled by Pius XII. The task of announcing the Pope's death was therefore carried out by Cardinal Tisserant, as Dean of the Sacred College. According to ancient custom, after having called the dead man by his family name in a loud voice, he should have tapped him three times on the forehead with a silver hammer, but this macabre ceremony did not take place; it had been abolished at the end of the nineteenth century.

Immediately after the official announcement the Court goes into mourning and the violet clothes of the prelates give way to mantles and amices of black silk. The palace gentlemen change into the customary mourning coats with black ties. No decorations, either Vatican or foreign, are worn. Then comes the first rite to indicate that the papacy is vacant—the breaking of the Fisherman's Ring, the seal used by the Popes on their letters and edicts. This is a big gold ring with an engraved amethyst or topaz. On the stone is depicted St. Peter in a boat and on the inner part of the setting the arms of the reigning Pope are engraved. Today in practice the ring is never worn; it is kept in a drawer of the Pope's writing desk. It is put there in the first few days of the new papacy and it stays there until the Pope dies, when the Chamberlain, or in his absence the Dean of the Sacred College, takes it and smashes it with a special hammer. A mission then goes to the Apostolic Chancellery and the Chamberlain supervises the destruction of the steel stamp used on the lead seals of papal documents during the reign of the deceased Pope.

Until the election of the new Pope the Chamberlain has full power, which in ancient times included the right to have money coined by the Vatican mint without accounting for it to anyone. Today he can issue postage stamps marked "Vacant See."

Each Cardinal is allowed to enter the Conclave with two trustworthy persons, one priest and one layman, but these privileged ones may not be prelates, monks or relatives of any of the Cardinals. Others admitted to the Conclave are the Monsignor Sacristan and a large clerical and lay staff to provide for the everyday necessities of the Cardinals and others.

In the last Conclave, apart from the fifty-one Cardinals, there were about two hundred people, including two doctors, a surgeon, a

chemist, nurses, valets, porters, four firemen, four barbers, two architects and various workmen such as smiths, carpenters and a plumber.
The cooking was in the hands of seven Daughters of Charity of Saint
Vincent de Paul, who are notorious for not excelling in the culinary
art, and this fact alone led one wit to predict that the Conclave would
be a short one.

Even if Cardinals arrive late they have the right of entry and
voting. This right also belongs to excommunicated Cardinals, assum-
ing that they can exist in these days as they did in the times of Boniface VIII (1295-1303). The French writer Charles de Brosses records
in his chronicle of the Conclave in which Prospero Lambertini, Pope
Benedict XIV (1740-1758) was elected, that admission was even
granted to the Neapolitan Cardinal Coscia who had been condemned
to life imprisonment for his crimes, and was locked up in Castel
Sant'Angelo.

The Cardinals generally go into the Conclave in the afternoon. But
the first day passes without any voting. They arrange their cells, pray,
pay one another visits, meet for dinner in the common refectory (last
time the Borgia Room was used), take a stroll in the internal court-
yards or pay another round of visits and then go to bed.

The next morning the Conclave really gets under way with the first
voting in the Sistine Chapel. In this can be seen the results of the
pre-Conclave discussions and the informal meetings of the previous
evening, and at this point the various forces and tendencies begin to
emerge, and the greater or lesser popularity of the candidates.

The election can take place in three ways—by inspiration, by compromise and by secret ballot—but the third way is the most common.
This is the method which modern democracy claims to have invented,
but historically it is at least seven centuries old. It consists of the
ballot-box, secret votes, the counting of the votes, and the sealing up
of voting papers or ballots.

The first two forms of election as they were codified by Pius XII
in his Apostolic Constitution of December 8, 1945 are worth noting.
The first, "by inspiration," occurs when all the Cardinals, moved
almost by the intervention of Divine inspiration, declare someone to
be Supreme Pontiff unanimously and out loud. This method also
must take place in Conclave behind closed doors, but actually it is
somewhat rare. One of those present, according to the suggestion
made by Pius XII, should stand up and speak, and the form of his
words should be something like this: Most reverent gentlemen, in
view of the personal virtue and probity of X, we consider him worthy
to be elected Supreme Pontiff, and for my part from now on I elect
him Pope.

After this, if the election is to be valid, all the other Cardinals must in a loud and clear voice pronounce the word *eligo*. (Anyone who is unable to speak must write it down.) Another condition that must be observed is that there is to be no special agreement beforehand, though this in practice would be rather difficult to ascertain.

The second system is the one by "compromise." This takes place when all the Cardinals entrust the task of choosing the new Pope to some of their number, which may be as few as three, five or seven. In this case too absolute unanimity is called for in the nomination of this small committee. The exact limits of the mandate must also be established. This means, to give some practical examples, whether the choice is to be accepted automatically as valid or whether it has to be confirmed by the Sacred College; within what time limits it has to be reached; whether the committee must decide unanimously or by majority; finally, whether someone outside the Sacred College can be chosen, as in the last election might have happened with the Archbishop of Milan, Monsignor Montini.

The Cardinals on the committee can discuss the possible candidates only in writing. "This condition is necessary," Pius XII explains with unwitting humor, "so that polite and respectful words may be used without prejudice between the electors." He knew whom he was dealing with and realized how easy it is, especially for Latin temperaments, to get heated in argument, and for the discussion to develop into something of a row.

The third system, by ballot, which was used in the election of Roncalli, had since the time of Gregory X required a majority of two thirds. Pius XII raised this to two-thirds-plus-one "so as to prevent any possibility of the two thirds including the vote of the person elected; (for no one may elect himself, or cast his vote in favor of himself) either by ballot or by compromise." Before this innovation, introduced by Pius XII, the ballots or voting sheets had to be checked, to make sure nobody had voted for himself, which was a little humiliating for the newly elected Pope.

At the time of voting only the Cardinals remain in the Sistine Chapel. Each one fills in his paper, writing the name of his candidate and attempting to disguise his handwriting as a further measure of secrecy. Then they all approach the altar, holding the paper with two fingers of the right hand, held up in such a way as to be plainly visible. Each kneels before the altar, remains for a short time in prayer and then, in a loud and clear voice, swears an oath according to a formula written on a slate: "I call to witness Christ the Lord, my judge, that I am electing him who I believe should be elected by God's will."

Then he places the paper on a paten and in the presence of the three scrutineer Cardinals, he puts it in a large chalice which is on the altar. The first to vote are the Dean and the Cardinals nursing those who are ill, who take a little box with a narrow slit, like the ones used for collecting alms, and visit those Cardinals confined to bed in their cells, and collect their ballots. When all the papers have been given up, the first of the Cardinals responsible for counting the votes covers the chalice with the paten and shakes it to mix up the ballots. The third scrutineer Cardinal then takes them out one by one, transferring them to another chalice and counting them out to check that all the Cardinals have in fact voted. Finally the actual count begins.

The first of the scrutineer Cardinals opens a ballot, reads it to himself and passes it to the second, who reads it to himself and passes it to the third. The third reads the name out aloud and all the Cardinals sitting in their chairs under canopies along the walls of the Sistine Chapel make a mark on the printed form, containing the names of all those present, which lies on the table in front of them. To avoid giving the Cardinals the trouble of adding up the marks, this is done by the scrutineers, who write on a separate sheet as follows: "The very Reverend Cardinal X has received 20 votes, the very Reverend Cardinal Y has received 15 votes," and so on. The ballots are then pierced one after another with a big needle and strung together. This remarkable garland is then tied in a knot and put aside. The votes are then counted again to find out whether a two-thirds majority has been obtained or not. If not, a second vote follows immediately, at the end of which the ballots are burnt in a stove, together with those of the first vote.

If the Pope has been elected the papers only are burnt, and the smoke that comes out of the chimney above the Sistine Chapel, to the right of Michelangelo's dome, as seen from the Piazza San Pietro, is whitish and does not last long. If on the other hand the result is negative, damp straw and pitch are burnt with the papers. In this case the smoke lasts longer and is darker in color.

The smoke signals of the last Conclave gave rise to a series of misunderstandings due largely to errors of interpretation and to the television. To say "white" or "black" smoke is not really exact. The smoke is capricious and changes color in unexpected ways, from white to gray, from gray to reddish or even to black according to the way the stuff is burning, the outside temperature, the humidity of the atmosphere, the light and other factors. The only precise criterion is how long it lasts. If the signal is short, then the Pope has certainly been elected, while if it is long (and on one occasion in the last

Conclave it lasted twenty minutes) it is certain that no one has received the necessary majority.

Interpretation of the late afternoon signals during the last Conclave, when the sun was already low and darkness was beginning in the Piazza San Pietro, was made more difficult by the television lights. In that vivid artificial light even the darkest smoke seemed much whiter and brighter than it really was. To tell the truth the two signals on Sunday, December 26, at any rate for the first few puffs, were undeniably white. And so it was that twice in succession, while the crowd was shouting "Long live the Pope," the great purveyors of world information gave out the news that a new Pope had been elected. Among those who made this mistake was even Father Pellegrino, the Vatican Radio announcer, who ought to have known that it was the duration that counted more than the color. What happened was that after the first triumphant snow-white puffs, a sinister, sluggish smoke began to belch from the chimney, gray at first but later decidedly black. Father Pellegrino, the newspapers, the television, were all forced to eat their words, not without some embarrassment; while the crowd, also taken in at first by the white smoke, began to drift away from the Piazza San Pietro, slowly and in disappointment.

As soon as one of the candidates has reached the necessary majority, the youngest of the Cardinals opens the door of the Sistine Chapel and calls for the Secretary of the Sacred College, the Prefect of Apostolic Ceremonies and the two Masters of Ceremonies.

Then the Dean (Tisserant in the last Conclave) asks for the consent of the elected candidate, in the name of the entire Sacred College, as follows: *"Acceptasne electionem de te canonice factam in Summum Pontificem?"* (Do you accept your election as Supreme Pontiff, legally carried out?)

Once the consent is given, at the end of a certain period decided on by the Cardinals by majority vote, the elected candidate becomes Pope and immediately acquires full and absolute jurisdiction over the whole Catholic world. His authority is such that anyone who questions decisions made by him even before his coronation is automatically excommunicated.

As soon as the consent is given the Dean asks the new Pope, *"Quo nomine vis vocari?"* (By which name do you wish to be called?) The Pope tells the name and generally makes a short statement to explain why he has chosen that particular name. A notary's instrument is at once drawn up, in which the Prefect of Apostolic Ceremonies acts as notary while the Secretary of the Sacred College and the two Masters of Ceremony act as witnesses.

At the same time all the canopies along the walls of the Sistine

Chapel, under which the Cardinals have sat, are lowered, with the exception of the new Pope's. The new Pope then sits on the throne and the Cardinals make their first act of obeisance, kissing his hands and feet. The Pope rises and embraces them. After this ceremony the Pope is dressed in robes which fit somewhat approximately. The Vatican tailor, naturally unable to tell beforehand who will be elected, makes vestments of three or four different cuts before the beginning of the Conclave, and these are hastily adjusted to the new Pope's size, if necessary with safety pins.

Finally the solemn moment comes when the Cardinal Pro-Dean, who in the last Conclave was Cardinal Canali, appears on the balcony of the loggia of Paul II and announces the name of the newly-elected Pope to the people gathered in St. Peter's Square. First he pronounces the traditional Latin phrase: *"Annuntio vobis gaudium magnum. Habemus Papam..."* (I bring to you glad tidings. We have a Pope), which is followed by the name which the new Pope had as a Cardinal and also the one which he has taken as Pope. Immediately afterward the Pope himself appears and imparts his first apostolic blessing *"urbi et orbi,"* to the city and to the world.

The secret of the Conclave which resulted in the election of John XXIII has not yet been violated.[1] Perhaps in the future someone may talk, in spite of the threat of excommunication, or maybe, as has happened in the past, the Pope himself, who is the only one able to authorize such a thing, may give one of the Cardinals permission to tell what happened. However, something is known, and from this and from an examination of the forces at work in the pre-Conclave discussions it is possible to reconstruct approximately what happened.

Of prime interest is the composition of the Sacred College, the fifty-one Cardinals that were locked up in the Vatican on Saturday, October 25, 1958. The Italian press, which has recently become well attuned to and pretty well informed about Vatican affairs, spoke of currents and tendencies within the Sacred College and the Roman Curia, of "right wing" and "left wing," of "Pacelliani" (followers of the rigid and intransigent line laid down by Pius XII) and "Montiniani" (supporters of the policy of Monsignor Montini, which is more open and elastic, especially in the social field). Other parties in the news at that time were "Capranicensi" and "Lateranensi" (dividing the Cardinals according to whether they had attended the

---

[1] An Italian weekly magazine published a table purporting to show exactly how each Cardinal voted in each of the votes. This is obviously based on imagination, and Roncalli himself poked fun at it in the audience given to Italian and foreign journalists after his election. He said, "The power of the press is very great . . . but the secret kept by the Cardinals is greater still."

aristocratic Collegio Capranica or the more democratic Lateran Seminary); the "pentagon" (consisting of Cardinals Canali, Ottaviani and Pizzardo, together with the two laymen—Prince Carlo Pacelli, the nephew of Pius XII, and Enrico Galeazzi, the five who at the time monopolized the key posts of the Curia and the Vatican finances). There was also reference to "reactionaries" and "progressives," "conservatives" and "reformers." These are all arbitrary categories, however, because Church affairs cannot be measured with the yardstick of lay politics. In the Church the distinctions are more subtle, and inseparable from political and social considerations there are matters of theology and doctrine.

One classification, however, must be made, if the matter is to be fully understood. The terms "right" and "left" and also, to get as close as possible to the truth, "center" must be included. Each elector, whether right, left or center represented ten million Catholics.

On the right wing there were to be found ten Italian Cardinals: Canali, Pizzardo, Ottaviani, Tedeschini, Micara, Fumasoni-Biondi, Ruffini, Mimmi, Cicognani and Siri; three Spaniards: Pla y Deniel, Quiroga y Palacios and De Arriba y Castro; two Americans: Spellman and McIntyre; one Portuguese: Cereira; two Argentinians: Copello and Caggiano; the Cuban Arteaga y Betancourt; two Brazilians: De Barros Camara and Da Silva; D'Alton of Ireland; Frings and Wendel of Germany and McGuigan and Léger of Canada. That is, twenty-six Cardinals in all.

On the left wing there were at least four Italians: Lercaro, Dalla Costa, Valeri and Ciriaci. To these must be added the six Frenchmen: Tisserant, Lienhart, Gerlier, Rocques, Feltin and Grente; Van Roey of Belgium, Tien Ken-sin of China, Gracias of India, De Vasconcellos of Brazil, Caro Rodriguez of Chile, Wyszynski of Poland, the Armenian Agagianian and Tappouni of Syria—eighteen in all.

Of those who belong in the center first of all comes Roncalli (who actually leaned somewhat to the left), Aloisi Masella (who on the contrary inclines to the right) and Fossati. Among the non-Italians were Gilroy of Australia, Luque of Colombia, De La Torre of Ecuador and De Gouveia of Portugal—a total of seven.

The right-wing group was the strongest, but not strong enough to obtain the two-thirds-plus-one majority it needed to elect its own candidate. It was also, if my information is correct, rather tired, undecided and resigned. The left-wing group was the most stable, strengthened by the compact bloc of the six Frenchmen and the Polish Cardinal who, in the absence of Stepinac and Mindszenty, represented the so-called Church of Silence—the Catholics behind the Iron Curtain. The center group, however, was convinced that a change was necessary, and consequently inclined rather more to the left than to the right. But not even the left and center together would have been able to obtain a majority and so, even before the Conclave, it was evident that a "center" candidate was needed. People were talking of a Pope of "compromise" as regards policy and of "transition" as regards age. The names of Aloisi Masella and Roncalli were most often mentioned.

It is worth noting that it was the non-Italian Cardinals themselves who wanted an Italian Pope. Indeed, to choose a French or Australian Pope, for example, could have offended all the other nations and aroused chauvinistic feelings, while to elect an Italian meant to remain in the tradition without causing prejudice. It was for this reason that some people favored Agagianian who, though Armenian by birth, has become Romanized.

A few things have leaked out about the Conclave. It is known from excellent sources that there were eleven votes. At the end of the first day, that is on Sunday evening, the Pope seemed as good as elected. That meant that the four votes of the day had gone in favor of a small number of candidates and that one of them had begun to show a lead over the others. This was probably Aloisi Masella, the one of the center group favored by the most powerful group, the right. But on the Monday, to use the expression of one of those present, "we were all at sea again."

This probably means that the left-wing group, supported by the center, had refused to budge or go back on its determination to see changes made, and that consequently Aloisi Masella failed to get his majority. Monday's voting was the most stormy and bitter; it is said that the opposing positions were further entrenched, with the right pushing its best candidate, the young and vigorous Archbishop of Genoa, Siri, and the left putting up Agagianian, perhaps in the hope of attracting the votes of non-Italian Cardinals.

But by Tuesday morning it had become clear that neither of the two extreme positions could prevail. They returned to a man of the center group, or of the left-center, such as Roncalli, who by his tact, moderation, qualities and personality would be able to draw a large number of votes. The entire left and center backed him, and finally certain less rigid elements of the right voted for him.

In the two morning votes the movement in favor of Roncalli had become evident, so that by midday the voters already knew for certain who was going to be Pope. In fact only one afternoon vote was necessary to give the Patriarch of Venice his majority, which, as far as is known, seems to have been considerably higher than the required minimum.

5

From Peasant to Pope

WHAT SORT of man is this Angelo Giuseppe Roncalli, who has risen somewhat unexpectedly to the throne of Peter and become the spiritual head of nearly half-a-billion Catholics? And what kind of life had he led up to this moment of his election? One could not do better than let him introduce himself. In 1953, as soon as he had been nominated Patriarch of Venice, Roncalli, at his first meeting with his new flock, said, "For goodness' sake don't look at your Patriarch as at a politician or a diplomat, but seek in him only the servant of God. Seek for the shepherd of souls who has been called to carry out his mission among the humble, a shepherd who in any case is unworthy of that great shepherd, Christ, and of Him whom he represents. Also when I mixed with the most powerful people, this is all I sought after."

And again, "I come from a poor family. Providence chose to take me from my native place and send me traveling throughout the world, from East to West, to bring me into contact with the most serious political and social problems. And now the end of my long experience has brought me here to Venice, between land and sea, to a city familiar to my forefathers and still more to me as a student."

These words give an idea of the simple, even humble manner of speaking of the Pope, a manner that can be understood by all. At the same time they sum up his life, except for the fact that when he

73

uttered them he was far from having come to the end of his experience. The supreme experience of being Pope had yet to come.

"I come from a poor family." His father was, in fact, a sharecropper on the estate of Count Mordani and worked a farm near Sotto il Monte, a village of about 2,000 inhabitants situated on a hill about nine miles from Bergamo, between the last foothills of the Alps and the plain of the River Adda. In this connection the Pontiff himself once remarked: "There are three ways of ruining oneself: women, gambling and farming. My father chose the most boring way." All the same, even if the Roncallis have never been rich, neither have they ever known stark poverty and, as a matter of fact, the brothers of the Pope, hard workers and savers, have been able to buy from Count Mordani the land around the farm which their father had cultivated as a sharecropper.

The Bergamo region is remarkable for large families and for the number of priests and nuns who come from it. The Roncalli family is no exception. The Pope's parents, Giovan Battista Roncalli and Marianna Mazzola, had thirteen children, ten of whom lived while three died soon after birth. Angelo, the third child and the first of the boys, was born on November 25, 1881. Three of his four brothers are still living—Zaverio, Alfredo and Giuseppe—but of his five sisters only Assunta, now a widow, has survived, and lives not far away at Longuelo. The Pope has eighteen nephews and nieces. One of them, Giovanbattista Roncalli, is parish priest of Fusignano, near Faenza, and two, Angela and Marianna, are nuns in Ethiopia and Rome, respectively.

The first day of the future Pope's life was marked by an incident that is typical. His parents, both very devout, did not wish to wait even a day before having their newly-born son baptized. Marianna Roncalli left her bed a few hours after his birth and walked with her husband to the parish church carrying in her arms her son wrapped in a blanket. The priest was away and the young couple waited for him until late at night while a freezing wind, mixed with rain and sleet, swept across the countryside and through the deserted streets of the village. This is an episode that gives an idea of the stuff of which these Bergamask peasants are made.

It would seem that it is the fate of great men never to be born near a school. All their biographers describe how, as boys, they had to cover, on foot naturally, an absurdly large number of miles to get to school. Something similar happened to Angelino, as he was then called (a diminutive that means "little angel"), when, at the age of six, he was sent to the elementary school at Sotto il Monte, about a mile and a quarter from his home. The distance grew to two miles when, having finished the elementary grades, he began to take private lessons from the priest of Cavico to prepare him for the higher classes. Angelo was rather a dullard and the priest did not spare the rod, a practice, incidentally, to which anyone who has ever had to study under priests in Italy can testify. Latin was the great stumbling block and, as Roncalli himself has admitted, "it stuck in my head only at the rate of one clout for each word."

The two miles became three (that is, six a day, there and back) when Angelo, at the age of eleven, began to attend, as an outside pupil, the grammar school at the college of Celana. But, either because he was still a little slow or because the instruction given him by the good priest of Cavico had not been sufficient, the fact is that the first year for the young student was a real flop. A glance at his final grammar school report is enough (in Italian schools the marks go from 10 to 0, 10 being the best one can get. At least 6 is required for promotion): Italian (written) 4; Italian (oral) 4; Latin (written) 5; Latin (oral) 5; geography 4; arithmetic 4; religion 7. In spite of this, perhaps because of his evident deep religious fervor, in 1892 he was admitted to the Bergamo seminary. Here at last he began to study well and to make progress. Indeed, he so distinguished himself compared to the other students that he was sent to complete his studies in Rome, at the Lateran University.

The Catholic Church, though completely based on the principle of authority and hierarchy, has never conceded much to snobbery. On the contrary, it is an organization in which persons of humble origin can make a brilliant and rapid career. In this respect it resembles American democracy rather than European countries, where the climb to the top of the social ladder is normally slow and often takes more than one generation. The Church is a good talent-scout and she takes a lot of trouble and goes to great expense to train and develop promising individuals. Usually young seminarists who have in them the makings of bishops, generals of religious orders, heads of Congregations, diplomats, theologians, rectors of colleges, and so on, are sent to Rome to finish their studies. It is in Rome that the general staff of the Church is formed. This applies to Italians as well as to Negroes, Chinese, rugby-addicted young Englishmen or football-playing American boys. In the shadow of St. Peter's the future leaders acquire the feeling of the Church's universality plus a common denomination—a spiritual Roman citizenship.

In 1904 Roncalli passed his examination in theology and was ordained priest in the church of Santa Maria in Monte Santo in Rome. On returning to Bergamo he was given a post that was to be of fundamental importance for his career and, above all, in shaping his personality and his political leanings. The famous Bishop of Bergamo, Mgr. Count Radini-Tedeschi, who inspired the Catholic labor movement, engaged him as his secretary. Roncalli has throughout his life retained a feeling of unbounded admiration and veneration for this man, whom he likes to recall in many of his addresses.

During the time that he worked with this bishop, Roncalli taught ecclesiastical history, apologetics and patristics in the Bergamo seminary. He also began historical research on San Carlo Borromeo, studies which he was to continue for the rest of his life and to which he still devotes time. This work led him to frequent the Ambrosiana Library at Milan and gave him an opportunity of meeting the then Prefect, Mgr. Achille Ratti, a future Pope and a former fellow-student of Radini-Tedeschi.

Then came the First World War. In 1915 Angelo Giuseppe Roncalli was called up and made a sergeant in the army Medical Corps. A few days after being elected Pope he recalled this fact. To an officer of the Palatine Guard who had knelt before him, John XXIII said smilingly, "Get up, get up. After all you are a captain and I am only a sergeant." During the early part of his military service, Sergeant Angelo Roncalli grew a huge and martial mustache. ("It was a weak moment on my part," as he was to confess afterward.) A few months later, after attending an officers' training course, he was given the rank of lieutenant chaplain, had his mustache shaved off and served at various military hospitals in Bergamo. He never got to the front but was most active in the rear areas. His duties included spiritual assistance to the troops and the mobilization of civilians, and he founded two organizations to encourage soldiers and students to attend Mass. Soon after the end of the war Roncalli organized at Bergamo Alta the first Students' Home, an institution that was afterward extended to the whole of Italy. He also gave several lectures at the People's University, was a Councilor of the Union of Catholic Women, and founded the first clubs of the women's section of Catholic Youth.

The fame of the dynamic priest of Bergamo reached the Vatican and in 1921 the Pope called him to Rome and sent him to the *Opera della Propagazione della Fede*, an institution for the propagation of the faith that was born in France but was subsequently taken over directly by the Vatican. He immediately distinguished himself as an organizer and, shortly afterward, was appointed President of the National Council of the *Opera* and a member of the Higher General Council. In this position he visited the most important centers of the *Opera* at Lyons, Paris, Brussels, Aachen, Munich and other European cities.

The Jubilee Year of 1925 found Roncalli engaged in his indefatigable and fruitful work for the *Opera*. At the same time he taught
patristics at the Lateran Pontifical Seminary and was a member of
the central committee for the organization of the Jubilee. Both Achille
Ratti, the former Vatican Librarian who had become Pope Pius XI
in 1922, and his State Secretary, Cardinal Gasparri, appreciated the
work and the qualities of the son of the Bergamo peasants and saw
that he had in him the makings of a diplomat. On March 19, 1925
Roncalli was consecrated bishop and sent, with the title of Apostolic
Visitor, to Bulgaria. He thus began a diplomatic career that was to
last for twenty-eight years.

The young and inexperienced diplomat found a very difficult situation to handle. When he arrived in Bulgaria there were 47,000 Catholics, of whom 40,000 belonged to the Pauline rite (similar to the
Armenian) while the others followed the Byzantine rite. The crum-
bling of the Ottoman Empire and the readjustment of frontiers that
followed the First World War had caused a lot of confusion. The
Vatican had decided in 1923 to submit the whole of Bulgaria to the
jurisdiction of an apostolic administrator, who died in 1924 before
he could be consecrated a bishop. The first task of Roncalli was to
find a new administrator. He took several months to make his choice
and finally decided on Mgr. Cyril Kourtev, who was then only thirty-
four years old. It proved a very good choice. Kourtev showed great
wisdom and even greater courage in face of Communist threats and
persecutions and held the fort until 1958, when he was arrested.

Another accomplishment of Roncalli in Bulgaria was the reorganization of the Byzantine-rite Catholics. He gave them a hierarchy,
grouped them in a single diocese, and founded a seminary which he
entrusted to the Jesuits. However, the most outstanding episode, from
the point of view of relations between the Holy See and Bulgaria,
was the marriage of King Boris to Princess Giovanna of Savoy. The
King belonged to the Orthodox Church while Giovanna was a
Catholic. The negotiations, in which Roncalli took an active part,
were very laborious and it was finally agreed that the marriage should
be celebrated according to the Catholic rite only and that the children
should be baptized as Catholics. The wedding was, indeed, celebrated
with great solemnity at Assisi, but a few days later, after the royal
couple had returned to Bulgaria, King Boris decided they should be
married again with equal solemnity, but this time according to the
Orthodox rite in the cathedral of Santa Sofia. Likewise, when the
first child, Maria Luisa, was born the King had her baptized according to the Orthodox rite. It was a blatant violation of the agreement
that had been reached and Pius XI, in a speech to the College of

Cardinals, did not hesitate to voice his indignation at this breach of trust.

Various curious details about this event were revealed some years ago by Signor Piacentini, the former Minister, who then represented Italy at Sofia. In the initial phase the discussions about the wedding took place between King Boris and Victor Emmanuel III through Signor Piacentini without the knowledge of the Vatican representative. Piacentini was summoned to Rome and had a long conversation with Victor Emmanuel. The diplomat pointed out to the King that the Bulgarian constitution explicitly established that the heir to the throne must profess the Orthodox faith. But Victor Emmanuel, who was anxious first and foremost to strengthen the dynastic bonds of the House of Savoy, did not seem unduly perturbed by this religious obstacle and handed to Piacentini a letter for King Boris in which he gave his consent to the marriage. Piacentini, alarmed by the possible complications that he already foresaw, frankly told the King, "Your Majesty, I respectfully venture to point out to you that I have two masters. One is my Minister, Count Grandi. But I am not worrying much about him. But the other is Mussolini and . . . well, you know what I mean." The King replied, "Don't worry. Leave it to me to arrange things with the head of the Government."

Before returning to Sofia, Piacentini was received by Mussolini. They spoke at length about Balkan problems and, at the end of the conversation, when Piacentini had already reached the door, Mussolini said to him, "And so I hear that this wedding cannot take place." Piacentini, who had in his brief case King Victor Emmanuel's letter of consent to King Boris, was taken aback by this unexpected remark which showed that Mussolini had been left in the dark. Not knowing how to get out of it, he smiled vaguely, raised his arm in the Fascist salute and hurried out of the room. He returned to Sofia, handed to Boris the letter of King Victor Emmanuel, and the royal engagement was announced shortly afterward.

Immediately after the second wedding celebrated by Boris and Giovanna with royal splendor according to the Orthodox rite, Piacentini received the visit of Roncalli. The Apostolic Visitor was deeply upset and protested to Italy's representative at what had occurred. Piacentini, with the skepticism and easygoing style typical of the Romans, replied, "Don't take it too seriously, Your Excellency. Actually King Boris professes the Orthodox faith and the matter is one for his conscience. As to Queen Giovanna, who is a Catholic . . . well, it means that she will go to confession." On hearing these words, Roncalli, as can well be imagined, flew into a rage. The conversation became very heated and ended only when Piacentini rang a bell and told the footman to accompany the Vatican representative to his car. Mussolini, however, always had a grudge against Piacentini because he had kept from him the fact that Victor Emmanuel had already given his consent to the wedding, and in subsequent years he did much to hamper the career of the diplomat.

During his stay in Sofia, Roncalli got to know many of the prelates who are now behind the Iron Curtain. In this connection, the painter, Franco Ferrari, who did a portrait of Roncalli when he was Patriarch of Venice, has related, "One day after a sitting he invited me into his study, opened a drawer and took from it the photographs of several bishops of Eastern Europe whom he had known during his diplomatic missions. He gazed at them with eyes filled with tears. 'This one, poor chap,' he said, 'who knows if he is still alive? This one, alas, was killed. And you see this other one? He was a saint. Here's another, but I've had no news at all of him. He's probably been arrested.' Before replacing the photographs of his ministers in the drawer, the Patriarch caressed them for some time, just as if each face were real, living flesh."

At the beginning of 1935 Roncalli was transferred from Sofia to Ankara, as Apostolic Vicar and Delegate to Turkey, to which was added the post of Delegate to Greece. He remained there for the next nine years, making frequent journeys from Ankara or Istanbul to Athens. In view of the traditional hostility between the two countries, he had to tread as skillfully as a tightrope walker so as not to arouse any suspicion or resentment on the part of either government. A fact that complicated things was that the faithful of the two countries in which he represented the Holy See belonged to various religious rites—Greek, Armenian, Coptic, Slav and Syrian. It was during this period that he was able to acquire a profound knowledge of the problems of the Eastern Church and to understand what Rome can do to promote a return of the schismatics to the bosom of the mother Church.

During Roncalli's stay in Turkey, Kemal Ataturk introduced various drastic reforms, which included the closing down of both Coptic and Koranic schools and a prohibition on the wearing in public of ecclesiastical vestments of any religion whatsoever. In this connection Roncalli relates, "I was half a civilian for nearly ten years. I had to change my clothes every time I entered or left a church."

When the Second World War broke out, Ankara and Istanbul became hotbeds of spies. The Apostolic Delegate was closely watched by agents of the Intelligence Service, the *Deuxième Bureau*, the *Gestapo*, the Russian NKVD and the Fascist secret service SIM. "I learned to recognize them all," Roncalli recalls smilingly, "but I have never really known whether they were keeping an eye on me or whether they were watching each other."

The former German Foreign Minister, von Papen, whose place in Hitler's good books had been taken by von Ribbentrop, was packed off as Ambassador to Ankara with the difficult task of keeping Turkey neutral and, as usual, he became the center of a network of intrigues. At Ankara, too, was Sir Hugh Knatchbull Hughessen, the British Ambassador, with his still more famous valet, Cicero, perhaps the greatest spy of all times, who filched from the British Embassy the most secret documents to sell to von Papen. That subsequently, because of the rivalry between von Ribbentrop and von Papen, between the SS and the Ministry of Foreign Affairs, the Germans never made use of the information secured by Cicero to the extent that it warranted, is another story. The fact is that Roncalli, who in his mission, as was his duty, steered a skillful course between the Greeks and Turks, Germans and Allies, also used to visit the British Embassy and certainly encountered the legendary spy there.

He was also in contact with von Papen. This old German fox, who had realized that Germany would lose the war, had, with consummate foresight, begun even at that time to separate his own responsibility from that of the Nazis. In his conversations with the representative of the Holy See, von Papen was already thinking of the future by making it very clear indeed that he was taking no share in the crimes of Hitler's henchmen and that he was carrying out his task of ambassador solely in the hope of being able to shorten the war. It is highly probable that if he had not created such an alibi, which was confirmed by Roncalli, and if the Holy See had not intervened in his favor during the Nuremberg trials, he too would have shared the fate of the other Nazi criminals instead of getting away with a short term in prison and today living hale and hearty.[1]

[1] How close the friendship between Roncalli and von Papen was is shown by the letter that the Papal Nuncio wrote on August 4, 1944 from Büyükada to the German Ambassador when the latter was recalled to Berlin, in which he said:

"You can well believe how sad my heart is that you are leaving Turkey. In accordance with the spirit of my duty I was always careful to keep myself aloof from the conflicting parties. I shall therefore carefully refrain from passing judgment on the present circumstances. I prefer to trust that these too are determined by Providence for a greater good.

"During the years you have stayed in this country, Excellency, I have always felt a deep pleasure both in realizing personally and in hearing eulogized without exception your standing as a most distinguished diplomat and as an exemplary Catholic. Thus you have carried out a highly exemplary mission for your country and rendered a most precious service to the Catholic Church.

"Allow me to thank you once again, Excellency, for the continuous, patient and manifold favors shown to the Apostolic Delegation in these years, with a particular

In December 1944, while he was in Athens, a telegram in code reached him from the State Secretariat. The code clerk happened to be away and Roncalli sat down patiently to decipher the text. The telegram contained the order to proceed immediately to Rome as he had been appointed Nuncio in Paris. He could not believe his eyes and thought that he must have made some mistake in using the key to the code. But on his return the code clerk confirmed the accuracy of the message. Roncalli went to Rome and called at the State Secretariat. Here he expressed his doubts about his capacity to carry out so important a mission. The reply was, "You can't see yourself as the Nuncio at Paris? To be frank, neither can we. But we think the others are even less suitable than you."[2]

The post was indeed important and the moment extremely delicate. General de Gaulle had assumed power and had asked that the Nuncio, Valerio Valeri, should be removed because he was guilty of having stayed in his appointment under the collaborationist government of Pétain and Laval; he was also accused of having had too

reference to my ministry as Apostolic Delegate to Greece, and also for the service connected with the religious interests of the German-speaking Catholics in Turkey. For this, too, your memory here will remain dear and blessed.

"Once the storm that is disrupting everything has passed, calm days will return and I trust that we shall meet again and find consolation together in the fruits that have resulted from the present tribulation. I would like my humble name to remain with you as that of a friend who will never belie the purity of his feelings, as that of a bishop of the Church of God whose prayers and whose benediction will always be extended to you, to your loving family and to everything that is nearest to your spirit. I love to recall with particularly pious affection your worthy wife, the Lady Ambassadress Martha, your good and distinguished daughters and also your beloved Franz, who deserves the more to be respected since he carries in his limbs the marks of his sacrifice as a noble son of Germany.

"Excellency, I would like to say to you once again: courage and faith. The numerous testimonies of respect, admiration and of good wishes that in these days you are receiving are the just and grateful expression of a human sentiment. May my very simple words be acceptable to you as the touch of something that comes from God and possesses the virtue of soothing and reassuring the most sacred recesses of your religious soul in its twofold aspiration toward the greater good of Germany—the always great Germany—and toward the peace and prosperity of the Catholic Church, common mother of souls and of the peoples.

"May the Lord preserve you, you and your dear ones, from all evil and keep you for a new task *pro aris et focis*. I will not say good-bye to you. But I say again, moved and confident, au revoir."

(Roncalli's prediction that they would meet again after the storm came true fifteen years later. On January 19, 1959 von Papen was received in private audience by John XXIII.)

[2] In a letter to a friend, commenting wittily on his appointment to Paris, Roncalli quoted the Latin saying: *"Ubi deficiunt equi trottant aselli"* (Where there are no horses, donkeys will do).

many and too cordial contacts with the notorious Abetz, von Ribbentrop's representative at Paris.

At the beginning of 1945, soon after Roncalli had taken up his
post, General de Gaulle presented him with a pretty long list of
bishops whom he wished to see replaced because they too were
regarded as guilty of collaboration with the Germans. Roncalli gave
an evasive reply and asked to be furnished with a dossier on each
prelate. A few days later he returned the papers to the French Government with the notation, "I have found here only cuttings from
the newspapers. I would like well-founded documents. Will you
please let me have them." Such documents, of course, never came to
hand and, in the end, only three bishops were replaced since in the
meantime the purge frenzy had calmed down. This is a typical
example of the temporizing tactics of Roncalli, who is in the habit
of saying that time of itself solves almost all problems.

During his eight years in Paris, the Nuncio, who hates red tape
and prefers personal contacts, dictated only one diplomatic note to
his secretary. On the other hand, he made a circle of friends which
anyone might envy. His first meeting with de Gaulle was most cold
and formal. Roncalli let a day or two pass, then made his call and
during their very frank conversation put his cards on the table. The
General was highly impressed by the clear, courageous and direct
position taken up by the new Nuncio and from then onward they
were friends. The Nunciature very soon became an important meeting place, a political and also literary *salon*. Roncalli's luncheons
became famous throughout Paris. His cook was a certain Roger, who
subsequently became well known after opening in the Rue des Grands
Augustins a restaurant called *La Grenouille,* the specialty of which
is, in fact, fried frogs' legs. Among its patrons are the Duke and
Duchess of Windsor and all the film stars who pass through Paris.
It has a slight underworld atmosphere that seems to stimulate the
appetite of its patrons. Speaking of the Pope, Roger says, *"Il était
gros comme un curé mais il mangeait comme un oiseau. C'est pas la
nourriture qui le rembourrait, c'étaient les livres"* (He was as fat
as a curate but he ate like a bird. It was not the food that stuffed him
out but his books). Roger naturally did not mean to say that Roncalli
literally devoured books but that his excessive reading, the sitting too
long at his desk and his lack of exercise made him put on weight
despite the fact that he eats little.

Besides exquisite food Roncalli used to offer his guests excellent
wines, renowned liqueurs, which he hardly tasted himself, and choice
cigars, which he never touched, though now and then he smoked a

cigarette. Among the habitual visitors to the Nunciature were Herriot, Léon Blum, Auriol, Schumann, Pinay, Monnerville, René Mayer, Bidault, Pleven, in short, the whole of what can be called the general staff of French politics. And they were attracted not solely by Roger's excellent cuisine, by the fine cigars and liqueurs, but also by the personality of the Nuncio, by his cordial manner, by his wit and by the restful feeling that he inspired. Schumann said of him, "He is the only man in Paris in whose company one feels a physical sensation of peace."

In his addresses Roncalli was fond of quoting La Fontaine, and he did so once when presenting to the President of the Republic, Auriol, the New Year good wishes for 1950, in the name of the Diplomatic Corps. At the end of the speech Auriol wished to congratulate him and said with a smile, "Fine, fine. I recognized La Fontaine in spite of the accent." Whereupon Roncalli came back, "I understand that, your Excellency. It took me a long time, too, to get used to yours."

Paris still remembers an episode that shows the tact and at the same time the finesse of the Nuncio. On the eve of one of the many elections held in France the clergy had indicated that the M.R.P. was the Catholic Party and had ignored the fact that de Gaulle's party had also proclaimed itself to be Catholic. Pierre de Gaulle, brother of the General, was then Mayor of Paris and relations between him and Rome were somewhat strained. The Nuncio was invited to attend a ceremony to celebrate the bimillennium of the capital. In his speech Pierre de Gaulle pulled a fast one on Roncalli by saying, "The Nuncio's presence with us is proof that the Church has changed its opinion and that it considers the Gaullist party, too, as Catholic." Roncalli did not bat an eyelid; he said nothing. A few minutes later, however, during the opening of an exhibition of antique books, he took from a shelf a volume, showed it to the Mayor of Paris and said to him with a slightly malicious smile, "This was written by a Bergamask like me and deals with good manners. Read it." The book in question was by Gasparino da Barsizza, a humanist of the fifteenth century and had been printed in France.

Another Parisian who experienced the quick though never nasty wit of the Nuncio was an anonymous carpenter who had been called to put up a new bookshelf in the Nunciature. As he was driving a nail into a plank the hammer slipped and hit one of his fingers. The carpenter started yelling and using blasphemous words. Roncalli heard him from the next room, tiptoed right behind him, tapped him on the shoulder and told the startled carpenter: *"Alors, que ce que*

c'est ça? Vous ne pouvez pas dire merde comme tous le monde?"
(Well now, what's this? Can't you say "filth" like everybody else
does?).

When Roncalli was made Cardinal by Pius XII on January 12,
1953, it was his old friend, Auriol, who, as President of the Republic,
placed the Red Hat on his head. Three days later the Pope nominated
him Patriarch of Venice and Roncalli left Paris amid general regret.
At the moment of leaving he remarked, "I sincerely hope that you
may be able to say of me, when you remember my stay in Paris, 'He
was a loyal and peaceful priest. Always, and on every occasion, a
sound and sincere friend of France.'"

From the purely religious point of view Roncalli's stay in Paris
coincided with the experiment of the worker-priests. Roncalli's attitude toward this sad and dramatic development among the French
clergy is not known with exactitude, but something can be divined.
A few months before Roncalli reached Paris, two courageous French
Abbés, Godin and Daniel, had published the results of a striking
investigation into the decadence of religious feeling in the country.
The book was entitled "France a Missionary Country?" and Cardinal
Suhard, after reading it, crossed out the question mark from the title
with a red pencil. A subsequent inquiry by Canon Boulard confirmed
the gravity of the situation: Among the workers, religion was something almost unknown and the same applied to several particular
zones in the agricultural areas, the result being that out of every
four Frenchmen, three no longer went to church. In certain industrial
centers the proportion rose to an appalling degree: Out of ten, sometimes fifteen thousand inhabitants, the churchgoers would not exceed
two hundred. There was a scarcity of priests and the number of
parishes without a priest had by 1943 risen to 15,416. This was a
truly alarming state of affairs that had to be energetically faced, with
enthusiasm, with new methods and without prejudice.

The more militant among the French clergy accepted the challenge
and threw themselves ardently into the struggle. The first factory
parishes were established, the liturgy was revised so that it could be
understood even by those who had not received any religious instruction and did not know any Latin, and the first worker-priests were
sent out from the famous seminary of the *Mission de France.* These
priests went into the factories and there shared the hard toil with
the workmen. They wore overalls or civilian clothes, lived in the
workers' tenements and often in the hovels of the *banlieu,* went with
their fellow-workers to the taverns, celebrated Mass wherever they
could, often at a factory bench or at a kitchen table which was made
to serve as an altar. On the whole the first results were encouraging.

A breach began to be opened in the massive barrier of working-class atheism, the intellectuals resumed a speaking relationship with the Church that had long been abandoned and a wave of enthusiasm swept through the French clergy.

Naturally, dangers were inherent in all this. First of all there was the risk that the worker-priests, immersed so deeply and inexorably in the everyday life of the common folk, might succumb to the temptations of the flesh (and, in fact, several of them did leave the priesthood and got married). Then there was the danger that, instead of influencing their environment, they might end by becoming its victims. Various scandals resulted and the climax seemed to have been reached in 1952 when two priests of the *Mission de France* were arrested, together with many Communists, while leading a violent demonstration in the streets against NATO and General Ridgway; or when the Abbé Barreau accepted the nomination as secretary of the Paris Steel Workers' Federation, which was linked with the Confédération Générale du Travail and was controlled by the Communists.

Roncalli certainly must have informed Pius XII of these dangers. But although the worker-priests were looked upon with suspicion by the Vatican, they were allowed to go on. It was only after Roncalli became Pope that the Holy Office issued a decree that put an end to this courageous experiment.

But the most splendid and happiest period of Roncalli's career is that which lasted for five years, when he was Patriarch of Venice. He entered Venice, a city that he already knew and loved, on March 16, 1953, joyfully acclaimed by the population. Only the windows of the Town Hall remained closed as he passed, for the municipal council was in the hands of the Communists, who preferred to ignore the event. Roncalli smilingly remarked, "We shall have those windows reopened." From the very beginning a great, spontaneous sympathy was established between the Patriarch and the Venetians, a kind, tolerant, soft-spoken, somewhat skeptical people, who immediately appreciated the geniality and spontaneity and good humor of their new pastor. The Venetian clergy, who had been kept on tenterhooks by his brusque and authoritarian predecessor, Mgr. Carlo Agostini, nicknamed Roncalli "the calm after the storm."

This does not mean, however, that the new Patriarch just folded his arms and watched and let things slide or go on as others wished. With tact, with discretion, with courtesy, but always knowing exactly what he was aiming at, he completely reorganized his vast patriarchate (which, in addition to Venice, embraces also a large section of the mainland) and showed a sound instinct in choosing his col-

laborators and assigning the various tasks to those most competent
to carry them out. Roncalli's discretion came out also in small things.
If by chance he met an unshaven priest he would send him the gift
of a razor. To another who was wearing a collar that was not exactly
white and spotless he would say with a smile, "My dear————,
I've a dozen collars that have become too tight for me. If you have
no objection, I'll make you a present of them."

As regards the daily life of his flock, he made a point of being
present at all the municipal events and in a short time he came to
be recognized as the first citizen of Venice, even more so than the
Mayor. Indeed, from certain points of view, he was a kind of
Renaissance prince. In contrast with his predecessor he did not pretend to ignore the two greatest events of the Venice season, the Film
Festival and the Biennial Art Show. He never failed to visit all the
pavilions of the Art Show, including those where the nudest of nudes
were shown, without making any comment. As regards the Film
Festival, while obviously he did not attend the actual projections,
he each year gave a splendid and luxurious reception at his Palace,
to which were invited indiscriminately Soviet producers and actors
and several film stars who had been the center of shocking scandals.

In the Patriarch's Palace there was a continuous coming and going
of people. Roncalli received everyone; it seemed as if he was never
in a hurry yet at the same time he managed to get through an enormous amount of work. Many illustrious men whom he had met
during his diplomatic career came to Venice to see him. Among them
were President Auriol and Cardinal Feltin of France. To honor his
guests on these occasions Roncalli had the "Marseillaise"—the anthem
of the French Revolution—played in St. Mark's Square by the municipal band.

When Cardinal Wyszynski, the Primate of Poland, was released
from jail by Gomulka and allowed to pay a visit to Rome, he was
met at the Mestre railway station by Roncalli. As the train was sched-
uled to stop for three-quarters of an hour, Roncalli suggested to his
Polish colleague a short sightseeing tour of Venice by motorboat. The
Primate of Poland was so enraptured by the beauty of the Grand
Canal that he did not notice that time was flying. Suddenly he
looked at his watch and exclaimed in anguish, "Good heavens! my
train has left." Roncalli smiled and reassured him, "Don't worry.
You see that gentleman sitting at the back of our motorboat? Well,
he's the Mestre station master and I kidnaped him. While he is with
us the train cannot leave."

But if in his relations with the world he showed himself extremely
tolerant and fond of social life, he never compromised where the

protection of morality or the behavior of his parishioners was concerned. There is a letter of his to the faithful, dated August, 1957, in which he advised priests and members of religious orders not to come to Venice during the summer when crowds of tourists, often too scantily dressed, besmirch the true face of the city. In December of the same year, in his diocesan bulletin, he condemned the purchase of television sets by priests and set forth the following reasons:

"(a) A television set is a luxury object that conflicts with the poverty and want of many of the faithful; (b) it represents a true attack on the priest by worldly things and by all their seductions; (c) it brings with it a great danger of waste of time, of dissipation, and of spiritual decadence; (d) it lowers the prestige of the priest in the eyes of the faithful, who can be disturbed by the mere thought that their priest, who celebrates the Holy Mysteries, has, without any sound reason connected with his pastoral duties, been watching television programs."

During his stay in Venice Roncalli was very happy. He loved the unique beauty of the city. He had a terrace built on the top floor of the archiepiscopal palace, where he used to go toward 5 o'clock in the morning, read his breviary, listen to the voice of the church bells, which he learned to recognize individually, and delight in the spectacle of the city and the lagoon in the early sunlight. He loved the Venetians for their kind and cordial character, so similar to his own, and he often stopped for a chat with the gondoliers and the citizens he met on his walks. It is only natural that a host of anecdotes should become linked with his name. Thus the story is told in Venice of the time when he saw his secretary give one hundred lire to a needy person and benevolently reproved him, pointing out that as things are today a gift, if it is to be of any real use, should be at least a thousand lire. According to another story, a very stout man once ran so hard to catch up with him that he reached Roncalli puffing like a grampus, whereupon the Patriarch remarked, "The Lord is bound to be particularly tolerant with us fat men."

While very few witticisms have been linked with the name of Pius XII, a whole crop of them have been gathered from the lips of John XXIII. His own stoutness is one of the subjects about which Roncalli is always ready to joke. In addition to the episode just mentioned, there are several others. On the eve of the Conclave, to a flatterer who told him he thought he had lost weight, Roncalli replied, "Not at all. But do you know what I do when I feel I'm too fat? I just go and stand next to Cicognani and then I feel I've become as thin as a rail." Cardinal Cicognani, in fact, is the most bulky and rotund of the whole Sacred College. According to another story,

John XXIII, some days after his election, paid an unannounced visit to the Vatican carpenters' shop. The nervousness and awe felt by the workmen soon disappeared when Roncalli sent for a bottle of wine and drank a toast with them. At a certain point he turned to one of the carpenters and suddenly said, "I bet you belong to the same party as I do." The man hardly knew what to say and so as not to commit himself said, "Holy Father, I haven't joined any party." Roncalli's reply came pat, "There's no need to join the party I'm speaking of. You're a member automatically. I mean the fat men's party."

Speaking to a group of French paratroopers he said, "Well, boys, while you're busily engaged in falling from the sky, I wouldn't like you to forget how to get up there." Another wisecrack from his Paris days was made by Roncalli at a party. When a shapely young woman in a low-cut dress entered, the Nuncio was heard to remark, "I wonder why, when a pretty woman comes in, everyone, instead of looking at her, watches me to see what sort of a face the Nuncio is making." He has shown no trace of being shy of women and, during his career as a diplomat, he often met women of high society, whose company he seemed to enjoy and with whom he had not the slightest difficulty in carrying on brilliant and witty conversations. To someone of little tact who during a reception had put an embarrassing question to him about the Church, Roncalli remarked, "When I am at a party religion is a subject I prefer not to touch upon." To anyone who complimented him on his diplomatic ability Roncalli used to reply, "I confine myself to speaking the truth. Perhaps that is why I am taken for an accomplished diplomat. But if I am a diplomat, I am so unintentionally."

His good humor is difficult to repress. The story goes that after the death of Pius XII a delegation of Venetian notables called on him to present their condolences. All of them looked sad and downcast. Roncalli listened to them for a while, then clapped his hands and smilingly said, "*Su, su, morto un Papa se ne fa un altro*" (Come on now, when a Pope is dead they make another), and he then started to tell them an anecdote. This episode reveals something of the personality of Roncalli, and is in keeping with the idea that, for a true believer, death is but a release, the passage to a better life and not, as it is for the faithless, something sad and definitive to be feared.

Since he has taken up residence in the Vatican, Roncalli has made but little change in his habits. He was already accustomed to a life of intense work, methodical and orderly, to granting frequent audiences and to making speeches. The fact that he needs little sleep helps him to get through a notable amount of work. The present Pope, by contrast to Pacelli who used to go to bed very late, retires about 10 P.M. but rises at three or four in the morning. Sometimes he sleeps only till 1 A.M. He then gets up, works or reads in the deep stillness of the night until about 6 o'clock, when he returns to bed until 8 o'clock.

The place of Mother Pasqualina and the Bavarian nuns who looked after Pius XII has been taken by four nuns of the *Poverelle* order of Bergamo. Instead of the regular nun's garb they wear what may be called working clothes, the main items of which are a long, gray-striped skirt and a short, black cape over the shoulders. They wear no coif and their hair is done up into a bun at the nape of the neck. The kitchen and the clothes of the Pope are under the care of Sister Pierpaola, a slightly-built woman of about sixty, while the cleaning is done by Sister Primarosa and Sister Nazarita, the three being under the direction of the housekeeper, Mother Saveria Bertoli, an active and intelligent woman who worked for nine years at the College for the Propagation of the Faith. Roncalli's valet at Venice, Guido Gusso, was also transferred to the Vatican together with his wife and has been appointed an assistant in the Pope's household. Although as has already been remarked his corpulence might lead one to think the contrary, the Pope is a very small eater and pays little attention to what is set before him. Sister Pierpaola relates that during the five years she worked for him in Venice, not once did Roncalli ask her to prepare a special dish. The Pope himself once revealed to a friend the secret of his good health and his unfailing good humor. "I don't suffer from either liver or nerves. I like to meet people and I never feel embarrassed."

And he certainly doesn't, as anyone who has been admitted to a papal audience with him can testify. He is so relaxed, so completely free of self-consciousness, that automatically he puts you at ease too. In the presence of Pacelli, whether one was a Catholic or not, one could not help feeling, despite his benign manner, a certain awe. When one is confronted with Roncalli it is like meeting an old, very kind, very dear uncle one has always known and whom one can trust. In this respect a special mannerism of John XXIII probably gives a good clue to his character and his approach to his fellow-men. All Popes refer to themselves as "fathers" of the faithful. Roncalli does this too but, almost invariably in the course of the same speech, and very often in the next sentence, he adds "and the brother."

6

Pope John XXIII,
Un Papa Simpatico

OF JOHN XXIII it has been said that he was both a transition and a compromise Pope. *Transition,* because of his seventy-seven years of age at the time of his election; *compromise,* because he was not clearly identified with any of the trends or types into which the College of Cardinals is divided: right or left, conservatives or progressives, diplomats or shepherds of souls. It must be admitted that while Pius XII was still alive nobody thought of the then Patriarch of Venice as a future Pope. Roncalli was liked and highly thought of in Venice, but his name was hardly ever in the news in Italy and he was practically unknown in the rest of the world. By contrast, there were in the College of Cardinals several powerful personalities—such, for example, as the Frenchman Tisserant, or the Armenian Agagianian, or the two Italian Cardinals, Giuseppe Siri and Giacomo Lercaro, Archbishops of Genoa and Bologna, respectively—who stole the limelight and in the Vatican jargon were labeled as "papabili," that is, the most likely successors to Eugenio Pacelli. Some of the American newspapers were even putting forward the candidature of Cardinal Francis Spellman, Archbishop of New York, but in the Vatican this was never taken too seriously.

It was only after the death of Pius XII, when it became clear that none of the trends or types inside the Sacred College was strong enough to impose its own candidate and obtain a two-thirds majority, that the Cardinals began to look for a less strong personality, for a man who was likable, middle-of-the-road, without too many enemies, not too young, and around whom agreement could be reached. It was then that the names of Benedetto Aloisi Masella and Angelo Giuseppe Roncalli started creeping to the fore as possible compromise candidates. As has been noted, it took the College of Cardinals four days and eleven polls before a two-thirds majority could be formed and Roncalli became the new Pope.

A compromise Pope, a transition Pope, then? The first acts of John XXIII looked as if he meant to say, "I'll let you have this compromise; I'll show you all about transition." From the very first days of his pontificate, Roncalli has shown such an ease, such a frank and direct style of facing problems and of coming immediately to the point that one can safely say that those who backed him as a compromise and transitional figure have been disappointed. In fact, one is inevitably reminded of the historical precedent of Sixtus V (1585-1590), who, after entering the Conclave in poor health and leaning on a stick, and being elected precisely because it was expected that he would not last long, as soon as he ascended the throne of Peter threw away his stick, summoned the executioner and began one of the most splendid and also one of the most ruthless pontificates in the history of the Church. It is true that he reigned for only five years, but in those five years he pacified the pontifical State by exterminating banditry, he reformed the Church from top to bottom and he gave Rome a new face with a building program, the daring and magnificence of which arouses astonishment to this day.

This is not to say that the easy-going, benevolent Roncalli is a new Sixtus V. But it is certain that from the first hours of his pontificate he showed himself to be a man who knows what he wants and does it without hesitation. It is therefore useful to make an examination of his reign so far in order to understand his policy and to guess at what the future is likely to bring.

Immediately after his election, Roncalli assumed the name of John XXIII. It is a name that had fallen into disuse for six centuries and had been discredited for five, that is, since 1415, when an antipope, the Neapolitan Baldassarre Cossa (1410-1415), who had taken the very name of John XXIII, was deposed and imprisoned by the Council of Constance. Roncalli did not hesitate to break the long and monotonous tradition of the Piuses, the Gregorys, the Leos, the Benedettos and to defy the ghost of the old antipope.

While Roncalli was being robed with the pontifical vestments for the first time, he removed from his head the Cardinal's skullcap and placed it on the head of the Secretary of the Conclave, Mgr. Alberto Di Jorio, thus creating him a Cardinal "on the field," so to speak. The gesture was a return to a tradition that had been allowed to lapse by the four preceding Pontiffs; it showed a desire to get moving, and quickly.

He kept the Cardinals in Conclave until the morning of the day following the election. The fifty high ecclesiastical dignitaries were thus compelled to pass another night in the uncomfortable and chilly cells of the Vatican instead of returning to their hospitable colleges, convents and hotels in Rome. A gesture that was justified by the fact that the extension of the Conclave gave him the chance of speaking, no longer as a colleague, but as Pope, with many of those who otherwise would have dispersed to various parts of the world without his being able to see them again for a long time. In any case, it was a gesture by which he at once asserted his will and his authority.

He immediately re-established the *di tabella* audiences, that is, those that are held on fixed days at fixed hours, and at which the Cardinals, the heads of Congregations and of orders, and other high functionaries of the complex administrative machine of the Holy See are entitled to be received by the Pope. These particular audiences had been suspended in 1954 during the serious illness of Pius XII, and had never been resumed. In effect, it had become more difficult, just to give an example, for Cardinal Tisserant to be received by the Pope than it was for, say, Clare Boothe Luce or Gary Cooper when they might happen to be passing through Rome. In this connection, the story goes that an American prelate, a judge of the Sacred Rota, after several months had passed in vain waiting, since the time when the body of which he was a member had asked to be received by Pius XII, finally suggested, "Let's all dress up as football players. Then we'll certainly be received right away."

The resumption of the *di tabella* audiences signified that Roncalli thought that the Pope should no longer be isolated the way Pacelli had been, but should be accessible, in direct and frequent contact with his collaborators and a source of wise counsel for the men responsible for the affairs of the Church. Connected with this change of style is his order to re-open the Vatican Gardens to whoever may wish to use them (while, as already observed, in Pacelli's time they were forbidden to all, and not even the gardeners could show their faces when the Pope was taking his walks), as well as his surprise and informal visits to the Vatican Radio, the carpenters' shop and other offices of the minute State. Another significant detail is that

Roncalli has abolished the tradition that the Pope should eat alone. Practically every day, both at lunch and at dinner, he has one or two guests at his table, and usually treats them to superior French champagne.

Furthermore, to show even more clearly the individual style of John XXIII, there is the fact that his collaborators find it very difficult to keep him in the Vatican. The self-imposed "imprisonment" of the Roman Pontiffs lasted from 1870 to 1929, when Mussolini and Pius XI settled the differences between the Church and the State by the Lateran Pact. But the habit had become established, and Pius XII left the Vatican only very seldom and whenever he did, it was quite a State affair. John XXIII, on the contrary, likes to slip out at the slightest provocation to visit a hospital or a jail, to inaugurate a new college or convent, to call on an old friend who has been taken ill. And once he is on the road, to the despair of the Italian police on motorcycles who escort him, he likes to deviate from the appointed route to take a look at an old church or at a view or, very often, just for the fun of it. His frequent and unexpected excursions outside the Vatican have led Anglo-American correspondents in Rome to nickname him "Johnny Walker."[1] To complete the pun and to stay within the province of whisky, somebody suggested that his private telephone number should be VAT 69!

Roncalli certainly has been moving fast. In his twenty-year reign Pacelli held only two Consistories to appoint new Cardinals. In less than seventeen months Roncalli held three, and nominated so many Cardinals (thirty-eight) that he far exceeded the *plenum* of seventy established by the pugnacious and despotic Pope Sixtus V, who had also threatened to excommunicate anyone who should dare to exceed the number. But Popes are not bound by the wishes or orders of their predecessors, and after the third Consistory was announced by Roncalli in March, 1960, the College of Cardinals reached the record number of eighty-five.

In his first Consistory, January 15, 1958, shortly after his election, John XXIII made twenty-three new Cardinals, thirteen of whom were Italians.

[1] Roncalli has always been very fond of traveling by car, which he prefers to trains or planes. Evidence of this is found in a letter he wrote in 1950 from Paris to a baroness from Bergamo who had asked him to officiate at the wedding of her daughter. "This time, too," Roncalli wrote, "I shall come to Bergamo with my car. Enrico is busy somewhere else and much to his regret he will not be able to drive me. I will go with my usual driver, Dino, who is also very good and who deserves the title of 'Dino the African' as he has driven me for forty days across the whole of North Africa, including the return journey from Morocco and across Spain, covering 10,000 kilometers without the slightest hitch."

The thirteen Italians were: Giovan Battista Montini, Giovanni Urbani, Paolo Giobbe, Giuseppe Fietta, Fernando Cento, Carlo Chiarlo, Amleto Cicognani, Carlo Confalonieri, Alfonso Castaldo, Domenico Tardini, Alberto Di Jorio, Francesco Bracci and Francesco Roberti.

Italians now hold all the key posts of the Curia. The exceptions confirm the rule: the Argentinian Cardinal Copello was placed at the head of the not so important Chancery while the brilliant and controversial French Cardinal Eugene Tisserant was removed from the Oriental Church Congregation he had successfully led for twenty-three years and left with the rather insignificant Congregation of the Ceremonial and the honorary title of Librarian of the Holy Roman Church.

The ten non-Italian Cardinals appointed by John XXIII in his first Consistory to fill the gaps abroad were: the Bishop of Berlin, Julius Doepfner, who was only forty-five years old, and thus became the youngest member of the Sacred College; Francis Koenig, Archbishop of Vienna, who is deeply versed in the history of religions; José Bueno Monreal, Archbishop of Seville, who has taken the place of the late, and pugnacious Cardinal Segura, so well known for having rebelled not only against Franco but also against the Holy See; Richard John Cushing, Archbishop of Boston, author of studies in the social sphere; Paul Maria Richaud, Archbishop of Bordeaux; John O'Hara, Archbishop of Philadelphia, who is very popular in the United States; William Godfrey, Archbishop of Westminster; Anthony Maria Barbieri, Archbishop of Montevideo; Joseph Garibi y Rivera, Archbishop of Guadalajara, the first Cardinal Mexico has ever had; Andrew Jullien, who, though French, has passed most of his seventy-six years in Rome, and who was the Dean of the judges of the Sacred Rota.

In his second Consistory, held December 14, 1959, the Pope gave the red hat to three Italians, Paolo Marella, Gustavo Testa and Francesco Morano, and to five non-Italians, that is the German Jesuit Father Augustin Bea (former confessor of Pius XII and the first Jesuit for a long time to become a Cardinal), the English William Heard (former Dean of the Sacred Rota, a lawyer converted from the Church of England); the Spaniard Father Arcadio Larraona of the Claretiani; the American Nuncio to Berlin, L. J. Muench; and the Archbishop of Chicago, Albert Gregory Meyer. These appointments, with the exception of the Chicago Archbishop and of Cardinal Marella who remained Nuncio to Paris, were made with the Ecumenical Council in mind. All are experts in theology or Canon Law and are being employed by the Pope to prepare the forthcoming universal congress of the Catholic Church.

The third Consistory of March 1960, in which John XXIII nominated two Italian and five non-Italian Cardinals, proved to be the first time in the history of the Church that the dignity of the purple was conferred on either a Negro, a Japanese or a Filipino—an example of Roncalli's disregard for precedent. The Negro Cardinal, Laurian Rugambwa, bishop of Rutabo, Tanganyika, one of the youngest members of the Sacred College, was born in 1912. The appointment of Peter Tatsuo Doi, formerly Archbishop of Tokyo, is a reward to a Catholic community which, although small, is one of the oldest and is celebrated for its numerous martyrs. The Filipino Cardinal, Rufino J. Santos, formerly Archbishop of Manila, studied theology in Rome. The other Cardinals appointed are: Luigi Traglia of Rome; Luigi Bacci, of the State Secretariat; Joseph Lefebvre, formerly Archbishop of Bourges, France; and Bernard Jan Alfrink, formerly Archbishop of Utrecht. The Pope nominated as Secretary of State Cardinal Domenico Tardini. This caused some surprise since, in view of the friendship between Roncalli and Montini and bearing in mind the political tendencies of the latter, it was widely expected that the important post would go to the Archbishop of Milan. On second thoughts, however, the wisdom of John XXIII's decision can only be admired. The nomination of Tardini—a man standing much further to the right than Montini, and known to have strong monarchist leanings—represents a friendly gesture toward that group of the Sacred College, that is, the extreme right, which had opposed the election of Roncalli to the very last. The new Pope clearly wished to restore harmony among his closest collaborators, while Montini at the head of the State Secretariat would have meant an exacerbation of the conflict. In the formal sense, too, Tardini's nomination is correct, for at the time of Pacelli's death he was the highest official of the State Secretariat.

No doubt the most sensational and far-reaching initiative of the present Pope was his decision to call an Ecumenical Council in 1963. In the whole twenty centuries of Church history there have been only twenty-one such Councils and they were all called either to settle fundamental theological disputes or in moments of dramatic crises. The last was held in 1870 and was interrupted after the Piedmontese occupation of Rome. It is somewhat ironical that such a history-making decision should have been taken by John XXIII, who has been defined as a Pope of compromise and a Pope of transition. The calling of the Council means that the present Pope feels that the Church is at a vital crossroad and that the normal consultative methods (Consistories, meetings of the heads of religious orders, international congresses, etc.) are not enough. The main problems

facing the Church today are the Communist danger, the spreading
of atheism, the lukewarm attitude of many Catholics, the re-organiza-
tion of the Church to meet modern conditions, and the reunion of the
Eastern Churches with Rome.

According to newspaper reports the Pope intends to invite as many
bishops as possible, including the Protestant ones. But Vatican quarters in general do not think that this is possible. The Holy See, they
point out, makes a fundamental distinction between the schismatics
or dissidents on the one hand and heretics on the other. The schismatics believe in more or less the same dogmas and principles as the
Roman Catholics but they do not recognize the authority of Rome.
The heretics preach something entirely different from the Catholic
creed. Roughly speaking, all Protestants are considered heretics and
the Eastern or Orthodox Churches schismatics. The Church of
England is in an intermediate position. It is very near Rome on theological grounds, but the fact that the Queen of England is also the
Head of the Church complicates matters and makes a reunion difficult. The Church of England communion service is, of course, based
on the Mass and many members long for union with Rome and many
would accord to Rome some sort of primacy. On the other hand
many others repudiate Rome very strongly.

Theoretically all the bishops of the Eastern Churches have a right
to take part in the Ecumenical Council (one must remember that
most of the Ecumenical Councils of the past had the aim of recon-
structing the unity of the Church which had been shattered by
theological disputes and schisms) without being individually invited.
It is believed, however, that the Pope will make it clear that all the
Eastern bishops will be welcome in Rome. It is also possible that some
Church of England or other Protestant bishops particularly favorable
to Christian unity will be invited to attend as observers.

All this seems to be confirmed by the wording of the *Osservatore
Romano* communiqué announcing the Ecumenical Council. According to the Vatican organ one of the Council's aims was to gather
"separate communities for the search of unity," a phrase which, in
Catholic parlance, could not have referred to Protestant heretics.

As to the number of participants, the figure of 3,500 was put out
tentatively by the Vatican. It would include all the Roman Catholic
bishops, abbots, titular bishops (those who do not have an actual
diocese of their own), heads of religious orders, generals, etc., plus
a large percentage of the Eastern bishops. This, too, is an indication,
for if the Protestant bishops were to have been included, the figure
would have been almost double.

The fact that the Council will attempt to bring about a reunion of the Eastern Churches with Rome is supported by the fact that the Pope has been meeting very often with the Armenian Cardinal Agagianian, who has dedicated practically all his life to this problem. The obstacles, as seen from the Vatican, are more of a political than a religious nature. They say that there is nothing in the doctrines of the Orthodox or Eastern Churches to prevent them from accepting the last dogma proclaimed by Pius XII, that of Mary's bodily Assumption into Heaven (which the Protestants find so difficult to swallow). The Church of Rome on her part is willing to permit the priests of the Eastern Churches to marry. She already does this with Catholic priests of the Eastern rite, though the practice is discouraged. More serious obstacles are the dogmas of the Immaculate Conception, which is still disputed by Eastern theologians, of the Pope's infallibility, and of divorce, which some Eastern Churches grant fairly easily on grounds of adultery.

But the real stumbling block is of a political nature. Most of the Eastern Churches are divided from Rome by the Iron Curtain. Moreover, the Russian Orthodox Church and the national Orthodox Churches in the satellite countries are collaborating rather closely with the Communists. To complicate matters there is an acute rivalry between those Orthodox behind the Iron Curtain, who look for guidance to the Metropolitan of Moscow, Sergej, and those Orthodox outside the Curtain, who consider the Patriarch of Constantinople, Athenagoras, their spiritual leader. Should Sergej come to Rome and take part in the Ecumenical Council (a move that, in view of Khrushchev's appeasement tactics and keen sense for spectacular propaganda gestures, is not to be ruled out), a clash between fellow-traveler Sergej and anti-Communist Athenagoras would be inevitable.

The fact that the Holy See entertained official diplomatic relations with the Lithuanian Government-in-Exile could have proved a further obstacle to the coming to Rome of Orthodox bishops in the Soviet-dominated countries. John XXIII, who is extremely keen on the success of the Ecumenical Council and on paving the way for a reunion of the Eastern Churches with Rome, has preferred to remove the obstacle, even at the cost of bringing sorrow to the hearts and doubts to the minds of many true Catholics and staunch anti-Communists on both sides of the Curtain.

Moreover, and even without taking into account the Ecumenical Council and the prospects of a reunion with the Easterners, the withdrawal of recognition from the Lithuanian minister is a move that fits within a larger plan of the new Pope to detach the Catholic Church from politics. During the nineteen years of the reign of Pius

XII quite the opposite had happened. Pacelli had had no experience as a parish priest nor as a bishop; his entire ecclesiastical life had been spent in the diplomatic service, in the State Secretariat and on the throne of Peter. He was therefore very politically and diplomatically-minded and his influence had to a very great extent pervaded the Church. The constant spreading of Catholic Action and its growing political weight, the postwar successes of strong Catholic parties in Italy, Germany, France, Holland and Belgium, the close alliance established between the Church and the dictators of Spain and Portugal had done the rest. The present Pope, at least according to what the people who are closest to him say, would like to disengage the Church from political commitments as far as possible, place her above the battle and reinforce her leadership in the spiritual and moral provinces.

Another trend to be noted in the policy of John XXIII is the rehabilitation of the secular clergy. Faced with a shortage of priests, the Church has come to rely more and more for the accomplishment of special tasks, particularly of a political, educational and cultural nature, on Jesuits, Dominicans, Franciscans, Salesians, Barnabites and other religious. These in turn have come to regard the "stick-in-the-mud" parish priest with that air of benevolent superiority which the commando or the marine reserves for the infantry. As in a chain reaction the more intelligent, able and ambitious young Catholics, who felt the call of the Church, preferred to enlist in the religious orders that promised them an exciting activity and a brilliant career, rather than to become priests. The standard of the parish priest thus tended to deteriorate. It is a vicious circle which John XXIII is determined to break by restoring the dignity, the standing and even the poetical and mystical appeal of the simple priest.

Quite significant in this respect was the long and moving encyclical which the Pope dedicated to St. Vianey, the Curate of Ars, a very humble French parish priest, in which he made it quite clear that the secular clergy is the backbone of the Church and that there is no better way of serving Christ than by being a priest. Also significant is the fact that the Pope has promoted to the rank of university the Lateran Athenaeum, frequented by the secular clergy, where he himself studied. And while Pius XII had two German Jesuits as his secretaries and a third German Jesuit as his confessor, John XXIII employs as his secretary a priest, Mgr. Loris Capovilla, and confesses to an old priest in his seventies, Mgr. Alfredo Cavagna.

According to Vatican gossip, Roncalli dislikes the Jesuits, but this, of course, is impossible to prove. It's a fact, however, that such influential Jesuits as Father Lombardi, nicknamed "God's Loudspeaker"

Eugenio Pacelli as
Vatican Secretary of
State with Premier
Benito Mussolini and
Fascist dignitaries at
the time of the
Concordat

Angelo Roncalli, as Papal Nuncio in Paris, with his four brothers

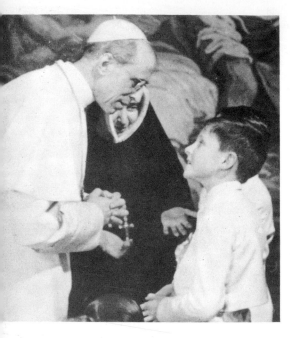

Sister Pasqualina, German nun, who was personal housekeeper to Pope Pius XII—*Wide World*

Pope Pius XII talking with a child in one of his frequent general audiences

Pope Pius XII addressing a crowd after a bombing in July, 1943

LEFT, ABOVE. Swiss guard recruits taking the oath of allegiance—
Attualità Giordani

RIGHT, ABOVE. Palatine Guard officer decorating guardsman—
Attualità Giordani

The Noble Guard in St. Peter's Square—*Attualità Giordani*

Air view of the Vatican

President Charles de Gaulle inspecting the Papal Gendarmerie—
Attualità Giordani

Eugene Cardinal Tisserant, Dean of the
Sacred College

Josef Cardinal Mindszenty, Catholic
Primate of Hungary—*Wide World*

Stefan Cardinal Wyszynski of Poland—*Wide World*

Part of the crowd outside the Sistine Chapel when the puff of smoke from the stove pipe announced the election of a new Pope, John XXIII—
Agenzia Farabola, Milan

Mother Dominic in street
clothes teaching a class—
Agenzia Mercuri, Rome

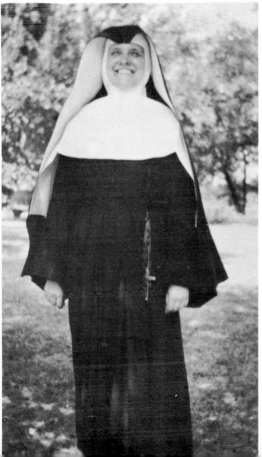

Mother Dominic in habit

Pope John XXIII on the day of his coronation—*Agenzia Rome Presse*

for his oratorical skill and his sensational preaching campaigns (a kind of Catholic Billy Graham), and Father Rotondi, creator of the "For a Better World" movement, a highly political organization, who were both very close to Pius XII, have scarcely any contacts at all with the present Pope.

It is too early to try and appraise the importance and the significance of Roncalli's pontificate. It will be the task of future historians to judge whether his courageous and ambitious initiative of holding an Ecumenical Council will be a success, whether his attempts to bring the Easterners back into the fold will have any results, whether he will be able to check the centrifugal tendencies of Catholics behind the Iron Curtain and in China, whether his decision to disengage the Church from politics will prove a wise one, and so on.

What I have tried to do so far is to describe the two Popes I have met, Pius and John, on the basis of my personal and necessarily limited experiences, impressions, reactions.

John XXIII, of course, doesn't possess the encyclopaedic culture of Pacelli, nor his phenomenal memory, his amazing gift for languages, his dignity nor his aristocratic deportment. Neither does he have Pacelli's capacity for work, his brilliant style in writing and resonant voice in speaking. And he does not lead such an ascetic life. But somehow I cannot help feeling that the son of the humble Bergamo peasants more than makes up for all these shortcomings by his human warmth, his sense of humor, his humility, his plain common sense and his spontaneity which have led the Italians to call him "un Papa simpatico."

7

How the Church
is Organized

THE POPE is the last absolute sovereign remaining in the world, and this prerogative he enjoys on two counts. First, he is sovereign over the Vatican City State, which confers upon him all the privileges and prerogatives enjoyed by other heads of State. Secondly, he is the Supreme Pontiff, that is, the spiritual head, of almost half a billion Catholics[1] spread throughout every country in the world. As absolute sovereign he holds in his hands the legislative, judicial and administrative powers, and to these must be added a fourth power of a more subtle and spiritual nature, that of laying down the doctrine and the

[1] Titles and appellations are something that the Pope certainly doesn't lack. In the Vatican Yearbook he is described as "Bishop of Rome, Vicar of Jesus Christ, Successor of the Prince of Apostles, Supreme Pontiff of the Universal Church, Patriarch of the West, Primate of Italy, Archbishop and Metropolitan of the Roman Province, Sovereign of the Vatican City State." He is also sometimes called "Father of Princes and Kings, Rector of the World upon Earth." Romans in general, and more particularly those who live in the Vatican, call him more simply "il Papa" (the Pope) or, even more colloquially, refer to him by his family name: Pacelli, Roncalli. When addressing him they prefer to say "Holy Father" rather than use the more formal "Your Holiness."

laws of moral behavior, which the Italians sum up in one word—
Magistero.

How does the Pontiff exercise these powers and what are the
channels through which he works? In other words, just what is the
central organization of the Church?

It must at the outset be understood that this is a highly complex
organism, which has evolved gradually for twenty centuries and which
preserves certain archaic institutions, even if they have been adapted
to new tasks, and above all an abstruse nomenclature which tends to
puzzle the man in the street. In this attempt to give a picture of how
the Church is organized, I have followed an admirably clear scheme
drawn up by Mgr. Pierre Canisius Van Lierde, an erudite Dutch
prelate, the Sacristan of the Holy Father, and author of an informa-
tive book entitled *Dietro il Portone di Bronzo* (Behind the Bronze
Door).

The tiny state of which the Pope is sovereign stretches over an
area of 440,000 square meters. It has thirty streets and squares, fifty
palaces, eight grand staircases, 200 smaller ones, about 10,000 rooms,
two churches (without counting St. Peter's), two jails (practically

always empty), a large garden, a small hill, a radio station, a railway station (used only occasionally for freight trains, never for passengers), a tiny astronomical observatory (not to be confused with the bigger observatory at Castel Gandolfo, the papal summer residence), a large garage with an underground car park, which is the most recent building, a printing shop and four publications: the daily paper *L'Osservatore Romano,* the *Acta Apostolicae Sedis* in which only official documents are printed, the Sunday paper *Osservatore della Domenica,* and the magazine *Ecclesia.* The printing shop is one of the most efficient I have ever seen. Typographical errors are as rare in the *Osservatore Romano* as in the London *Times.* But the real characteristic of this printing shop is its cosmopolitanism. As far back as 1870 the Vatican printers were able to produce the "Pater Noster" in 250 languages using 180 different alphabets.

The inhabitants of the Vatican City are about one thousand (official figures have never been given) and the citizens of this state about 1,200. The difference is explained by the fact that not all the citizens, such as the Cardinals and the Vatican diplomats, live in the Vatican. Then there are about 400 clerical and manual workers who reside in Rome but go to work in the Vatican.

The Vatican library, again one of the best in the world, has scores of valuable Egyptian papyri, 60,000 codices and one and a half million volumes.

The art treasures concentrated in such small space are simply fabulous. To quote just a fraction we shall recall that the great architects Bernini, Bramante, Maderno, Sangallo have left the imprint of their genius in St. Peter's and the Vatican palaces, that Michelangelo figures prominently as architect, painter and sculptor (he designed St. Peter's dome, he carved the Pietà—the Madonna holding the dead body of Christ in her lap—to be seen in the basilica, painted the frescoes in the Sistine Chapel), that Raphael has painted the loggias and the *stanze* and contributed oil paintings to the Vatican Museums. In the Museums there are Egyptian, Etruscan, Roman and Greek statues including the Apollo of Belvedere and the Laocoön. The enormous picture gallery ranges from the Italian primitives to the French impressionists and constitutes a striking memorial to the love for arts of the Roman Popes.

In the execution of his tasks the Pope relies first on the Cardinals, who are his most direct collaborators and who, gathered together in the Sacred College, form the Senate or House of Lords of the Church. Then he uses the Congregations, which assist him in carrying out his *Magistero,* in interpreting the laws and in directing the tribunals, to which the judicial power is delegated, and the offices, which take care of the administrative tasks. All these organs taken together are known by the generic name of the Roman Curia; the Roman Curia together with the Pope constitutes the Holy See. In addition there are several permanent commissions to which particular tasks are entrusted.

In any consideration of the various elements that make up the central administration of the Church, the first group is the Cardinals, who are, or at least ought to be, the pivot upon which the activity of the Pope turns. (By the way, the word *Cardinal* comes from the Latin *"cardo,"* that is, a *hinge.*)

The Cardinals are divided into three orders of priests, deacons and bishops, a classification which dates back to the first centuries of Christianity. In Rome there used to be different titular churches and the Bishop of Rome had appointed to each of them a priest, and it is from him that the Cardinal priest is derived. Even today, when a bishop of far-distant regions, whether he be Canadian or Australian, Polish or Indian, is named Cardinal, one of the titular churches of Rome is assigned to him. In this connection an odd fact is worth noting. The wealth of a Cardinal can be estimated in inverse proportion to the neglected and decrepit state of the titular church that is given to him. And this is a very wise and logical procedure. Clearly, if a broken-down church should be assigned to a Cardinal without means, it would be extremely difficult for him to put it in order and to restore it, while a wealthy Cardinal will leave nothing undone to ensure that his church shows up well as compared with the others. As an example there is St. John and Paul, a church which was once in a state of great neglect but which has been restored from top to bottom with dollars provided by Cardinal Spellman so that it has been transformed into a veritable jewel.

Again, in the early centuries of Christianity, Rome was divided into quarters, and every quarter had a deacon who busied himself with charitable works. The most important deacons assumed the title of *diaconi cardinales* and it is from them that the modern Cardinal deacons derive.

With the spread of Christianity, small dioceses, called suburban dioceses, began to be set up around Rome and several of the bishops of these dioceses became Cardinals. As time went on, naturally, ever-wider tasks were entrusted to the Cardinal priests, deacons and bishops as the Church of Rome gradually transformed itself into a universal church.

The Code of Canon Law, Canon 230, defines the position and functions of the Cardinals as follows: "The Cardinals of the Holy

Roman Church constitute the Senate of the Roman Pontiff and assist him as counsellors in the government of the Church." Some of them deal with the administration of the Vatican City State, of the Congregations and of the other offices of the central administration, and are Cardinals in Curia. The others, scattered throughout the world, carry out their pastoral duties and apostolates. Their maximum number, fixed at seventy by Sixtus V, remained unchanged up to and during the pontificate of Pius XII but as has been explained, has been exceeded by John XXIII. At present their dean is the French Cardinal in Curia, Tisserant. This title does not confer upon him any authority over his fellow-Cardinals but gives him the position of *primus inter aequales* and the privilege of addressing the Pope in the name of the whole Sacred College.

In carrying out his complex and vast tasks the Pope relies mainly on the Congregations, which roughly correspond to the Departments or Ministries of lay governments. Here is a list of these Congregations, with a short indication of their principal functions and characteristics.

Holy Office. This is the most important of the Congregations and accordingly has been given a separate chapter in this book.

Consistorial Congregation. The Consistorial Congregation originated from the Consistories, that is, from the meetings with the Pope of the Cardinals of the titular churches of Rome, at which were discussed the most important affairs of the Church. As a Congregation, that is, as a permanent organ, it was founded by Sixtus V. At present much of the business that was originally dealt with by this Congregation has been assigned to other Congregations or offices. It has however been left with complete and absolute jurisdiction over the bishops and over all dioceses throughout the world, with the exception of the mission territories, which come under the jurisdiction of the Congregation for the Propagation of the Faith, and of the dioceses of the Eastern Churches, which come under the authority of a special Congregation.

The Consistorial Congregation prepares the nomination of bishops, deals with the creation and territorial subdivision of the dioceses and with the grouping of the bishops in ecclesiastical provinces. In addition, it gives advice to the bishops in connection with the administration of their respective dioceses and takes care of spiritual assistance to emigrants.

The choice of new bishops is the most delicate and important task of the Congregation. Examination of the qualities of the candidates is carried on in great secrecy, with the assistance of the bishops in each ecclesiastical province, and of the nuncio or the apostolic delegate. A highly detailed report is then submitted to the Pope, upon whom rests the final decision and the act of nomination.

Congregation for the Eastern Church. Founded by Pius IX in 1862, but linked with the Congregation for the Propagation of the Faith, this Congregation was made autonomous by Benedict XV in 1917 and reformed by Pius XI in 1938. It exercises legislative, administrative and judicial powers over about 9,000,000 Catholics in Egypt, Cyprus, Greece, the Dodecanese, Persia, Lebanon, Israel, Syria, Transjordan, Turkey, Afghanistan and certain parts of India. While originally it interested itself only in the Catholics of the Eastern rite, since the pontificate of Pius XI it has had jurisdiction also over those of the Latin rite resident in those countries. It embraces the powers of all the other Congregations, except those exercised by the Holy Office and by the Congregation of Rites. It also carries on work for the return to Rome of the schismatic churches of the East, which number about 200,000,000 faithful. As has been noted, great progress in this sense has been made in the elimination of obstacles of an ideological and liturgical nature, and union could probably be achieved fairly soon were it not for the obstacle of the Iron Curtain.

Congregation of the Sacraments.[1] As its name indicates, this Congregation occupies itself with the seven sacraments. The bulk of its work concerns the granting of dispensations in the case of marriages that have been ratified but not consummated, and the granting of dispensations to priests who wish to withdraw from their vocation.

In the case of marriages not consummated, the bishop of the diocese to which the married couple belong must not express any opinion. He confines himself to collecting all the documents, testimonies, medical reports, etc., and transmitting them to the Congregation. This then institutes a kind of trial in two phases, before the "Defender of the Bond," who does his best to show that the marriage is valid. If, however, the Congregation has reached the conclusion that the marriage has really not been consummated, it presents a detailed report to the Pope, who alone is empowered to grant the dispensation.

This Congregation also deals with those marriages which are null and void owing to some original defect, but which the couple subsequently wishes to legitimize, and with cases of presumptive death, that is, when one marriage partner has disappeared for a long time and the other wishes to remarry.

Congregation of the Council. Created for the purpose of applying the decisions and reforms of the Council of Trent (1545-63), this Congregation is today mainly concerned with the supervision of the

[1] Also known as Congregation of Sacramental Discipline.

clergy and the laity, the spreading of the Catechism and the control of the financial affairs of the dioceses. Many Cardinals not in Curia are members of this Congregation. Since it has supervision over the laity, the Congregation is in charge of the problems of Catholic Action and therefore often fulfills a political role. The aspect of the Congregation as an administrative organ is dealt with separately in the chapter on Vatican finances.

Congregation of Religious. This Congregation controls a world that is vast, picturesque and complex—that of the religious orders. Under its jurisdiction come hundreds of orders having objects and characteristics of the most varied nature (monastics, contemplatives, nuns, mendicants, missionaries, teachers, nurses, simple-vow religious, pious associations without vows, secular institutes, etc.) with a total of about one million nuns and a quarter-million monks, friars and other male religious. It is one of the most complex of the Congregations as regards the volume of business handled and the number of its personnel. The religious will be dealt with in a separate chapter.

Congregation for the Propagation of the Faith.[1] This Congregation has charge of missions. It covers an immense territory which includes Africa, Asia with China, Japan, India, Indo-China, Korea, Formosa, the Pacific Islands, Australia, New Zealand, several regions of Latin America and, in Europe, the Scandinavian countries, Turkey and Albania. The missionaries number nearly 50,000, to which must be added 72,000 nuns and an unspecified number of laymen. The converts total over 31,000,000.[2] So important is this Congregation that in the Vatican its Prefect is nicknamed the "Red Pope" and this not only because of the color of his robes but also because of the blood that so often the missionaries are forced to shed. The Congregation for the Propagation of the Faith administers its own finances.

Congregation of Rites. This Congregation deals with liturgy and the causes of beatification and canonization. The liturgical section includes the masters of the pontifical ceremonies and the experts in strictly liturgical matters and in other matters linked with these,

[1] Also called Congregation *"de Propaganda Fide."*
[2] In this sphere too it is not easy to give exact, up-to-date figures. According to statistics published in 1956 by the American Institute of Management and referring to 1955, there were in the mission territories 74,065 churches, 11,643 parishes, 11,279 diocesan priests, 5,475 seminarists, 18,058 regular priests, 2,831 male religious communities containing 19,512 religious, 6,265 female communities with 72,110 nuns, 43,519 schools and colleges for boys with 3,522,494 pupils and students, 22,948 schools and colleges for girls with 2,196,446 pupils and students, 5,867 charitable organizations that were assisting 6,982,179 persons and 31,554,849 native converts to Catholicism in a total population in the missionary territories of about 1,200,000,000 souls.

such as history, archeology, geography, sacred music and so on. This is the Congregation which has studied the recent liturgical reforms, including the return to the old style of celebrating the Easter feasts, the evening Masses, concessions as to fasting before receiving the Eucharist, and the use of modern languages instead of Latin in certain parts of the ritual. It should be added that Pius XI attached to this Congregation a historical section whose task is to collect, study and preserve all those documents which in future might be useful in the cause of canonization. What part the Congregation of Rites plays in the causes of both beatification and canonization is dealt with in the chapter which describes how saints are canonized.

Congregation of the Ceremonial. Created by that great organizer, Sixtus V, the Congregation of the Ceremonial takes charge of the ceremonies and audiences at which the Pope is present, the visits of heads of States, princes, ambassadors and other VIPs to the Vatican, and concerns itself with questions of protocol, including precedence, etiquette and the like.

Congregation of the Seminaries and Universities. This supervises the seminaries (except those of the Eastern Church and of the native clergy which are under control of the Congregation for the Eastern Church and the Congregation for the Propagation of the Faith respectively), the Catholic universities, all the Catholic schools and institutes placed under ecclesiastical authority; the organizations that encourage priestly vocations. The Catholic schools are so numerous, diverse and widely scattered that it is impossible, within the limits of a short review, even to attempt a classification of them. To give some idea of the importance which the Catholic Church attaches to education, it can be pointed out that there are in the world thirty-eight Catholic universities, twelve Catholic "Atheneums" (equivalent to a university) and seven pontifical academies.

Congregation for Extraordinary Ecclesiastical Affairs. This is a committee of Cardinals, presided over by the Secretary of State which advises the Pope on questions of foreign policy. It is dealt with in greater detail in the chapter describing the State Secretariat.

Congregation of the Basilica of St. Peter. This Congregation looks after the upkeep of the Church. It employs three architects, including Count Enrico Galeazzi. A school and laboratory of mosaics is attached to it.

After the twelve Congregations, we come to the tribunals—the Apostolic Penitentiary, the Sacred Roman Rota and the Supreme Tribunal of the Apostolic Signature.

The Apostolic Penitentiary. It's not a prison, but it does handle problems of conscience, indulgences and those censures or ecclesiastical penalties reserved to the Pope which punish particularly serious crimes, such, for example, as profanation of the Host.

Any Catholic can apply directly to the Penitentiary and ask its assistance in solving a problem of conscience. Usually, however, the channel chosen is the Catholic's personal confessor who, in order to preserve the secret of the confessional, writes to the Penitentiary explaining the problem and using fictitious names. The reply is sent directly to the confessor but the letter contains a second envelope, closed and sealed, to be handed to the penitent person. The latter can ask his own confessor, or another whom he can freely choose from a list of names of priests approved by the bishop, to open this second letter. The more normal and more logical practice, however, is to have the letter opened by a habitual confessor, since he is already informed about the problem. The replies, which are brief, clear, and which waste no words, are given with the greatest possible speed with the object of putting worried minds at rest. The Penitentiary continues to function even while the papal throne is vacant, that is, between the death of a Pope and the election of his successor, a period when the majority of the other Vatican offices cease their activities.

In connection with this Congregation Mgr. Van Lierde records a rather amusing episode. It happens from time to time that a theologian or confessor will submit to the Penitentiary a fictitious problem, that is, a complete invention of his own, with the aim of obtaining an authoritative reply to some controversial point or to clear up some theoretical doubt that is worrying him. But the Penitentiary officials are old hands at the game who, in the majority of cases, see through such ingenuous little tricks. The questioner will then receive a little note with the words *"consulantur probati auctores"*—(go and read the approved authors).

As already stated, the Penitentiary also grants indulgences. According to Catholic doctrine the serious and mortal sins entail eternal punishment (Hell). This penalty can, however, be condoned, after sincere repentance and confession, by means of absolution. However, absolution does not cancel the temporary punishments (Purgatory) for sins committed, but they can be reduced or annulled by penitences, by good works, by suffering, by troubles borne with resignation, and, finally, by indulgences. Indulgences are generally linked with particular prayers, pilgrimages, visits to sanctuaries and, above all, to the Holy Places. In addition there are others which come through medals, religious objects, readings of the breviary, the Stations of the Cross, and so on. The Penitentiary examines the requests for new indulgences, and grades and distributes those already in existence according to place and time.

The Sacred Roman Rota.[1] This tribunal too, which is the normal tribunal of the Holy See and concerns itself, among other things, with annulments of marriages, is dealt with in a separate chapter.

Supreme Tribunal of the Apostolic Signatura. This originated from the "*referendari,*" counselors of the Pope, upon whom fell the task of drawing up verdicts and requests for pardon for the signature (*segnatura*) of the Holy Father. Today the Supreme Tribunal of the Apostolic Signature functions as a court of cassation, rather than a court of appeals, inasmuch as it does not judge which side is right or wrong but only whether the laws or the juridical forms have been properly observed. It is possible to appeal to the Apostolic Signature against the verdicts of the Sacred Rota and it is to this supreme tribunal that the task falls of settling the controversies between judicial organs of a lower grade such as the Rota and the diocesan and metropolitan tribunals. The verdicts of the Holy Office and of the Congregation of Rites are outside its jurisdiction.

Next to be examined are the principal offices of the Curia whose tasks are mainly executive and administrative.

Apostolic Chancery. This functions substantially like any lay chancery. Its officials are merely executors of orders which reach them either directly from the Pope or from the various Congregations. The Chancery, which takes its name from the magnificent palace, built by Bramante, in which the Rota also has its headquarters, draws up papal bulls and other documents of the Curia. However before sending them on to their destinations, the Chancery awaits further, explicit instructions. Here is one of the examples of the traditional prudence of the Church, the idea being to give to the Congregations and to the Pontiff himself a further period to reflect and, if necessary, to change their minds.

Apostolic Datary. The task of the Apostolic Datary, essentially, is to date the documents of the Pontiff. It was created after the great schism of the West, during a time of confusion and turmoil, to put an end to the circulation of false papal documents. In addition to this duty, which is now something almost mechanical that could quite well be left to the Chancery, it has the more delicate one of attending to certain special ecclesiastical appointments. As a rule the Catholic priest is rather poor but in some cases the parish owns (a

[1] Also called for short in Vatican terminology, the Sacred or Holy Rota, which includes the Spanish branch.

heritage of the good old feudal days) a lot of farmland or even buildings in city areas. In other cases the parish, and the parish priest on its behalf, is the beneficiary of trusts or legacies left by wealthy Catholics. The same applies to dioceses, colleges and other Church institutions. As a result, some of the posts entail the collection and administration of vast incomes. All such posts fall within the jurisdiction of the Datary. The abilities and qualities of the candidates are carefully weighed and they themselves are even submitted to a written examination to make sure not only that they are men of absolute integrity but also that they have a certain nose for business. The Datary also fixes the contributions which the nominees must make to poorer parishes, charitable institutions, etc., and the pensions they must pay to local people, usually mothers or sisters of priests who died in poverty.

Apostolic Camera. Originally the Apostolic Camera administered the revenues and properties of the Holy See, and, in theory, this is still its function. In practice, however, as can be seen in the chapter on Vatican finances, this administrative task is carried out by other bodies and the Apostolic Camera functions only while there is a vacancy in the Holy See. At its head is the Cardinal Chamberlain or *Camerlengo,* who exercises very wide powers during the interval between the death of a Pope and the election of his successor.

Secretariat of State. This was the last of the offices to be created, and is placed last both in the Code of Canon Law and in the Vatican Year Book. In reality it is so important and its tasks are so complex that in this volume it has been given a chapter of its own in which the Vatican's foreign policy is also dealt with.

To complete this over-all picture of the central organization of the Catholic Church the permanent commissions must also be briefly examined. These commissions are concerned with subjects that require specialized knowledge and study and, moreover, that could not be adequately handled by the Congregations since these are already short of staff and overburdened with work.

Pontifical Commission for Biblical Studies. Founded by Leo XIII, the object of this Commission is to promote the study of the Bible and to ensure that these studies are kept free from errors. It is composed of a varying number of Cardinals and of thirty-one advisers, seventeen of whom live in Rome, with the others spread over the world. The Commission is also empowered to confer academic titles (diplomas and degrees) on those prelates and laymen who have distinguished themselves in Bible studies.

Pontifical Commission for the Authentic Interpretation of the Code of Canon Law. This was instituted by Benedict XV on September 15, 1917, only four months after the promulgation of the Code. The codification of the rules of Canon Law, a gigantic work undertaken by order of Pius X and completed under Benedict XV was, above all, the achievement of Cardinal Gasparri, ably assisted, as has been related, by the young official of the Secretariat of State, Eugenio Pacelli. Although the Code is well framed and drawn up with great clarity, it cannot, nevertheless, foresee and meet all the particular circumstances and situations that can possibly occur in the various parts of the world. The Commission's task, therefore, is to give an authentic interpretation of the Code to those among the clergy and the faithful who may need it. It answers the questions submitted by the various departments of the Roman Curia and by the superiors of the religious orders and congregations.

Pontifical Commission for the Compilation of the Code of Eastern Canon Law. As already noted, the Congregation of the Eastern Church is completely autonomous and this autonomy extends also to Canon Law. This is essential since the Eastern Church embraces the faithful of both the Oriental and the Latin rites and since it is necessary to eliminate all controversies of minor importance and keep to essentials, in doctrine as well as in worship. The Commission was instituted by Pius XI in 1935.

St. Jerome's Abbey for the Revision and Emendation of the Vulgate. It was St. Jerome who prepared the Vulgate or Latin version of the Bible. Over the centuries errors and alterations have occurred as a result of the transcribing by hand of this text. Pius XI founded the Benedictine Abbey of St. Jerome and set those monks the task of preparing a critical edition of the Vulgate.

Pontifical Commission of Sacred Archeology. This Commission has charge of the ancient Christian cemeteries, and encourages excavations, investigations and studies, lays down the rules for the admittance of scholars and the public to these cemeteries, and indicates which crypts of the Catacombs can be used for religious ceremonies. It also co-ordinates the work of the Roman Pontifical Academy of Archeology and the Pontifical Institute of Christian Archeology.

Central Pontifical Commission of Sacred Art in Italy. The object of this Commission is to keep alive everywhere, and especially among the special commissions set up in all the dioceses, the feeling for Christian art, and to preserve and increase the artistic possessions of the Church.

Cardinals' Commission for Supervision of the Pontifical Sanctuary of Pompeii. This is the Commission in charge of the spiritual and material administration of this famous sanctuary, one of the greatest in the world, the goal of continuous pilgrimages with which are connected various charitable organizations.

Pontifical Institute for the Preservation of the Faith and for the Provision of New Churches in Rome. The preservation of the faith in the Eternal City, spiritual capital of the whole Catholic world, is more important than in any other city, and the churches are one of the principal instruments for this task. The Institute also deals with the civil authorities in cases where sacred buildings are expropriated in the public interest.

Permanent Commission for the Guardianship of the Historic and Artistic Monuments of the Holy See. This was created by Pius XI in 1923 and its name clearly indicates its objects.

Heraldic Commission of the Pontifical Court. The purpose of the Heraldic Commission is to supervise the coats-of-arms of the members of the Pontifical Court and of the Cardinals and to see that they are in accordance with heraldic regulations and artistic standards, so as to avoid designs which might be open to irreverent criticism.

Pontifical Committee for Historical Sciences and Pontifical Commission for the Ecclesiastical Archives of Italy. These two bodies have been set up recently, with the task of encouraging historical studies. The Archives Commission keeps in touch with the bishops and instructs them on the preservation of diocesan archives, particularly those documents which are of importance for the history of the Church.

Pontifical Commission for the Cinema, Radio and Television. This is one of the most important and interesting of the permanent Commissions and was created by Pius XII in 1948. Pacelli always realized to the full the great importance of the modern means of recreation, education and information such as the press, radio, cinema, television and sport. This Commission, headed by an American bishop, is charged with the task of co-ordinating the activity of Catholics throughout the world so as to prevent immoral films being shown to the public, and radio and television transmissions which are contrary to the ethical principles of the Church. There exist in various countries special committees of listeners to radio and of viewers of television (these are particularly strong in the United States, Belgium and Holland), which are very active in their protests to and with their pressure on the radio and television transmitting companies. The influence of the Commissions is so powerful that a number of companies consult the top members of the Commission before putting certain programs on the air. The Commission also endeavors to promote the production of films with a Catholic background and to give support to radio and television directors of sound

Catholic faith. The Commission is headed by Martin J. O'Connor, Archbishop (of Scranton, Pa.), who also heads the North American College in Rome.

Pontifical Organization for Social Assistance. This was created by Pius XII in 1954. It co-ordinates the activities of the organizations and individuals who handle social assistance, and adapts them to local needs. It is, above all, the poorer classes who are the target of Communist and atheist propaganda and the endeavor of this organization is to counteract such efforts by means of material aid and spiritual assistance.

The newest commissions set up are the *Pontifical Commission for Latin America* (1958) and *The Pontifical Antepreparatory Commission for the Ecumenical Council* (1959).

In addition there are another thirty-one international Catholic associations of laymen that concern themselves with workmen, intellectuals, seamen, teachers, youths (both boys and girls), children and university students and that have set themselves many other tasks such as the fight against heavy drinking, the strengthening of the family, Catholic philosophical studies, physical education and so on. As, however, they do not always depend directly on the Vatican and have their central headquarters abroad, they do not come within the scope of this book.

Now that an indication has been given on how the Vatican administration works, several questions naturally arise. Does the Catholic Church function well or badly? Is she in a position, with her antiquated structure, to face up to the needs of modern life? And what grade of efficiency has she reached?

It is hard to tell what would be the opinion of the administrator of a lay government Department or Ministry or that of a managing-director of some vast industrial enterprise, or even that of an ordinary accountant, were they to be asked to find their way through the maze of the Vatican's bookkeeping system. But in this connection there is at hand a fairly rare and curious document that can perhaps provide some enlightenment. It is a study prepared for its members in 1956 by the American Institute of Management. The Institute, a typical product of American pragmatic mentality, concerns itself with studying the efficiency of business and industrial firms and giving advice on making economies and on advertizing campaigns, investments, methods of increasing production, changes in office structure, simplification of bookkeeping systems and similar problems.

The American Institute of Management, on its own initiative and without pay, applied the yardstick of Yankee efficiency to the Catholic

PLAN OF ORGANIZATION OF THE CATHOLIC CHURCH

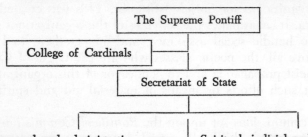

The Supreme Pontiff

College of Cardinals

Secretariat of State

Temporal and administrative power

Congregation of the Ceremonial
Congregation of the basilica of St. Peter
Apostolic Camera
Apostolic Chancery
Apostolic Dataria
Secret Archives of the Vatican
Administration of the Properties of the
    Holy See
Special Administration
Institute for Religious Works

Vatican City State:

Governor's Palace
Technical and economic services
Health services
Vatican Library
Vatican Museums
Pontifical Villa of Castel Gandolfo
Swiss, Noble and Palatine Guards and
    the Gendarmery
Vatican Radio
Vatican Observatory
Tribunal of the Sacred Roman Rota

Spiritual, judicial and doctrinal power

Congregations:

Holy Office
Consistorial
For the Eastern Church
Of the Sacraments
Of the Council
Of the Religious
For the Propagation of the Faith
Of Rites
Of the Seminaries and Universities

Tribunals:

Sacred Rota (of Appeal)
Apostolic Penitentiary
Apostolic Signature (of Cassation)
Holy Office

Permanent Commissions:

Biblical Studies
Interpretation of Canon Law
Preparation of the Code for the Orien-
    tal Church
Revision of the Vulgate
Historical Sciences
Sacred Archeology
Sacred Art
Cinema, Radio and Television
Sanctuary of Pompeii
New churches in Rome
Monuments of the Holy See
Heraldry
Social Assistance
Latin America
Ecumenical Council

Apostolic Nuncios and Delegates
Archbishops, Bishops and Catholic Ordinaries
    in the various dioceses and ecclesiastical
    jurisdictions

The Clergy

The Community of the Faithful

Church. It made a thorough study of both the Church's central and local administrations, and distributed the conclusions it has reached to its 15,000 clients, with the aim of showing what lessons private firms can draw from the Vatican. The Institute applies a certain system of points based on a total of 10,000, subdivided into the different sections of a firm's organization. It is all a bit complicated but suffice it to say that the Institute allotted to the Catholic Church a total of 8,800 points out of a possible 10,000—which is extremely high. In all the various sections except one, she was classified as "excellent" or "above excellent." The one in which, according to the Institute, she didn't make the grade was the Board of Directors, which in the Church's case is the College of Cardinals. The criticism levelled by the Institute against the Red Hats is that they are too old on the average and that they tend to look too much to the past instead of to the future; they tend to look too much to Rome and Italy instead of concerning themselves more with Catholic dioceses all over the world.

There is still another criticism, as regards Vatican finances. The men who administer the Pope's money are accused of concentrating too much on Italy and of not realizing that there are many other countries with better financial prospects. But as a whole, even the appraisal of the Vatican's financial abilities is entirely favorable and the Institute comes to the significant conclusion that no other organization manages to do quite so much with so little.

8

The State Secretariat

A FEW DAYS after he had been elected Pope, Roncalli visited the offices of the State Secretariat. On this occasion he said: "Here in the Vatican there certainly isn't a lack of substitutes. As a matter of fact we have had far too many." It was a way, typical of his direct and amusing style, of announcing the appointment of Cardinal Domenico Tardini as State Secretary, a post which Pius XII had left vacant since 1944, that is, since the death of the State Secretary Cardinal Luigi Maglione, who proved to be the last for fifteen years. It was also a way of saying that too many important posts of the Roman Curia had been entrusted to substitutes and that he was going to put an end to this.

For Tardini it was the climax of his career, the end of a series of ups and downs, of a kind of Tantalus torture which for fourteen years had placed the Red Hat of a Cardinal and the coveted job of State Secretary within reach of his hand without letting him attain either the one or the other. It's been a strange story in which he has been closely linked with Cardinal Giovan Battista Montini, Archbishop of Milan. Montini and Tardini. Tardini and Montini. In the Vatican world these two names always used to go together, like those of Gilbert and Sullivan, Laurel and Hardy.

When Maglione died, Pacelli started acting, if not officially at least factually, as his own State Secretary and the two Monsignori, as has already been noted, became his closest and most trusted collaborators. Tardini, who was older and had a longer service record, was made Secretary for Extraordinary Ecclesiastical Affairs and Montini Secretary for Ordinary Affairs.

But first, let me try to explain just what the State Secretariat is and how it works.

First of all, it must be made clear that the foreign policy of the Vatican is handled by two different bodies. One is the Sacred Congregation for Extraordinary Ecclesiastical Affairs and the other is the State Secretariat proper. The Congregation was formed in 1814 by Pius VII (1800-1823) and is therefore the youngest of the Congregations (age is a relative matter behind the Bronze Door). It is presided over by the Secretary of State, with the title of Prefect, and it is made up of a variable number of Cardinals (usually a dozen). It's a high-level advisory body which the Pope can consult—when he feels like it—through the Secretary of State, on questions of an ecclesiastical character which involve relations with other States. To give a few examples, this Congregation can be summoned when the Holy See is planning to reach a Concordat with another State or when there is a question of appointing new bishops or of creating new dioceses, providing that to do this it is necessary to embark on diplomatic negotiations with the countries involved. The Congregation gives its opinion on the general line of conduct but the negotiations and the settling of details is left to the State Secretariat. During Pacelli's reign, in the absence of a State Secretary, Mgr. Tardini acted as Pro-Prefect to this Congregation.

The State Secretariat, in its present form, was founded by Pius X in 1908. For all practical purposes, besides being a kind of Vatican State Department or Foreign Ministry, it has become the Pope's personal office, through which he, as head of the legislative, executive, administrative and spiritual power, deals with the most important and urgent questions, an office which supervises and coordinates the work of all the Congregations and all the other offices, tribunals, committees directly under the jurisdiction of the Holy See. The State Secretariat is the Pope's right arm and the State Secretary is, after the Pope, the most powerful man in the Vatican.

The State Secretariat is divided into three sections: the first corresponds roughly to the State Department or Foreign Ministry of a lay State, the second to the Department or Ministry of the Interior, while the third has minor, complementary functions.

First Section: Extraordinary Ecclesiastical Affairs (not to be confused with the Congregation for Extraordinary Ecclesiastical Affairs which, as has been noted, is an advisory committee of Cardinals). It concerns itself with carrying out the negotiations and preparing the text of Concordats with foreign countries; with the choice of bishops when the *placet* of local governments is necessary (otherwise, the appointment of the bishops is made by the Consistorial Congregation) and, generally speaking, with all ecclesiastical questions which can interfere with relations between the Holy See and other countries (freedom of religion, education, divorce, etc.). They are in other words the great problems which concern the fundamental policy of the Holy See and which require the utmost caution, a great deal of study and far-reaching vision. About thirty prelates, all of them Italian, make up this section. During Pacelli's pontificate Tardini was at its head.

Second Section: *Ordinary Affairs*. This section deals with all current and ordinary affairs that do not fall under the jurisdiction of the First Section. It works together with the Consistorial Congregation for the appointment of bishops, but only when there are no difficulties of a diplomatic nature. It keeps informed on the most important issues dealt with by the Holy Office. It suggests to the Pope the names of prelates most suited to represent the Holy See abroad as nuncios, apostolic delegates or visitors. It gives instructions and advice to Catholic Action and other lay organizations and thus has an influence on the internal politics of other countries. It concerns itself with the distribution of relief, alms and subsidies and with conferring Vatican honors and titles on ecclesiastical and lay persons. For the honors to be bestowed on ecclesiastics it consults the Consistorial Congregation; for those to be given to laymen it gets in touch with the Congregation of the Council. This section is made up of sixty Italian prelates and twelve of other nationalities whose job is mainly that of translators. During Pacelli's reign Montini was at the head of this section.

While the First Section is more ponderous, sedate and concerned with international problems at the highest level, the Second Section is busier and faster moving as it has to keep up with world events day by day. For example, should an earthquake wipe out a city during the night, it would be the task of the head of the Second Section to inform the Pope first thing in the morning and discuss with him what help the Church can offer. It is the Second Section that prepares a daily résumé of the world press and of agency reports for the State Secretary and the Pope, and that studies political trends in the various countries.

Third Section: *Apostolic Briefs*. This section has a secondary function, its task being that of putting into suitable handwriting the papal documents prepared by the other two sections.

Two further minor offices are directly under the State Secretariat. One is the *Secretariat for the Briefs to Princes* and the other the *Secretariat for Latin Letters*. All the letters the Pope addresses to kings, presidents of republics and members of royal families (whether reigning or in exile) are written in Latin and signed by his own hand. The Secretariat for the Briefs to Princes was headed by the present Cardinal Bacci, one of the world's greatest Latin language experts. He not only translates into Latin the letters to the heads of States, but he also answers the pleas addressed to the Pope for the creation of new saints and, when the Pope dies, he it is who pronounces in St. Peter's, on the eve of the Conclave, a Latin oration for the election of the new Pope, *"De eligendo Summo Pontifice."*

Usually such an oration is an academic affair in which the qualities and virtues the future Pope should possess are brought out in a conventional way. But the speech that was pronounced by Mgr. Bacci before Roncalli's election in 1958 contained some rather startling and even controversial points. It embodied a not-too-veiled criticism of Pius XII, charged with having become aloof from the Curia and inaccessible to the Cardinals, and the recommendation that the new Pope should have had experience as a shepherd of souls as well as being versed in diplomacy and politics and that he, above all, should be like a father to the faithful—a recommendation which fitted Roncalli very well.

Naturally Mgr. Bacci didn't prepare such an oration entirely on his own and without consultation. Before writing it he consulted a number of Cardinals and then submitted the final text to the Dean of the Sacred College, Cardinal Tisserant, who approved it, thus imparting a kind of official seal both to the criticism of Pacelli and to the advice on the choice of a new Pope.

The Secretariat for Latin Letters has the task of translating into a Ciceronian Latin the Pope's less solemn and less momentous letters, such as the letter the Pope writes to a Catholic congress or to congratulate a bishop or some other Church personality celebrating an anniversary.

The State Secretariat has under its jurisdiction the Vatican diplomats who represent the Holy See all over the world. There are various grades in the Vatican diplomacy, just as there are in the diplomatic services of other countries. The apostolic nuncio corresponds to an ambassador and, by tradition, is automatically considered the dean of the diplomatic corps of the capital in which he resides. The

Holy See has normal diplomatic relations with and is represented by a nuncio in the following countries: Argentina, Austria, Belgium, Bolivia, Brazil, Chile, Colombia, Costa Rica, Cuba, Eire, El Salvador, Ecuador, France, Germany, Holland, Luxembourg, Guatemala, Haiti, Honduras, Italy, Lebanon, Nicaragua, Panama, Paraguay, Peru, the Philippines, Portugal, Dominican Republic, Spain, Switzerland, Uruguay and Venezuela. In other countries the Vatican is represented by an internuncio, who is the equivalent of a minister plenipotentiary. Such countries are Ethiopia, Egypt, Formosa, India, Indonesia, Iran, Japan, Liberia, Pakistan and Syria.

The Holy See also has representatives abroad who don't have any diplomatic status and who are not responsible to the State Secretariat but to the Consistorial Congregation, the Eastern Church Congregation or *Propaganda Fide*. They are called apostolic delegates, they have no official relations with the governments of the countries they are sent to; they represent the Pope in dealings with the local Catholic authorities. They supervise Church affairs and they report directly to the Pope. The apostolic delegates in Canada, Great Britain, Mexico and the United States are responsible to the Consistorial Congregation. Those in Greece, Iraq, Israel and Turkey to the Eastern Church Congregation and those in Australia (including New Zealand and Oceania), the Belgian Congo, French Africa (Dakar), Indochina, Korea and South Africa (Pretoria) report to *Propaganda Fide*.

The Vatican diplomatic service is dominated by the Italians. The thirty-eight nuncios and internuncios are all Italians except three, while out of fourteen apostolic delegates nine are Italians.

A motive for sincere regret in the Vatican is the fact that the United States has no diplomatic relations with the Holy See. During World War II President Roosevelt had appointed a personal representative to the Pope, a post which was held with great tact and success by Mr. Myron Taylor, who had succeeded in creating a good understanding and a fruitful collaboration with Pius XII. The fact that Rome was spared from massive Allied bombings and that it was subsequently declared an open city is due to a great extent to the good relations established, through Myron Taylor, between the Pope and the American President.

It was hoped in the Vatican that the Taylor mission would have been the first step toward the establishment of normal diplomatic relations. However the opposition of American Protestants, who represent more than 60 per cent of the population, has proved stronger than any other consideration and neither President Truman nor President Eisenhower has wanted or dared to follow the example of their predecessor in the White House.

As a matter of fact, in the Vatican they are quite upset about the suspicions and prejudices, still somewhat alive in the United States, against popery and the alleged capacity for political intrigue of the Church of Rome. An episode of this hard-to-die suspicion and animosity took place during the last Conclave. Some American Protestant quarters asked the State Department to withdraw American citizenship from the American Cardinals who had taken part in the election of John XXIII. They pointed out that the American Constitution forbids American citizens from taking part in foreign elections. In the Vatican it was held that such an attitude was not only ridiculous but also contradictory. If, they argued, with their customary subtlety, one admits that the election of the Pope has a political character—that he becomes not only the spiritual head of the Church, but also the temporal head of the Vatican City State—then one must admit the existence of such a State from the point of view of international law. And once this has been admitted there is no reason why the United States should not have normal diplomatic relations with such a State.

Great Britain is in a particular situation as, while the apostolic delegate to London has no diplomatic status, the British minister to the Holy See is fully accredited. The difficulty here, as has already been pointed out, is that the Queen is also head of the Church of England. In that capacity she couldn't very well accept the credentials of a diplomatic representative of a rival faith. Against this, of course, it has been argued that her spiritual (and somewhat symbolic) power should not be confused with her temporal power and that, as Queen, she is also the head of the British Catholics. However, in the State Secretariat they are quite pleased with the state of relations between the Holy See and the United Kingdom and they have no intention of making an issue of the fact that they have to keep in London an apostolic delegate rather than a nuncio.

The countries that are represented at the Holy See by ambassadors and ministers are Argentina, Austria, Belgium, Bolivia, Brazil, Chile, Colombia, Costa Rica, Cuba, the Dominican Republic, Egypt, Eire, El Salvador, Ethiopia, Ecuador, Finland, Formosa, France, Germany, Guatemala, Haiti, Honduras, Holland, India, Indonesia, Iran, Italy, Japan, Lebanon, Liberia, Luxembourg, Monaco, Nicaragua, Pakistan, Panama, Paraguay, Peru, the Philippines, Portugal, San Marino, Spain, Syria, United Kingdom, Uruguay and Venezuela.

But to go back to the Tardini-Montini pair. It's difficult to imagine two more different personalities. Tardini is a Roman, friendly, jolly, plump, witty, a gourmet and a good teller of jokes. Montini is a

Lombard, thin, serious, ascetic, punctilious, reserved, without the slightest sense of humor. They are both extremely able with the difference that while Tardini often hides his intelligence behind his easy-going manner, Montini's is enhanced by his earnestness and application.

Tardini comes from a poor family (he was born in Rome in 1888), had an unhappy childhood, knows what it means to go hungry and had to fight his way into the exclusive Vatican diplomatic service. Montini is the offspring of a wealthy and influential family (born at Concesio, near Brescia, in 1897). His father was a Catholic member of Parliament and his brother Ludovico, also a member of Parliament, is a very rich man and the head of the Catholic international relief organization. Contradicting their social origins, Montini is interested in working-class problems and is considered to be a bit to the left, while Tardini is much more conservative and has monarchist sympathies.

These two individuals always complemented each other in remarkable fashion and for many years Pacelli was well satisfied with his two top collaborators. He actually preferred Montini, with whom he had a certain affinity of temperament, and although Montini was younger and head of the Second Section (theoretically less important than the First which was headed by Tardini) he consulted Montini more frequently and gave him particularly delicate and difficult tasks to perform.

In 1946 Pacelli held a Consistory, at which neither Tardini nor Montini got the Red Hat. It was said at the time that Pius XII didn't want to lose his precious collaborators. Had he made them Cardinals he would then have been morally obliged to appoint one of them State Secretary and give to the other a diocese or some job in the Curia. But Pius XII believed that nobody would be as good as himself as State Secretary and preferred to leave the post vacant.

Next came the 1953 Consistory and with it the sensational official announcement that Tardini and Montini had both declined the cardinalate so as to be able to remain at the Pope's side in a more humble capacity. To compensate them for their attachment Pacelli nominated them both Pro-Secretaries of State, a new and purely honorary title which didn't alter the substance of things at all.

What had happened? No one will probably ever know for certain. At all events at least three different versions leaked out of the Vatican, and these three I shall relate impartially.

According to the first version the Pope had told them that, although he had decided to make them Cardinals, neither of them would have gotten the post of State Secretary which would continue to be left vacant. They had preferred to stay in their key posts, which gave them an effective power superior to that of most Cardinals, rather than to satisfy their vanity but be forced to leave the heart of the Church administration.

The second version was worthy of Machiavelli. Tardini, it said, had realized that the Pope's preference went to his younger colleague. Therefore, once they had both become Cardinals, Montini would have leapt over Tardini's head and become State Secretary. Tardini then made the great gesture of renouncing the purple and Montini, not to appear more ambitious and less devoted to the Pope, was compelled to follow suit.

The third version has to do with Vatican finances. As I shall explain in a later chapter the handling of the Church's money was firmly in the hands of two laymen—the Pope's nephew Prince Carlo Pacelli and the Pope's close friend Count Enrico Galeazzi. The functions of the State Secretary include the control of finances; thus a clash with the two lay financiers would have been inevitable. As these two were very dear to Pacelli, the new State Secretary, whether he was going to be Tardini or Montini, would have found himself in an extremely difficult and embarrassing position. Whatever the reason, the fact remains that both Tardini and Montini had twice missed the Consistory nod.

At the end of 1954 another *coup de théâtre* took place. The Pope, quite unexpectedly, appointed Montini Archbishop of Milan and his old colleague, friend and rival Tardini was left the key figure of the State Secretariat. In this case too there were conflicting interpretations. It was said that Pacelli wanted to offer Montini the chance of acquiring experience as a shepherd of souls (of diplomatic and political experience he had had quite enough) thus reinforcing his chances as a *papabile*. In other words, it was a way of indicating that Pacelli favored Montini as his successor. As a matter of fact the respect and repute Montini enjoyed in the Vatican, his thorough knowledge of Church affairs, the sympathy most foreign Cardinals showed for him—all these combined to make him Candidate Number One.

As the years went by and Montini was never made a Cardinal this theory began to totter. Milan is, after Rome, the most important Italian diocese and by a well-established tradition its Archbishop was always a Cardinal. The Milanese took it almost as a personal affront that their Archbishop had not been made one, and they got into the habit of addressing Montini as "Your Eminence" although he had no right to this title which is reserved to Cardinals. The removal of Montini from the State Secretariat no longer looked like a reward and a prelude to the pontificate, but as the consequence of a mysterious clash of opinion between Pacelli and the man who for so many years had been his closest adviser and collaborator.

The rumors at the time were that Pacelli and Montini were no longer seeing eye to eye so far as Italian politics were concerned and also that Montini had been gaining such an influence in the Vatican that the Pope feared that the control of the State Secretariat might slip out of his own hands. It's quite possible, of course, that there was no truth in these rumors and that the Pope never meant to slight Montini. In this case the explanation (not altogether convincing) is that the Pope intended to make Montini a Cardinal, but that he just kept postponing it year after year until he died. As things went, at the death of Pacelli the scion of the Church found himself still outside the College of Cardinals and thus missed the chance of being elected Pope by the 1958 Conclave.

If the Tardini-Montini story has been dealt with somewhat at length it is not for the love of gossip, but because it affords the occasion of catching a glimpse of Vatican mentality, of showing that, even behind the Bronze Door, personal friendships and antagonisms, luck, circumstances and subtle maneuvering play almost as important a part as in lay politics. Moreover, I have a feeling that the Tardini-Montini story is not quite finished yet, that more will be heard about these two top Church personalities and that the reader might like to have this insight into their backgrounds.

John XXIII immediately remedied the somewhat unfair situation in which Montini had found himself. He gave him the Red Hat and put his name at the top of the list of new Cardinals. But, at the same time, as has been noted, he also made Tardini a Cardinal and gave him the key post of State Secretary.

In the last year of Pacelli's reign Tardini appeared to be a tired and disillusioned man. Often he was ill, went around with a thick woolen scarf wrapped about his neck and didn't turn up at his office for long periods. It was even reported that he intended to resign and dedicate himself entirely to his hobby, which is a college for orphans and boys from poor families. He gives all the money he earns—and that which he can squeeze out of his friends—to this institution and he spends all his spare time among his boys. Tardini, as has been said, has known poverty through personal experience and his dream is that of providing poor children with an education and a standard of living equal to that of the rich. Another aim of the college is to promote priestly vocations, but here Tardini has been disappointed as only very few of his boys have chosen to become priests.

After he was made State Secretary, Tardini seemed to take a

new lease on life. His ailments disappeared for a while, the woolen scarf has been thrown away, his usual jollity and pungent wit have returned and he dedicated himself to his work with renewed enthusiasm and energy. And he needs them both, as the problems that confront John XXIII and his State Secretary are truly formidable. Let me try to outline these problems briefly.

For the Roman Catholic Church the main danger is, without doubt, communism. Since the Soviets have seized power in Russia a relentless war, which is often subterranean but which from time to time explodes into sensational dramas, has been going on between the smallest and the largest States in the world, between a power which is essentially spiritual and one which is based on materialism, between those who promise Paradise after death and those who dazzle their followers with the promise of Paradise on earth. After the first centuries of Christianity, when the Church suffered endless persecutions, one can say that the greatest dangers the Church of Rome has had to face have been Islam, the Reformation, the French Revolution and now communism. Rome has always managed to come out on top, sometimes almost miraculously, and to those who predict its end at a more or less early date the prelates of the Vatican reply with an anecdote concerning Napoleon. The future Emperor, then Commander in Chief of the French army in Italy, once had a violent clash with Cardinal Ercole Consalvi, the State Secretary.

"Don't you know," shouted the fiery Corsican, "that I could destroy your Church?"

To which Consalvi had answered with a smile,

"I doubt it. Not even we priests have succeeded in doing so during eighteen centuries."

The story is reported from Poland that at the beginning of 1959 a Polish adventurer was charged with swindling. He had bought 20,000 portraits of Engels from a State library, painted a halo round the head, touched up the clothes and sold the final products as images of St. Joseph. Since religious feelings continue to be as strong as ever in Poland, he was able to sell his St. Josephs at ten times the price he had paid for Engels and thus pocketed a small fortune. Interestingly enough, a Warsaw court acquitted him.

I am relating this episode because it epitomizes a situation. A thing like this (I refer specifically to the acquittal!) could not have happened three or four years earlier in any Communist country, not even in Poland. The fact is that the struggle between the Vatican and the Kremlin has entered a new phase. It is no longer a question of ruthless persecutions on one side and of anathemas, excommunications, and heartrending prayers on the other. Naturally the Vatican and the Kremlin are still implacable foes, but instead of hitting out at each other in a blind rage or in desperation, they are playing a much more subtle chess game, moving their pieces carefully, studying each other's moves, calculating possible losses and gains on a long-term basis.

The denunciation of Stalin's crimes and the debunking of his myth, the policy of relative liberalization and appeasement inaugurated by Khrushchev, the Hungarian revolution and the near-revolution of Gomulka in Poland have brought about a change in the situation. Today the position of the Catholic Church in the Communist countries varies greatly—from the relative freedom and collaboration established in Poland between the Church and the national communism of Gomulka to an uneasy collaboration in Hungary, to a forced collaboration in Czechoslovakia and East Germany, down to the outright old-style persecutions which Catholics are still suffering in Rumania, Bulgaria and, above all, in China.

A rough-and-ready but effective rule permits one to say that the persecution is stronger where the Church is weaker and vice versa. This means that the Communists while still hating the Catholics fear them and do not dare to persecute them rigorously unless they are sure the Catholics cannot hit back. Where the Catholics are still strong and united, the Communists prefer to come to terms with them and to try and disrupt them from within, little by little. Before taking up the latest developments and the attitude of the new Pope, John XXIII, let me briefly outline the situation of the Church in the various Communist countries.

CHINA. There are about three million Catholics in China, but they represent only a small fraction as compared with the total population of 580 millions. When Mao Tse-tung took over power in 1949 he at first gave his support to the Catholic Church, but it turned out to be an idyll of very short duration. Relations between them deteriorated rapidly and by 1951 persecution was in full swing.

China had 120 bishops, of whom only thirty were Chinese, all the rest being of foreign origin. Today all the foreign bishops have been expelled, the majority after suffering imprisonment, while of the thirty Chinese, fifteen are in prison. Then 3,015 priests, 2,315 nuns and 775 friars, all of them foreigners, have been either expelled or put in jail, so that the native clergy and members of religious orders have been left to face the Communist assault alone.

The religious orders have not been officially dissolved (except the Legion of Mary, which, because of its title, has perhaps been mistaken for a paramilitary association!), but their apostolate has been seriously hampered by the fact that friars and nuns are all compelled to work at menial labor. This applies also to the priests, even if they are of very high rank. A number of bishops are working as peasants or in textile factories, one is a carpenter, while another has become a photographer. No priest can celebrate Mass after 8 in the morning. All must wear civilian clothes. The churches are open but are used also by the Party as dance halls and for other celebrations, which often take place while in another part of the church Mass is being celebrated.

The clergy who have survived are so few that many Catholics die without being able to receive extreme unction. The seminaries were closed and then re-opened in 1956, but the students are obliged to attend courses in Marxism and, generally speaking, they end up by being so indoctrinated that they are more useful to the Communists than to the Church. In spite of all this, the faith still burns strongly, especially among the young, perhaps as a reaction to the widespread conformity around them. In the Catholic families, which follow both the Catholic and the Chinese pattern and are very large, it has become a habit to keep a suitcase ready packed in case one of the men of the household should be arrested by the political police.

The work of internal disruption of the Church has met with greater success in China than in the other Communist countries. This is probably due to the complete isolation of the country, to the long distance—this is also spiritual in a certain sense—that it is from Rome, and to the nationalistic fervor which has seized the Chinese and hence also a part of the Chinese Catholics. The Communists have organized an association of "patriot priests," who held their first conference in Peking in August 1957. The "patriot priests" have declared that, while remaining faithful to Rome for all that concerns Catholic dogma, doctrine and morals, they consider themselves independent, from the political and administrative point of view. It is over this last point that the very grave dispute with Rome has developed, so grave that John XXIII has been compelled, during a speech at a Consistory, to use the ominous and almost forgotten word "schism." In fact, the philo-Communist priests in China have started to elect their own bishops, asserting that they have thus gone back to olden times, to the practices of the first Christians. Already in June 1958, Pius XII had declared that this constituted an act of rebellion against the Holy See and that such bishops had incurred excommunication, unless they had been compelled to accept under duress. John XXIII, after recalling the persecutions to which the Catholics of China are being subjected, added in his speech at the Consistory, "Unfortunately we have to say to our sorrow that there have been several who, more afraid of the injunctions of men than of the holy judgment of God, have given way in face of the impositions of the persecutors and reached even the point of accepting a sacrilegious episcopal consecration, from which they cannot derive any jurisdictional authority since it was conferred without the apostolic mandate."

Among the high prelates who took part in the Peking conference and who are supporting the patriot priests are the Archbishop of Siangyang, Mgr. Pu Ciu-ce, the bishop of Chunking, Mgr. Paul Wang, the vicar general of Nanking, Mgr. Li Wei-wang, and the vicar capitular of Shanghai, Mgr. Francis Xavier Chang. It would also seem, though it is hard to say with certainty in view of the difficulty of receiving trustworthy news from that enormous country, that Communist propaganda has also made headway to some extent among the Chinese Franciscans.

BULGARIA. Here there are only 53,000 Catholics in a population of 7,700,000 and persecution has been most violent. The Bishop of Nicopolis, Eugeni Bossilkoff, was condemned to death in 1952 on the charge of plotting against the State. The sentence was afterwards commuted to imprisonment for life and he was deported to Siberia. It is not known whether he is still alive. With him twenty-eight other priests were tried. The brothers Siskov were condemned to death; the remainder received sentences of from one to twenty years' imprisonment. Smoking is allowed in the churches. Religious teaching has been prohibited in the schools since 1948. All Catholic priests are compelled to join the Partisans of Peace movement.

RUMANIA. The Catholics number 2,650,000 and represent 14 per cent of the population. The persecution, arrest and sentencing of priests began as early as 1946. In 1948 the Concordat with the Holy See was denounced and in November of that year the whole Catholic Church was incorporated by decree into the Orthodox National Church, which is very submissive to the Communists. Those who refused to obey the injunction were subjected to ferocious reprisals. Eight bishops have been imprisoned and five died in jail; fifty-five priests have been murdered, 250 deported; 200 sent to labor camps; 200 imprisoned. All the religious houses (with 318 monks and 1,826 nuns) have been closed and the same has happened to the 228 Catholic boys' schools (28,000 pupils), to the 152 girls' schools (23,000 pupils) and to all the Catholic cultural and charitable institutes.

CZECHOSLOVAKIA. Although 70 per cent of this country is Catholic, its inhabitants have accepted the Communist regime (as they formerly did the Nazis) without any great show of resistance, a fact that has allowed the Soviet leaders to submit the Church to violent and unrelenting pressure. The Archbishop of Prague, Mgr. Giuseppe Beran, has for many years been detained in an unknown place and the bishops of the six Czech and the six Slovene dioceses are either in prison, or under house-arrest or are prevented from exercising their mission. All the Catholic schools have been confiscated by the State. All the religious orders (which comprise about 2,000 men and 5,000 women) were dissolved in 1950 and their members have been sent to labor camps or to homes if they were too old or ill. The seminaries, which numbered twelve, that is, one for each diocese, have been reduced to two, and the students have to take courses in Marxist teaching. The teaching of religion is allowed in the State schools, but in practice it is hampered and discouraged, so much so that only 10 per cent of the pupils attend these lessons. Very many priests have been enrolled as members of the Communist Party.

HUNGARY. If the heroic fighters for Hungarian freedom did not succeed in winning independence for their country, they at least were successful in creating in the Communists a certain respect and fear. The Communist authorities no longer dare to put into practice the high-handed and brutal methods of the old days and the Church has been able to gain something from this new atmosphere. In this country a *modus vivendi* has been reached and there is a certain amount of collaboration between Church and government.

Here too, however, as with relations between the Church and Communism in general, religion is affected in a dozen different, and sometimes curious, ways. Cardinal Mindszenty, after being arrested, tortured, compelled to confess to imaginary crimes, condemned to imprisonment for life and later liberated by the revolutionaries, is still living as a refugee in the American Legation in Budapest. When the Conclave was summoned the Kadar Government declared that if the Cardinal should attempt to leave his place of asylum in order to go to Rome, he would be arrested just as if he were an ordinary Hungarian citizen who still had a sentence to serve.

But Archbishop Joseph Groesz, who, in the forced absence of the Primate and having been chosen for the diocese of Kalocza, finds himself automatically in the position of head of the episcopate, is in a very different position. He takes part in official ceremonies and when Khrushchev visited Budapest after the revolution had been crushed by Russian tanks, Groesz met him, gave him a smile and shook his hand. On the eve of the elections of November 1958 the Hungarian episcopate launched an appeal to the faithful, inviting them to do their duty as citizens and to go to the polls. Seeing that, as is the case in all the dictatorial regimes, only one list was put before the voters, this clearly represented Church support for the State.

The Vatican was deeply embarrassed by this move but did not dare to disavow the Magyar bishops, just as Pope John XXIII, in his allocution at a recent Consistory, dealt solely with China and made only a passing reference to other Catholics who are suffering persecution, but without entering into details or mentioning political systems or countries. However, the *Osservatore Romano,* in a rather cautious article, commented on the appeal of the episcopate and led the reader to understand that the bishops were compelled to put their signatures to it.

And it is just here that the heart of the question lies. It is necessary to know how far these Hungarian Church leaders have been forced and intimidated by threats of physical violence (death, torture, trials, imprisonment, arrest) and how far by blandishments, promises, concessions of help to the Church (the Hungarian Communists have financed the reconstruction of many church buildings destroyed during the war and have replaced the bells that the Germans melted down to make cannons), more freedom for the clergy, permission to print parochial periodicals, reviews, as well as other advantages. The bishops and the clergy who live in the country are faced with a tragic dilemma. On the one hand they can follow literally the official point of view of the Holy See according to which all Communists are demons incarnate and those who collaborate with them are traitors. In this case they would all have to share the fate of Mindszenty, become martyrs and resign themselves to seeing the Church return to the period of the catacombs. On the other hand they can do what many of them are now doing, that is, endeavor to survive, to save what can still be saved, to pretend to respect the Moloch of the Communist State and try to obtain in exchange as many advantages as possible. It is also necessary to know how far the Vatican, while unable officially to admit this policy, may not tacitly, I would say almost secretly, approve it as the only possible one.

It is, in any case, a strange and risky game in which both sides have something to lose and something to gain. The Communists obtain, if not the sincere support, at least a sort of neutrality on the part of vast masses of the population, the bulk of them rural, who are still deeply religious and who by their nature would be hostile. They lose in having to admit implicitly that their atheism and materialism have become bankrupt, that there is another power besides that of the Party, by allowing an organization to exist that they will never be able completely to control, and by permitting the entry into the interior of the State of a potential Trojan horse. The Church obtains some practical advantages, a chance of surviving and greater liberty of action, but loses on the moral plane, since she is compelled to come to terms with her persecutors, to shake hands with those who have murdered so many priests and people faithful to her and who have thrown into prison an even greater number.

But it must not be thought that all the Hungarian bishops are in the same position as Groesz. Only four of them have fallen into line and are functioning regularly. They are Mgr. Ferenc Virag, Bishop of Pécs, Mgr. Endre Hamvas, Bishop of Szeged, Mgr. Lajos Shvoy, Bishop of Szekesfeherhvar, and Mgr. Sandor Kovacs, Bishop of Szombathely. After the death three years ago of the Bishop of Eger, Mgr. Czapik, his Vicar, Mgr. Brenoczay, went a step further than Groesz in collaboration with the Communists and associated himself with the movement of the Partisans of Peace. On the other hand, however, the Bishops of Györ and Vac, Mgr. Kalman Papp and Mgr. Jozsef Petery, respectively, have been banished to the village of Hejce, and the Bishop of Veszprem, Bertalan Badalik, is under strict police surveillance and cannot exercise his ministry. Mgr. Papp has been repeatedly arrested and submitted to very close questioning by the AVO secret police on the matters he discussed with Mgr. Zagon, an envoy of the Vatican, who visited Hungary during the revolution.

In Hungary, as in other satellite States, the Communists are still trying to disrupt the Church from within. A very small number of priests have broken away from Rome and have joined the "Priests of the Peace" movement, thus incurring excommunication. The Communists are also trying to organize a lay Catholic Action movement, of which the notorious Father Balogh was nominated president in September 1958. Balogh is a priest steeped in intrigue, who likes to enjoy the good things of life, is greedy for wealth and power, and who, from the very beginning lined up on the side of the Reds and was suspended *a divinis*.

In every Hungarian diocese there is a seminary that functions after a fashion but the number of students is very limited (from ten to twenty for each seminary) and the scarcity of priests is beginning to make itself felt. An encouraging factor, however, is the existence of a very intense religious life; the churches are crowded and many declared Communists, after being married according to the civil rite, undergo another marriage ceremony in church in secret. Hungary has a population of a little under ten million, of whom 69 per cent are Catholics.

POLAND. As the joke repeated at the head of this chapter indicates, this country represents a real exception as regards the Catholic

Church behind the Iron Curtain. There are in Poland thirty million fervent Catholics who comprise nearly the whole population and who, even during the period of the worst persecutions, when Cardinal Wyszynski was tried and imprisoned, have always remained a compact body and have compelled the Communists to concede to the Church a freedom of which their unfortunate co-religionists beyond the Curtain have never dreamed and perhaps will never dream. Since the return of Gomulka to power and his liberation of Wyszynski, the position of the Church has become further strengthened. There is complete freedom of religion, the bishops and the clergy can do as they please without having to render an account of their actions to the Party. There is a Catholic university at Lublin that is still active (although the attendance has fallen to less than half—from 3,095 in 1951 to 1,352 in 1958), religion is taught in all the schools for one hour a week, there are several Catholic secondary schools with a total of 600 pupils, youths who wish to become priests can come to Rome, study in a seminary, and then return to their country, and Catholics have been allowed to publish various reviews.

In Poland too, the Communists had tried fifth column tactics by creating the "Pax" movement, which directed its appeal above all to the Catholic intellectuals and which had its own publishing house. But since Gomulka has been in power, financial support for this movement has been reduced and it has lost much of its influence.

Gomulka himself realized that from the point of view of Communism he had gone too far in his leniency toward the Church. During the ninth Plenum in May 1957 he justified himself in the following terms, "We have concluded an agreement with the Church and we have accepted optional religious teaching. In this field we in Poland have a situation that does not exist in any other Socialist State, and not even in France or the United States. This does not correspond to the ideology of our Party, but we cannot shut our eyes in the face of reality. We cannot exercise any pressure on the believers and we must take into account the fact that the recent conflict between the Church and the State has turned millions of believers against the people's regime. The Party accepts the principle that the idealist ideology (religion) will live a long time at the side of the materialist ideology (communism). And for a long time to come believers and nonbelievers, the Church and Socialism, the people's regime and the ecclesiastical hierarchy will go on existing side by side."

Wyszynski fully realizes that the position of the Catholic Church in Poland is wholly exceptional and also that Gomulka has powerful enemies not only in the Kremlin but also inside his own Party and that he might not remain in the saddle long. Hence he has persuaded the local clergy to exercise a strict control over their actions, not to take too much advantage of the freedom granted them so as not to embarrass Gomulka, and not to play the game of his Stalinist enemies. In this country collaboration between the Church and national communism is fairly sincere inasmuch as the two sides in question have a common aim: that of keeping Poland independent as far as possible without coming to a showdown with Moscow and the other satellite States, which could end as tragically as was the case in Hungary.

EASTERN GERMANY, LITHUANIA, ESTHONIA, LATVIA AND YUGOSLAVIA. Here the situation is more or less the same as that in Czechoslovakia, though it is perhaps slightly more oppressive in the Baltic countries that have been incorporated into the Soviet Union.

Conditions in Yugoslavia resemble those of Poland. After the initial persecutions and the imprisonment of the heroic and stubborn Cardinal Alojzye Stepinac, a kind of modus vivendi seems to have been found.

But to return to the Vatican and John XXIII. The dilemma with which the new Pope is wrestling is perhaps even more dramatic and difficult to solve than that of the bishops and the clergy in each of the Communist countries. The Pope cannot restrict himself to considering the situation in each country, one by one, and try to solve them in the best way possible. He must face the problem of communism as a whole, and on both sides of the Iron Curtain, as a political system, as an ideology, and, as has been noted, as the gravest danger that has threatened the Church since the advent of Islam and the French Revolution. A too rigid and intransigent attitude could lead to the loss of the advantages obtained in Poland and, to a minor degree, in Hungary and Yugoslavia, while if the Vatican were to show itself too accommodating this would provide the Communists with a powerful propaganda weapon, enabling them to proclaim to the world, "You see, the devil is not as black as he is painted. Even the Catholic Church has reached an agreement with us."

This, naturally, would give great pleasure to the Communists and, indeed, they have already made several attempts to gain this end. From 1956 on Khrushchev had given instructions to the Counselor of the Soviet Embassy in Rome, Dmitri Pogidaiev, to endeavor to establish some contact with the Vatican and to lay the basis for talks. Some very indirect soundings were made but matters ended there because of the reluctance of the Vatican to engage in such a very risky game and because of the rigid policy of Pacelli. Pogidaiev was later appointed Ambassador to Berne, and it is said that from there he made another attempt to get in touch with the Vatican. Until 1960 he was serving as Ambassador in Morocco. Soon after the election of Roncalli he was reported to be in Rome and there was talk of a mysterious meeting he had with a high prelate through the collaboration of a Bulgarian refugee. There has, however, been no confirmation of the story.

In January 1958 the Soviet Foreign Minister, Gromyko, made a first formal overture to the Vatican. He said, "The Soviet Union would welcome official contacts with the Vatican on all the questions that concern the defense of peace. The speeches made by the Pope on the questions of peace and on the industrial use of atomic energy for peaceful purposes coincide with the Soviet point of view." The offer, in view of its propagandistic character, was naturally ignored by the Holy See. According to authoritative Vatican circles, as things stand today, open and direct negotiations between the Holy See and the Kremlin are out of the question. It cannot be ruled out, on the other hand (and this is just what John XXIII will have to decide) that the Church may relinquish her pretense of ignoring the existence of the partial agreements reached by the local clergy with the Communist authorities of the various countries, and may attempt to obtain more substantial and permanent advantages in exchange for official recognition by Rome of what is, in effect, an established fact.[1]

Since Roncalli was elected Pope there have been a few straws in the wind to indicate a change of attitude in the Vatican. First of all, John XXIII has withdrawn diplomatic recognition from the Polish Ambassador to the Holy See, Casimir Papée, and from the Lithuanian Minister, Stanislaus Girdvainis. They were both representing the governments-in-exile of these two countries and under Pius XII they had enjoyed full diplomatic status to the degree that Papée was the dean of the Diplomatic Corps.

The old ambassador, as soon as he heard what was in store for him, wrote a short but rather moving and noble letter of protest to State Secretary Tardini, of which I was able to see a copy. Papée

[1] Roncalli's attitude, or at least mental approach, can perhaps be surmised from the following passage of a private letter he wrote as early as 1921 to his friend Don Chienze, a leader of Catholic Action. Referring to the political struggle raging in Italy, in which Catholic Action was deeply involved, Roncalli wrote, "Our elders used the motto 'Frangar, non flectar' (I will break but not bend). I, on the contrary, prefer this motto in reverse 'Flectar, non frangar' (I will bend but not break), especially when questions of a practical character are concerned: and I think that the whole tradition of the Church is with me."

underlined the great symbolical value of the Polish Embassy to the Holy See and the disastrous psychological effects that its closing down would have on the ten million Poles in exile and on all those Catholics behind the Iron Curtain who were still putting up a heroic fight against the Communists in the hope of future freedom. He reminded Tardini that the Communists had offered only promises in exchange and that history has shown that such promises were worthless.

The representatives of the Lithuanian clergy abroad—bishops, heads of religious orders, rectors, etc.—signed a plea to John XXIII imploring him not to close down the Lithuanian Legation, and Lithuanian politicians in exile and leaders of the communities scattered all over the world bombarded the Vatican with telegrams and letters. They were joined by political exiles from Hungary, Rumania, Czechoslovakia and other Communist-dominated countries, who used to look at the two diplomatic representations as a tangible proof that the Vatican would never sanction Communist domination over Eastern Europe. In view of this world-wide reaction the Vatican has tried to water down the measure as much as possible. The withdrawal of diplomatic recognition—said an article in the *Osservatore Romano*—had no political implications and was based merely on technical and juridical grounds. The two diplomats, it added, could go on functioning as *"gerenti di affari,"* a strange definition unknown in diplomatic language which can be loosely translated as *caretakers.* Both Papée and Girdvainis are still invited to official Vatican ceremonies but the *Osservatore Romano* regularly omits mention of their presence.

Girdvainis was received in private audience by the Pope, and again the *Osservatore Romano* omitted to report the news. I have been told that John XXIII, after having embraced and kissed him on the forehead, went to fetch a chair and made him sit down. He told him he was sorry for having withdrawn recognition but added he had had to do it in the superior interests of the Church. Stanislaus Girdvainis, a disillusioned old gentleman with a bad heart, tried to find out what his position was going to be in future but the interview came to an end before he was able to do so.

In Vatican quarters there is not the slightest doubt that the elimination of Papée and Girdvainis was the doing of Wyszynski. The Polish Cardinal delayed for two days his departure from Warsaw to attend the Conclave in order to wait for Gomulka to return from Moscow and discuss with him his trip to Rome. After Roncalli was elected Pope, Wyszynski had three very long interviews with him and remained in Rome much longer than was expected. He met

Tardini several times and discussed with him a 500-page typewritten memorandum on the subject that he had brought with him.

Wyszynski pointed out, and quite rightly from his point of view, the absurdity of the situation: While he and his clergy were collaborating with Gomulka and helping him to keep Poland as independent from Moscow as possible, the Vatican was still recognizing the Polish government-in-exile. This, he added, was an act of hostility toward Poland and weakened his position when dealing with Gomulka. Both the Pope, who has always been ready to face reality, and his State Secretary were convinced by Wyszynski's reasoning and sacrificed Papée on the altar of immediate and practical advantage.

The story, however, does not end here. The Vatican is rife with rumors about a further tightening of relations between the Holy See and Warsaw. They say that all the Polish bishops will come to Rome within a year to pay the routine visit that they had been prevented from doing since the end of the war. They also say that the Pope is contemplating the appointment of an apostolic visitor to Warsaw. An apostolic visitor does not have actual diplomatic status but something very similar. He is not officially accredited to the government of the country he is sent to but he does represent the Holy See and supervises all the activities of the local clergy.

Another rumor is that Gomulka has in store a peace plan, which he would produce in case the differences between America and Russia over Berlin should bring the West and the East to the brink of war. The plan is designed in such a way as to allow both the Americans and the Russians to withdraw from their positions without losing face. According to Wyszynski the Gomulka plan has some chances of success and the Vatican should not ignore it but, on the contrary, try to break into the diplomatic game with all the weight of its moral authority, both to help the success of the maneuver and to share the credit of having saved peace.

While the Vatican's attitude toward Poland is fairly clear and logical, the Lithuanian issue is a more tricky one. Unlike Poland, Lithuania has no government of its own and, together with the two other Baltic States, it was bodily incorporated into the Soviet Union. By withdrawing recognition from the Lithuanian Minister, the Vatican has indirectly sanctioned the loss of Lithuania's freedom. The United States, Great Britain, France, Western Germany and several South American countries have so far refused to recognize this incorporation of Lithuania. The Vatican gesture represents a breach in the Western anti-Communist front that probably could not have occurred under Pius XII.

It is therefore more difficult to see the reasons that prompted Roncalli to sacrifice the Lithuanian Minister. Some people feel sure that here too it was Wyszynski who has been maneuvering behind the scenes. The Polish primate is credited with the intention of getting the Vatican to transfer the Lithuanian Catholics under his jurisdiction. In exchange he promised he would secure them better conditions, similar to those the Polish Catholics are enjoying. Lithuanians abroad look with suspicion at this plan and accuse Wyszynski of "Polish imperialism."

With regard to the Far East, the great hopes that had been placed on Japan immediately after the end of the last war have not been fulfilled. Hostility and prejudice against the Catholic Church, which seemed to have melted in the fire of the lost war, have little by little reappeared. With an increase of population of 800,000 a year, Catholic baptisms are only 15,000. True conversions are very rare and limited to the big cities. For some years past the situation has deteriorated with a constant diminution of adults undergoing religious instruction before baptism.

In Latin America, the situation is causing great concern to John XXIII. The shortage of priests, which is a symptom and a consequence of the weakness of the Church in that part of the world, is the most urgent problem the Vatican must solve there. While the Catholics of Latin America represent 35 per cent of all the Catholics in the world, the Latin American priests are only 8.7 per cent of the total Catholic clergy. To be more exact, in South America there is only one priest for every 11,800 inhabitants, in Central America one for every 14,000 and in the Antilles one for 18,000. (In this connection one is inevitably reminded, by the way of contrast, of the situation existing in the Kingdom of Naples in 1789. This minute State then had twenty-two Archbishops, 116 bishops and no less than 61,000 priests!) The situation is made even worse by geographical conditions: some parishes are as large as a whole normal European diocese. Lack of communications, high mountains, tropical jungles, and floods make it very difficult for the priest to visit his parishioners. In some remote villages marriages, baptisms and first communions are celebrated en masse once or twice a year when the parish priest manages to get there.[1]

---

[1] The figures quoted do not relate to the total number of priests in Latin America but to those who actually look after their flocks. A few comparisons will help to define the situation. While in the Paris diocese there are 1,675 priests for 3,436,556 Catholics, in Mexico City there are only 305 priests for an even larger number, 3,880,500 Catholics. The New York diocese (1,491,000 Catholics) has 1,234 priests while Santiago (Chile) has but 296 for a Catholic population of 1,600,000.

Because of this very serious situation several areas of Latin America are still considered missionary lands and therefore fall under the jurisdiction of the *Congregation de Propaganda Fide*. "This Congregation has conducted a thorough inquiry into the causes of the Church's weakness in Latin America and its conclusions have been disclosed by the official organ of the Congregation, the international news agency *Fides*. The dangers the Church has to face have been listed as follows: illiteracy, Freemasonry, secularism, spiritism,[2] Protestantism and Communism.

"Illiteracy," [the agency wrote] "reaches very high peaks in Latin America; the average is about 40 per cent. The position is made worse by the shortage of teachers. Religious ignorance is also very worrisome: religious teaching in the State schools is authorized only in nine countries. Therefore the burden of religious teaching falls entirely on the priests who are already scarce and overworked in most countries."

As for Freemasonry the Vatican agency said that it "has been strong since the Latin American Republics became independent and has never ceased attacking the Church in Parliament using a subtle disrupting tactic and hiding its antireligious aims so as not to offend the religious feelings of the people. In this way freemasonry has caused damages in nearly all the Latin American countries bringing secularism into the schools and the families, favoring the birth of centers of spiritism, particularly in Brazil and Haiti. Instead of disappearing, freemasonry has strengthened its action in several countries. In Cuba, for example, 15 per cent of the students in State secondary schools belong to masonic lodges."

Fides added "Lay legislation has caused serious damages not only in the field of teaching, but also within the families, and its nefarious action has been made easier by the scarcity of the clergy. To the large number of marriages contracted without the religious sanction—in some countries illegitimate marriages reach 60 or even 80 per cent— one must add divorce, which is recognized in sixteen out of twenty Latin American States. In those countries where such law is in effect the proportion is sometimes of one divorce for every four or five marriages."

The Fides Agency then dealt with the spreading of the Protestant Churches. It wrote "Protestant infiltration into Latin America goes back to 1858, but has become more intense since the congress of

[2] By "spiritism" the agency means all those primitive rites—often contaminated by spurious elements of the Christian faith—exorcisms, witchcraft, obsessive dancing and chanting which also go under the name of "voodoo" and which are practiced by the natives of the West Indies and Latin America. Their total number has been reckoned by the Vatican at around five million.

Protestant Churches held in Madras in 1938. Since 1946 Protestantism has multiplied its sects in Latin America and in some cases has trebled its personnel. Having abundant financial means, they have overcome the difficulty of great distances and they have opened infirmaries, hospitals, schools, colleges and seminaries, thus attracting souls with the promise of material wellbeing.

"During the last decades Protestantism has made great progress: In the forty years from 1916 to 1957 their foreign missionaries have risen from 1,689 to 6,303; their South American auxiliaries from 2,180 to 14,299, of whom more than 8,000 are laymen; their believers have risen from 169,880 to 4,614,000 and their churches from 3,530 to 25,891."

However, according to this appraisal by the Vatican, "The last and the worst enemy of the faith and the true wellbeing of the peoples of Latin America is communism. The economic-social problem facing all these countries, especially Bolivia and Chile, provides the best ground for Communist penetration. The inhuman conditions of the workers, badly paid and badly lodged, and particularly of the agricultural workers who form two-thirds of the Latin American population, the bad distribution of property, the state of abandon in which the Indians have been left, the lack of a solid intellectual foundation of the students in high schools and universities, as well as laicism prevailing in such quarters, are all causes that have paved the way for Marxism which overcomes all obstacles and infiltrates in a thousand different ways. The fact that communism is officially banned in the majority of Latin American countries should not deceive us, as in reality it has everywhere more or less clandestine organizations."

Pacelli had already sensed the danger and had promoted the formation of a Latin American episcopate known for short as CELAM which was set up in Rio de Janeiro in 1955. Its aim is to co-ordinate the activities and efforts not only of the bishops themselves but of all Catholic forces such as the religious orders, both male and female, seminaries, the Catholic schools and universities, the lay organizations, the press, the special bodies dealing with the cinema, radio, cultural activities, etc. It is a kind of Catholic Cominform for Latin America. Before CELAM was formed the Catholic Church in that part of the world lacked unity of action and very often this resulted in conflicting and overlapping initiatives and in waste of effort and money.

Working in close cooperation with *Propaganda Fides*, CELAM is also trying to solve the problem of the shortage of priests. A close collaboration has been established with the Spanish clergy (particularly useful since there are no language difficulties) and Spain, by the end of 1958, had sent to Latin America 258 priests. The Belgian

Collegium pro-America Latina of Louvain has sent twenty, while a number of Canadian priests are working in the region of Pinheiro, Brazil. But this is a mere trickle when one considers that the Vatican has reckoned that Latin America would need 160,000 priests and that there are now only 30,000.

The remedies which CELAM is trying to bring into action include:

(1) To intensify the anti-Communist propaganda with all possible means.

(2) To exercise pressure on the various governments for more speedy and effective social reforms so as to snatch the initiative from the Communists in this field.

(3) To launch a fund-raising campaign, especially in the United States, to finance missionary and welfare activities of the Catholic Church in Latin America on a scale similar to that for the Protestant churches.

(4) To try to get more priests from Spain, Portugal, Italy and other Latin countries and in the meantime to stimulate local vocations.

(5) To encourage the lay Catholic organizations (Catholic Action, *Opus Dei*, etc.) which have proved very successful and which are flourishing all over the world.

Africa, too, represents a very vast field of action for the Catholic Church. It is the continent of the future to which all those who nurse ambitious long-range plans of economic, political and religious expansion are looking. Despite the intense and often heroic activity of Catholic and Protestant missionaries, the record of conversions belongs to the Moslems. In other words, there are more Negroes who abandon their pagan or animistic beliefs to embrace the faith of Mohammed than those who let themselves be convinced by the message of Christ. Moslem proselytizing, however, goes on rather by force of inertia, while the Christian missionaries are more active, better organized and should, in the end, come out on top.

There are in Africa 13,107 Catholic priests and the faithful constitute only 10 per cent of the total population. It is a field mainly reserved to the *Congregation de Propaganda Fide* but one in which the State Secretariat is also interested, particularly whenever special issues are involved. Among these issues the more topical and burning is the urge for independence of the colored peoples.

Admonished by the experience of the past (and particularly by that of Latin America, the republics of which gained independence against the opposition of the Church and in which a considerable fund of anticlericalism has been accumulated) the Vatican as a rule is backing the independence movement. The Vatican is applying this policy through directions imparted to the bishops, through

Catholic Action and, finally, by trying to constitute a strong native clergy and by placing the natives in posts of responsibility. But it is a very complex picture, complicated by Arab nationalism and by the fact that the communities of whites living in Africa (which in the French, Spanish, Italian and Portuguese colonies and ex-colonies are mainly Catholic) are strongly opposed to the independence of the natives.

But not everything is dark on the vast horizon of the Church. The Catholics have made enormous progress in the United States where they represent 22 per cent of the population and constitute the largest single religious community. When, at the end of the War of Independence, Father John Carroll was appointed Apostolic Delegate in the United States, Catholics numbered 25,000 in a population of about four million. A big leap forward was made from the middle of the 1800's to the beginning of the 1900's, that is, in the period of the great migrations. After a period of relative stagnation the tempo of Catholic growth has increased since the end of World War II. Twenty-two million Catholics in 1945, twenty-six million in 1948, thirty-four million in 1956 and forty million in 1958 in a total population which the last census placed at 175 million.

The Vatican is noting with pleasure that the typically Catholic communities of the United States, such as the Irish, the Italians, and the Spanish speaking Caribbean islanders are constantly improving their economic and social status and are acquiring more weight in the life of the nation.

The Church of Rome is also progressing in Great Britain. Catholics in the Westminster (London) Archdiocese in 1958 exceeded the half-million mark, an increase of 70,000 units compared with the 1954 figure. The increase of Catholics in the London district is due to several factors: the natural increase of population, which is greater in Catholic than in Protestant families as the former don't practice birth control, immigration from Ireland and conversions. In 1954 the English and Welsh adults who were converted to Catholicism were 11,920, in 1955 the figure went up to 13,291 and in 1956 to 14,077. The figures of later years were not disclosed to avoid unpleasant discussions with the Protestant press which charged the Catholics with manipulating their figures.

This quick excursion across the continents, was not designed to give a complete picture of the problems the Vatican is facing in the world, but just to try and give an approximate idea of the magnitude and character of the tasks entrusted to the State Secretariat, which is the pivot of the central administration of the Church.

9

Today's Apostles

IN ROME there is a nun who wears a fur coat, uses Elizabeth Arden cosmetics, has a permanent wave and a professional hair-do, and attends receptions given by Elsa Maxwell. You may ask: What sort of a nun is this? And yet Mother Dominic Ramacciotti, a vivacious, dynamic, intelligent Italo-American approaching her sixties, has been authorized by the Pope to do all these things.

Mother Mary Dominic is carrying out an interesting experiment in the education of young girls, an experiment closely linked with the now famous "Boys' Republic" at Civitavecchia, of which the founder and presiding genius is Mgr. Carroll Abbing. It must be admitted that especially in Latin countries the institutions of the Catholic Church for the assistance and education of youth—orphanages, colleges, seminaries and homes—have something antiquated, austere and often gloomy about them. Who has not noticed in the streets of Italian cities the files of orphans or school children with their pale faces and drab uniforms, their frightened air and lack of vivacity, their eyes mostly fixed on the ground? And what a contrast they offer to the boys of the "Republic" of Mgr. Abbing, who are frank, at ease, cheerful, sure of themselves, and who share in and are responsible for an active, alert communal life.

Generally speaking, the girls who leave a Catholic institution (and to a lesser extent this applies also to the boys) are ill prepared to face the conditions of modern life. The Catholic institutions as a rule turn out good wives, excellent nuns, fine servants and angelic aunts who always remain spinsters, but they rarely produce good employees or active professional or business women. The object of the "Girls' Village" founded by Mary Dominic Ramacciotti in the Via Trionfale, on the outskirts of Rome, is twofold—to give to the young girls an advanced social training and education in keeping with the times, so that they will be able to fill well-paid jobs; and to introduce suitable girls of sound Catholic faith into such circles as the aristocracy, the fashionable world, the wealthy classes which, in general, are losing touch with the Church.

The girls turned out by Mother Mary Dominic's institute will be able to speak English and French, play the piano, distinguish a Van Gogh from a Picasso, arrange flowers, mix a cocktail, lay a table with taste, give orders to the servants, keep household accounts and entertain guests with brilliant conversation. They will be able to find and hold positions as airlines hostesses, housekeepers or governesses in patrician homes or in any case with well-to-do families of the smart set, or obtain jobs in the wide sphere of public relations.

To give her girls the necessary training and education and to create a suitable environment, Mary Dominic considered it indispensable to set them an example. She therefore obtained from Pius XII—while maintaining all her vows and remaining a nun—permission to dress with a certain elegance, to go to the opera and the theater, to frequent fashionable circles, to use make-up within limits and altogether to behave like an elegant woman from whose ways the institute's pupils could learn what would be to their advantage. The Girls' Village, which at present houses only twenty-four girls from all social classes but which has plans for rapid expansion, strikes the visitor with its air of poise, gaiety, elegance and downright freedom from all prejudice as compared, that is, with the ordinary religious institute.

Born in Maryland of wealthy Italian emigrant parents, Mary Dominic Ramacciotti from childhood felt the call of the vocations of nun and teacher, and she responded to both. Entering the Order of Our Lady she took her degree in philosophy at Washington University in the capital city, and after teaching in various secondary schools was made a professor at New York University. Subsequently she directed the College of Our Lady at Baltimore and, finally, having met Mgr. Carroll and become imbued with the utmost enthusiasm for the original teaching methods of the founder of the Boys' Republic, she devoted herself to the task of imitating him in the feminine sphere.

This is an unusual example of what one member of a religious order is doing. But there is much besides to learn about the religious orders and secular institutes and what they represent in the Church of today.

Within the Church's fold there are nearly a million nuns and about 250,000 male religious. The number of men and women belonging to the secular institutes, which are rapidly and continuously expanding, is not known even in the Vatican.

Altogether they form a complex, picturesque, diversified world, evolving unceasingly with enormous energy, which constitutes one of the most significant and timely aspects, full of promise of development, of the Church of Rome. In the ranks of this immense and multicolored militia are to be found missionaries, the monks of the hospice of the Great St. Bernard Pass who brave blizzards with their famous dogs to search for travelers who have lost their way, the erudite Jesuits, editors of great periodicals and newspapers, bearded hermits isolated from the world, Dominicans who sponsor abstract art, Franciscans who go barefoot from door to door asking for alms, teachers of all grades from the elementary schools to the universities, the astronomers of the Castel Gondolfo Observatory, the friars who draw teeth at the Isola Tiberina, an islet in the Tiber, where for centuries they have been running a primitive but efficient dental clinic, the nuns who enter a convent never to leave it until they die, the sisters who edit and print the brilliant women's magazine *Così*, the nuns who run an elegant dressmaker's establishment at Monte Mario, those who look after lepers in the wildest regions of Africa, the Franciscan tertiary, Gino Bartali, a former world champion bicyclist, several ministers of State and various Spanish generals who are secretly members of the *Opus Dei*, in a word, a vast multitude of men and women who, whether in ecclesiastical or lay dress, are working for the Catholic Church and carrying out the most varied and unexpected activities.

It is easy to lose one's way in this *mare magnum,* so let me try to explain this whole matter of the religious and of the various secular institutes.

The outstanding characteristic of the religious, as distinguished from the regular clergy, is that they live within a community and obey particular rules established by the order, congregation, institute, society or whatever the community may call itself. The bond between the individual and the community to which he belongs is so strong that anyone who leaves it loses the title of a religious and is exonerated from his vows. The slight differences are numerous and not always easy to grasp by those who are not well acquainted with the rules of

Canon Law and with the historical formation of this militia of Christ. Another characteristic is that for anyone to be considered as a religious in the strict sense of the word, he or she must have taken the public vows—vows, that is, accepted by the Church—to which are added the three evangelical counsels, called general counsels; namely obedience, chastity, poverty.

Regular canons. The regular canons are given this name because they add to the dignity and office of a canon a life lived in common. Among them are the Laterans, the Hospitaller Congregation of the Great St. Bernard, the Premonstratensians and the *Crocigeri* (Cross bearers).

Monks. Historically the monks were the first religious to live in communities. Gradually, as centuries passed, they added other activities to the monastic life, such as the priesthood and the apostolate in their most diverse forms; these activities, however, are not necessary for qualification as a monk. Among the principal communities of monks are the Confederated Benedictines (about 11,500) who are grouped into fourteen congregations, the Camaldolese Benedictines, those of Vallombrosa, the Silvestrines and the Olivetans (less than a thousand in all), the Cistercians (1,623), the Trappists (6,323), the Antonians, the Certosians, the Basilians, and many other minor orders.

Mendicant Orders. The characteristic feature of the mendicant orders, which arose at the beginning of the thirteenth century, is the corporative poverty which complements their individual poverty. Theoretically the order can possess nothing. In practice, however, this rule has been relaxed in accordance with the necessities of the times. Another characteristic is the rigid discipline under a superior, who has the fullest powers, and the organization into provinces. Among the principal mendicant orders are the Dominicans (9,508), the Franciscans (26,162), the Conventual Friars Minor (4,348), the Capuchins (15,442), the Augustins (divided into three orders with about 4,900 members altogether), the Carmelites (4,236), the Fate-benefratelli (Goodworks-Brothers) (2,420), the Servants of Mary (1,549) as well as other minor orders.

Regular clerks. This order came into being between the end of the sixteenth and the beginning of the seventeenth centuries. The principal object is to combine the priest's apostolate with community life, naturally according to specific circumstances. The rules of this community life are rather strict. The most famous among these religious are the Jesuits who, with 34,293 members, form the largest order in the Catholic Church, one which is continuously expanding. Particular attention will be given to the Jesuits in a separate chapter.

Other members of this group are the Scolopi (2,358), the Ministers of the Sick (1,278), the Barnabites, the Teatines and the Somaschi.

Clerical religious congregations. These associations are composed of both priests and laymen, who live together in communities. Without claiming to be regular religious orders, they carry out (in addition to the task of perfecting their members in religious matters) charitable works and promotion of the faith. Their members either do not take vows (and these will be listed later under a separate heading) or else they limit the solemnity of their vows. This category includes sixty-seven different congregations, of which only the most important are mentioned here: the Passionists (3,870), the Redeemers (8,900), the Marists (2,200), the Congregation of the Holy Spirit (5,200), the Oblate Missionaries of Mary Immaculate (7,307), the Marianists (3,110), the Congregation of the Holy Cross (2,837), the Claretians (3,356), the Salesians (18,240), the Missionaries of the Sacred Heart of Jesus (3,000), the Priests of the Sacred Heart of Jesus (2,997), and the Verbites (5,232).

Societies of community life without vows. As has been indicated, the members of these societies either take no vows at all, or not all the vows, or if they take them they do so privately and not publicly. They lead a community life very similar to that of the religious and devote themselves to perfecting their faith, to promotion of the faith of others and to charitable works. Generally they specialize in teaching and in assistance to the sick. Among them may be mentioned the Lazarists (5,510), who besides teaching in the seminaries also direct the associations of the Daughters and the Ladies of Charity, the Pallottines (2,155), the White Fathers (3,396), that is, the famous missionaries of Africa who dress in white, and many other minor societies.

Lay religious congregations. They are given this name because the great majority of their members are laymen. The most important group is that of the Brothers of the Christian Schools, with 17,215 members, followed by the Marist Brothers of the Schools (8,974), the Christian Brothers of Ireland (3,500), the St. Gabriel Brothers of Christian Education (1,640) and many others.

Secular institutes. For some decades now various associations of laics, both male and female, have been springing up and developing to a surprising extent. Their members, while not living in communities but continuing to follow their normal professions and occupations, devote themselves to promoting the Catholic faith and have placed themselves entirely at the service of the Church. They are men and women who, in former times, would have become priests, friars or nuns but who today prefer not to give up their lay dress and ways.

How, one may well ask, can the extraordinary success of these associations be explained? And what are the motives that inspire this movement?

First and foremost, are the psychological ones. Not a few priests admit, and often complain, that the wearing of the religious garb is an obstacle—however paradoxical this may seem—in the carrying out of their mission. The mere fact that they are wearing a black gown often creates a barrier between them and those with whom they converse, a feeling of estrangement, if not of downright embarrassment.

Again, a great number of prejudices exist against priests (one of the most common in Latin countries is that priests bring bad luck, and it is by no means rare for persons, when they see a priest, to touch wood or the keys in their pocket or make some other little gesture to ward off evil) and many people do not like to be seen in their company. In addition, religious practices have become more and more neglected in modern times. There are millions of Catholics who do not go to Mass, never visit the parish house, do not pray, do not go to confession and have practically no contact with the clergy. It is above all to this great mass of the indifferent that the lay apostles intend to direct their efforts; it is this mass of human beings that they want to bring back to the Church.

It would, for instance, be very difficult for a priest or a friar to go into a workshop or a factory and begin talking about God. Yet this would be a very easy thing for an architect, an engineer or a foreman to do, provided he was discreet and tactful. Again, a doctor called, let us say, to the sickbed of a freethinker can, without appearing to, turn the conversation toward the possibility of a life beyond that of this world, can begin to talk in such a way that a dying patient might end up by being converted *in extremis*. Lawyers, teachers, nurses, shopkeepers, businessmen, commercial travelers, bankers and others are all persons who make an infinite number of contacts with their fellow-men and who are able to enter circles where the priest is rarely seen or perhaps never appears. Moreover, what the priest says may be received with instinctive or preconceived diffidence, while, on the contrary, the short, friendly chat with a colleague can be far more effective. These are all reasons which many priests accept and which, generally speaking, led to the courageous experiment—brought to an end by an official ruling of the Vatican in the summer of 1959—of the French worker-priests, who used to go and work in the factories, celebrated Mass in civilian clothes and to a very large extent shared the life of their flocks.

Another factor that leads laymen of deep religious faith not to change their status is a certain distrust of the clergy's educational methods. They feel that the young priests who leave the seminaries lack the necessary cultural background, the open-mindedness, the adaptability which the complex and ever more pressing tempo of modern life demands. Educated according to rigid and traditionalist criteria (up to a short time ago daily newspapers were not allowed to be read in the seminaries, the one exception being the *Osservatore Romano*) they can still serve some small country parish, teaching the Catechism to children, hearing the confessions of elderly women; but, unless they possess noteworthy innate gifts that they are able to develop on their own, they are generally doomed to feel like fish out of water when they come into contact with broad-minded, liberal university students, the sharp-witted workmen of the great cities, in short, with the elite of the faithful. It must also be added that the mystical sentiment has grown weaker even among true believers and that the new lay apostles prefer to get down to brass tacks by entering completely, with the authority that a good professional training gives them, into everyday life and developing their work in the circles they can most easily reach and where they are most at ease. In addition, the economic factor must not be overlooked. Priests, in general, are poorly paid and many of them lead a life that verges on want. The lay apostles by contrast more often than not hold well-paid positions and believe they can do more good by giving money to the Church than by managing on the meager resources which she can provide.

This blossoming of secular institutes has naturally been greeted in the Vatican with joy, which, however, was not free from initial anxiety and reservations. First of all, this represents an entirely new phenomenon and when faced with any novelty the Church always moves slowly. Moreover there were, and still are, rather serious and obvious dangers in the movement.

These lay apostles, just because of their position, are exposed to temptations that are far more frequent and pressing than those that must be faced by a priest or a monk sitting in some fine library of his abbey—temptations to amass wealth, to succumb to feminine fascination, to become over-proud, to allow themselves to be involved too deeply in the welter of worldly interests. It was feared, in short, that the members of the secular institutes, though not wearing priestly robes, might compromise the good name of the Church. One must consider, too, the great freedom they naturally enjoy, the absence of any constant discipline and the difficulty their superiors in the Church have in exercising adequate control over them. And last, but certainly not least, there is the political factor. The lay apostles inevitably tend to engage in politics, to identify their mission with the interests of a given party, and to involve the Church in situations of an unforeseen character, not always in conformity with her much wider and loftier spiritual function.

From the technical and juridical point of view, too, it was by no means easy to fit the secular institutes into the structure of the Church. Ought they to be left exclusively under the control of the bishop of the respective dioceses, or ought they to come under the jurisdiction of the Congregation of Religious, or, perhaps, since they were always laymen, under that of the Congregation of the Council? The problem was made more difficult by the fact that, in Canon Law, no rules were ever drawn up to regulate this new form of apostolate. For a certain time the game of "passing the buck" was indulged in. The question was submitted to the Holy Office, which studied it from the doctrinal aspect but without reaching any practical conclusions. The dossier was then passed to the Congregation of the Council which, after long consideration, washed its hands of the problem and passed it on to the Congregation of Religious. This, in its turn, was of the opinion that secular institutes could not be regarded as religious orders and declined to accept them. They were, so to say, like orphans of whom everyone declines to become the guardians. Finally the matter was somewhat resolved when Pius XII decided to interest himself personally in the question. For some time nothing further was heard; then the Pope announced his decisions in the Apostolic Constitution *Provida Mater Ecclesia* of February 2, 1947.

This document constitutes the official birth certificate of the Secular Institutes (the name given to them by Pius XII himself) and simultaneously represents their fundamental constitution. The Pope recognized that the way they live and work represents, too, one of the Christian "states of perfection" and, as regards their place within the Church's organization, he decided to place them under the Congregation of Religious. In addition Pius XII issued to these latest but promising offspring of the Catholic Church ample and detailed instructions as to their internal constitution, their method of working and their objectives.

This is the situation reached today by a movement which, strictly speaking, can be traced back to the Jesuits. They were the first to relinquish, in favor of a more active program and more intense apostolate, some of those rules which, at the time they were laid down, were considered essential for the qualification of a religious, that is, singing in a choir, the vow of seclusion, community living. The accusation launched against the Jesuits at that time was that they were not true religious, and the same accusation is today made—

ironically enough also by these very Jesuits—against the lay apostles of the secular institutes. Similar diffidence and hostility were encountered in the seventeenth century by Mary Ward, founder of the English Ladies, the first female religious to take up teaching. While she was alive her work was hampered and she was even admonished by the Holy See. After her death the order was approved and today is among the most flourishing.

How many secular institutes are there and what is the strength of their membership? No one, not even the directors of the Congregation of Religious, is in a position to answer this question definitively. To give an idea of the extraordinary growth of this modern form of apostolate, it may be mentioned that within the brief space of ten years—from 1949 to 1958—as many as 250 secular institutes have asked for the approval of the Holy See and that almost all of them are still awaiting this approval. They have, however, all been sanctioned by the bishops of the dioceses in which they have arisen. Once the approval of the Holy See has been given, they will acquire the qualification of institutes by pontifical right and will be included in the Pontifical Year Book. The 1960 edition of this listed only five—the Company of St. Paul, the Priestly Society of the Holy Cross (*Opus Dei*), the diocesan worker-priests of the Holy Heart of Jesus, and the Society of the Heart of Jesus and the Prado Institute.

This new form of apostolate, carried on by men or women, takes on the most varied forms. Some of the members take the simple religious vows, some take them for a period of three years and afterward take the perpetual vows, while others take no vows at all. The objects of the institutes are equally varied—education of youth, missionary work, proselytism among workmen, penetration among intellectuals (which is the declared task of the *Opus Dei*), social assistance in organized forms or else through private and unobtrusive channels, defense of family life, and so on. To give an example, a courageous female secular institute in Lombardy specializes in the apostolate among working women, especially among the rice gatherers. Young women of good family, often with a university degree, leave their comfortable homes and enroll themselves among the mob of peasant women, often coarse and foul-mouthed, who each year are taken on temporarily to gather the rice harvest. From dawn to dusk they work in the rice fields with water up to their knees, their faces scorched by the sun, snatch a meal in the farmyards, sleep in the communal dormitories, frequent the local dance halls, in short, plunge into that tough, violent, licentious world depicted in the Italian film *Bitter Rice*. The rice gatherers generally come from peasant or poor city families with little education, and the fact that they are living away from home, the absence of controls, the first taste of freedom, the reaction to hard work and the example of the more audacious among their fellow-workers often lead them to forget any moral training they may have received and so they fall easy victims to the rural Don Juans. The task of the young lay apostles is to set a good example, to remind the workers of moral and religious precepts and to prevent them from going astray.

But, of all the secular institutes the most powerful, the most mysterious is undoubtedly the *Opus Dei*. Founded in Madrid on October 2, 1928 by Mgr. Jose Maria Escrivá de Balaguer, a Saragozza lawyer who became a priest, the *Opus Dei* is a kind of fifth column of God, a freemasonry of half-monks. Although it is not actually a secret society, its members prefer not to make known that they belong to it so that they can do their appointed work better ("Let your state remain unrecognized like that of Jesus for thirty years," was the counsel given by the founder of the order). The result is that the strength of its membership is not known—one suggestion is 10,000 as a rough figure—and that the extent of its power, surrounded as it is by a halo of mystery, is probably exaggerated. But that it is powerful, above all in Spain, cannot be doubted.

The members of the *Opus Dei* have secured command of the key positions in the State and have infiltrated into all the vital organs of the Spanish nation. To mention only a few of the most striking cases, the *Opus Dei* counts among its members the Minister of Foreign Trade, Alberto Ullastres, the Minister of Home Trade and head of the new supermarkets, Matarraz, the Minister of Finance, Navarro Rubio, the Minister of Information, Casado, the Minister of the Interior, Arrese, another Rubio at the Ministry of Education, Carrero Blanco at the Secretariat of the Council of Ministers, Lopez Rodo at the directorate of administrative reform.

But in addition to these politicians and several generals who occupy key positions in Spain at the Ministry of Defense and on the General Staff, other men of the *Opus Dei* control the National Council of Research, all the universities and almost all the cultural institutes (it is said that 40 per cent of the professors belong to it and that the remainder are too intimidated to dare oppose them), the Cantabria Real Estate Society which handles building activities throughout the country, the *Banco Popular*, the *Credito Andorrà*, the daily newspapers *A.B.C.*, and *Informaciones de la Tarde*, the reviews *Nuestro Tiempo*, *Actualidad Española*, *Punta Europa* and various others, the most important cartel of film producers and the Rialp publishing house, to which have gone nearly all the literary prizes in recent years and which has printed 200,000 copies of the basic book of the

Opus Dei, Camino, written by its founder, Mgr. Jose Maria Escrivá.

Those who belong to this semi-secret militia, this religious-lay general staff, excel in all the activities they take up, certainly as regards zeal, assiduity in their work, persistence and honesty. They are at the head of the class in Spain and as such can hardly fail to be disliked. But they are also feared, and with good reason as, unhappily, various Catholics of liberal tendencies have been forced to realize, among them Ruiz Gimenez, Father Llanos, Lain Entralgo, Aranguren, who, because of the hostility of the *Opus Dei,* have no longer been able to publish their writings or to teach.

As always happens in similar circumstances in countries governed by a dictatorship, public opinion lets off steam by telling jokes and funny stories about the regime. The favorite target for these is the Minister for Foreign Trade, Alberto Ullastres. He is in the habit—and it is a practice that in Spain even more than in Italy is considered to be in very poor taste—of being the first to get to the office and of seeing that his staff arrive punctually. Hence he has been nicknamed *"el abominable hombre de las nueve"* (the abominable 9 o'clock man, which in Spanish sounds very much like "the abominable snowman") and also because of his austere appearance and gravity, "bonjour tristesse."

The members of the *Opus Dei* take the three fundamental vows of the regular monks—obedience, poverty, chastity. These, however, are all interpreted and adapted to fit their particular positions. The obedience is above all internal, a complete acceptance of the dictates of the Church and of those peculiar to the order, without their being a rigid control by those in charge, something which would be impossible in the circumstances. The poverty consists in "the use of goods under the control of a superior" according to the most recent definition of the Congregation of Religious. In point of fact the members of the *Opus Dei* must lead a sober and moral life which, however, must always be compatible with their social position. No economy is permitted that would place them in an inferior position within the environment in which they live. If they earn more than they need they hand over the surplus to the order, whereas if they earn less than is necessary for them to live on decently, it is the order which provides them with the funds they lack. The "chastity" does not rule out marriage and, for married couples, implies the fulfillment of their conjugal duties, always, needless to say, in the measure and in the manner approved by Catholic morals. You cannot apply to become a member of the *Opus Dei.* It is the order itself which, at the suggestion of one of its members, approaches possible candidates and proposes to them that they join.

Apart from the fact that it is the duty of these modern Knights Templar to conceal their membership in the *Opus Dei*, they must also seek to adapt themselves to the utmost to the environment in which they live, even if this may cost them moral sacrifices. Take for example what the founder has written in *Camino* in connection with smutty and vulgar conversation, "What talk! What filth and how . . . loathsome! And you have to live with them in the factories, in the universities, in the operating theater, in the world. If you ask them as a favor to cut it out, they make fun of you. . . . If you show anger, they will persist. . . . If you clear out, they will continue. . . . The solution is this: First, commend them to God; second, face the situation like a man and put into practice 'the apostolate of bad language.' When I meet you I'll whisper in your ear a good selection!"[1]

The protector of the *Opus Dei* is Cardinal Tedeschini. Its founder, Mgr. Escrivá, is also its President General, and the other principal offices are distributed as follows: Secretary General, Don Alvaro del Portillo; Procurator General, Don Giorgio De Filippi; Counsellors, Don Severino Monzò, Dr. Riccardo Rieman, Dr. Nuno Girâo Ferreira and Bernardo Fernandez; Prefect of Studies, Professor Giuliano Herranz; Administrator General, the lawyer Gioacchino Alonzo. The central headquarters is in Rome, in Viale Bruno Buozzi, 73.

In Italy the order is far less widespread than in Spain. In view of its, if not altogether secret, certainly circumspect character it is by no means easy to know who belongs to it. There is talk of a son of Signor Segni, a post-war Italian Prime Minister, various high officials of the civil service, university professors and bank managers. It is also said that a rather strong branch has been established in Palermo, and this would surprise no one in view of the tendency of the Sicilians to help one another and to establish secret bonds, a tendency which, in a diametrically opposite sphere, gave birth to the Mafia, the dreaded secret society. It seems certain that in Italy the *Opus Dei* is very far from having secured control of as many and as important key positions as is the case in Spain. Other minor branches are to be found in France and Latin America.

The *Opus Dei* has many enemies. In Spain itself a noteworthy majority of Catholics fear the possible future consequences of the close identification which the *Opus Dei* has with the power of the State and with the Franco regime. As long as there is Franco, who

---

[1] The reader must not expect to find in Mgr. Escrivá's book a lot of advice of a Machiavellian nature that might justify the power acquired by the *Opus Dei*. *Camino* is a small book, lively, snappy, somewhat ingenuous, made up of short, broken sentences in which exclamation points, question marks, dots, dashes and so on far exceed the number of ideas.

skillfully plays the Church against the Falange, and the Falangists against the Monarchists in a delicate but so far successful game of tightrope walking, everything goes more or less well. But the end of the dictatorship and a return of democracy could unloose a most violent popular reaction against the *Opus Dei*, that is, against today's masters, a reaction that would end by involving the whole of the Catholic Church. The less authoritarian and fanatical Spanish Catholics are, in fact, thinking of the future and plan to create the foundations for a Christian Democratic party similar to those in Italy and Germany which without great difficulty would be able to join in democratic and parliamentary activities. Their efforts have, however, been fruitless and twenty-seven of them have ended in prison. For the same reasons, and also because they see in it a competitor, not even the Spanish Jesuits are particularly fond of the *Opus Dei* and would like to limit its great power.

Other dark clouds threaten the order in the theological field. A French Dominican friar, Father Dubarle, is compiling a critical treatise on the "bible" of the *Opus Dei*, that is, the *Camino* of José Maria Escrivá. He proposes to show that the founder of the order has been guilty of Pelagian heresy by becoming a modern follower of the fourth century monk Pelagius who denied the doctrine of original sin. When, however, the authoritative approval given by Pius XII to this new form of apostolate is considered, as well as the pressing need to supplement the work of the scanty number of clergy with that of laymen, it is highly improbable that the thunderbolts that Father Dubarle is preparing to hurl will have any effect.

The *Opus Dei* with its cloak-and-dagger fascination must not distract attention from the rest of the religious orders, that is, the monks, friars, fathers, brothers and nuns who form the main body of the Church's militants. Here, too, there are changes in the air, similar in many respects to those which the secular institutes are experiencing and which, in substance, aim at modernizing these noble but ancient organizations, adapting them more and more to the needs of the life of today and rendering them more simple, efficient and elastic. In the words of an authoritative director of the Congregation of Religious, the object is to make a more thorough examination of the rules and bring them up to date so that every religious, every community and every order will see more and more clearly what are the essential and what are the accidental factors.

The new tendencies have in great part been summed up and regulated in three important documents of Pius XII who, in this field, will go down in history as a reformer. Here is a brief summary of these:

Provvida Mater Ecclesia, of February 2, 1947. This has already been dealt with in describing the secular institutes which Pius XII approved and regulated.

Sponsa Christi, of November 21, 1950. This concerns mainly the walled-in nuns. It has erroneously been said in some quarters that Pius XII aimed at abolishing their seclusion. This is not correct. Pacelli realized that not all sisters serving the Church are made for having contacts with the world, and that meditation, prayer, the ascetic life are aspects of the Church that must continue. He did, however, mitigate many rules to which the nuns in seclusion were submitted and which were too rigid, severe and sometimes downright cruel. Their convents were very often without any heating (this encouraged tuberculosis and, in particularly severe winters, caused a startling number of deaths from pneumonia among the elderly), without sanitary appliances or running water, the food scarce and not always suitable for the maintenance of good health; beds were lacking and planks or even slabs of bare stone took their place. All these defects have in great part been remedied, though a number of mothers superior, particularly severe and attached to tradition, put up passive resistance to each innovation.

The rules of seclusion have been somewhat relaxed. The so-called "buried alive" have received permission to go to the polls and vote, have been encouraged to open their convents to children and to run nurseries, schools and Catechism courses. They have also been encouraged to take up such work as embroidery, sewing, dressmaking and the like that can be done within the walls of the convent, thus contributing, even if only in modest fashion, to the general economy and helping to reduce the state of extreme and chronic poverty from which many of these convents suffer. In this connection it may be mentioned that near Rome there is a very small convent with about a dozen elderly walled-in nuns. Once a week Mgr. (now Cardinal) Tardini—at least before he became Secretary of State—had large baskets of dirty linen collected at his boys' home, loaded them into his car and personally took them to the nuns to be laundered. By paying them for this work he was literally able to save them from hunger.

Another reform introduced by Pius XII regards the novices. In the past the period of novitiate was always spent at the particular convent that the future nun had expressed the wish to enter; this was responsible for a notable waste of effort and of teachers. Today the novices study and prepare themselves for the conventual life in large groups, at special institutes and under the guidance of experienced teachers with appropriate training, to the great advantage of their religious and moral education.

A further disadvantage abolished by Pius XII concerns the fact that, formerly, when a seclusion nun entered a convent she never left it until her death. This tradition was the cause of great inconveniences. Some of the convents were vast and semideserted while others were small and overcrowded, since those wishing to follow the vocation did not everywhere come forward in the same regular flow. It was Pius XII who granted special permission to the walled-in nuns for moving and advised them to transfer from one convent to another, according to needs. In one case the result was that nuns in their nineties, for the first time in their lives, traveled in a train or saw an automobile. In Italy the seclusion nuns number about 15,000, divided among 550 convents.

Sedis Sapientiae. In this document of 1956 Pius XII regulated the studies and education of the religious. In this connection, let me recall the exhortation of Pius XII of September 23, 1950 on the reform of the seminaries, since it traces the fundamentals of this Pope's policy in the field of the studies for and formation of the clergy. First of all, one notes in it an effort to improve the quality of the priests. The Pope invited all priests to exalt the greatness, the dignity and the nobility of the priesthood, to encourage a greater number of young people to take up the vocation, either by approaching them directly or by endeavoring to influence their guardians or parents, and to make a far more rigid choice of candidates from the moral and physical point of view, arranging, if necessary, for a medical examination. As for the working of the seminaries, the general line laid down by Pius XII was that they should adapt themselves to the times. The teaching courses had to be brought up to date, greater proficiency was to be attained in literary and scientific studies ("not less," Pacelli urged, "than that of the laymen who follow similar courses") and, above all, greater importance was to be placed on the formation of character. An endeavor should be made in the seminaries to create a "homelike and tranquil" atmosphere, punishments were to be mitigated and given less frequently as the seminarists grow older. Particular attention is devoted to giving them a sense of responsibility and instilling in them "a horror of double-dealing." Seminarists who display unhealthy moral tendencies, which can develop easily in a community of men alone, are to be dismissed without recourse.

The subject on which the greatest insistence was laid throughout the Pontiff's exhortation is that of absolute chastity. Pius XII realized that in the life of today this virtue is subject to a greater threat than in the past. He therefore recommended that the strengthening of the ideal of chastity should be made a special point in the seminaries; he asked priests in general to share a communal life whenever possible; he advised special spiritual exercises, and he even got to the point of urging priests who direct associations of girls and women not to allow too much familiarity to creep into their relations with them.

While the reform of the seminaries aimed at creating a new type of priest—a priest more cultured, more open, more free and easy, resembling rather, in fact, the American type of priest impersonated on the screen by Bing Crosby than the timid Don Abbondio, the priest immortalized by Manzoni in his novel *The Betrothed*, the *Sedis Sapientiae* endeavored to achieve the same results with the religious. Here again there was to be far more thorough training, an adaptation to the times, a modernization of programs. This in order to prevent friars and nuns who, in their apostolate, have to direct associations of former pupils, university students, mothers, professional men and the like, from cutting a poor figure when they come up against the cultural background of their flocks. Within this framework comes the foundation of the new Theological School of the Lateran for the religious, the opposite number of which is the *Regina Mundi* Pontifical Institute, frequented by nuns from all over the world, chosen from those who are to hold important offices both inside the various orders and in connection with outside apostolic activities.

To complete this short review of the religious orders, mention must also be made of the federative movement which developed during the reign of Pacelli and concerns both the male and female orders. Its object is to coordinate the activities of the various orders so as to avoid waste of effort and means, duplications, overlapping, and sometimes even useless competition. The male orders, which gathered together for the first time at a world congress in Rome in 1950, in 1953 formed a Permanent Committee of Superiors, presided over by the General of the Jesuits, Father Janssens, and in 1956 a Committee of the Provincial Councils of the generals. The orders, both central and remote, through these organizations are in a position to have an over-all view of the various problems and to work in fraternal cooperation for the common end.

The nuns too have kept pace with this new spirit, both in internal organization and by encouraging a kind of emancipation of women inside the Church. The nuns number about one million throughout the world, divided among 1,700 orders, congregations and institutes of pontifical right, that is, officially recognized by the Holy See. But although they are four times as numerous as the men, they were, compared with the latter, up to recently in an inferior position and had little voice in the administration not only of the Church but of their own communities.

In Italy the nuns are grouped into three large federations, the F.I.R.O., (nursing sisters), the F.I.R.E., (teaching sisters) and the F.I.R.A.S., (social work sisters). Labor disputes have been partly responsible for the urgent creation of these organizations. To give an example, suppose the lay male nurses and servants of a hospital go on strike, what ought the nuns to do? Take orders from the General Confederation of Labor controlled by the Communists? Carry on as strike breakers? This was not something that could be decided case by case and the nuns' federations, in addition to settling internal questions, are also called upon to present a common front to the lay trade unions.

As to the emancipation of the nuns and their growing participation in the men's councils, in 1950 when the first world congress of the religious was held, this participation was limited to prayers said by them imploring that the work of the men should be crowned with success; an act undoubtedly edifying, though it would have failed to satisfy any Sister Carrie Chapman Catt or Sister Emily Pankhurst. In the second congress, however, 800 sisters representing 450 orders also took part. In 1951, too, the first international meeting of religious sisters was held in Rome, and in 1952 a permanent council of the mothers superior was formed, similar to that of the men. Finally, in 1957, for the first time the sisters voted and were elected to administrative posts in the F.I.D.A.E., a federation into which are grouped all the educational institutes responsible to the ecclesiastical authorities (altogether 1,076 schools, colleges and so on), all the Catholic elementary schools and children's homes. The movement is under way and it may well be predicted that the sisters will share in the work of, and make their influence felt in both the federated organizations and the counsels of the Church to an ever-growing extent and more and more in keeping with their numerical strength.

10

The Jesuits

IN A SPANISH ANECDOTE, the Lord was once looking for a secretary. Accordingly He staged a competition, asking the saints to submit their names as candidates by a certain day, together with a list of their particular qualifications and merits. The saints are said to have met in consultation, the upshot of which was that the only one who could worthily hope to hold such a high position of trust was St. Peter. In deference to the first of the Apostles, they decided, therefore, to refrain from presenting themselves as candidates and to let Peter, unopposed, present his own. This was done. At the last minute, however, St. Ignatius of Loyola came limping up and handed in his own application. There was understandable indignation among all the saints, and this turned to stupefaction when the outcome of the competition was announced, and St. Ignatius was named secretary. Even St. Peter himself was a little upset and, with great tact and deference, went to the Lord to object. Plainly somewhat embarrassed, the Lord replied, "I'm perfectly aware of how you must feel, my dear Peter. But then, what could I do?" and thumbing through St. Ignatius' application papers, he added, "You know how it is . . . a wounded war veteran . . . and recommended by the Jesuits."

I have related this little story because it sums up a lot of things— the notoriety for double dealing, cunning, unscrupulousness, and at the same time, the power which many people associate with the

Society of Jesus. It is a notoriety which, at least in our own times, is not applicable. The legion of Ignatius' followers is, in point of fact, far less underhand and far less influential than is generally believed. This, however, does not mean that the Jesuits are on the decline. On the contrary, they constitute, as was pointed out in the preceding chapter, the largest of all religious orders. And whereas the Church in general and most other orders in particular complain of the shortage of new recruits, the Jesuits are unique in having to worry about the overrapid swelling of their ranks.

A highly placed Jesuit has explained to me that the Society, ever since its inception, has been an élite, similar to what, in military terms, shock troops once were or what commandos are today. Quantity, however, risks compromising quality, in that selection and a rigorous and individual preparation of candidates becomes more difficult, with the result that its élite character becomes diluted.

I have compared the Jesuits with shock troops and commandos, and not entirely unjustly, in that the founder of the order, St. Ignatius of Loyola, was himself a valorous warrior. He impressed on the order courage, discipline and organization typical of military units. Faithful to its origins, the Society of Jesus has never known peace. Its history is an epic and adventurous one of struggles, of clamorous victories and grievous defeats, of death and resurrection. A never-ending battle fought in distant lands—from India to Peru, from Japan to Russia— in the corridors of the Vatican and in the shadow of all the thrones of Europe. A tale of intrigues, of trials, of death sentences and rehabilitations, of bans, persecutions, ignominious expulsions, and of cautious or triumphant returns.

One might well say that the Society of Jesus was born on May 20, 1521, when a cannon ball, fired by the artillery of Francis I of France at the town of Pamplona in Spain, rebounded from the fortress wall and broke the right shinbone of Captain Inigo de Onaz y Loyola.

Inigo was the youngest of thirteen children born to an insignificant provincial nobleman. As a young man, together with his brother Pedro, he had received the tonsure. But whereas his brother had continued his ecclesiastical career, Inigo had gone into the army. As an officer, he was brave, brilliant, somewhat of a braggart, a picker of fights, and a ladies' man—in a word, a Spaniard through and through. One night in 1515, during the carnival season, he and his brother took part in a fracas in which short work was made of a parish priest. Don Pedro aspired to the parish of San Sebastiano of Soreasu and considered the titular priest of the parish, Don Anchieta, an interloper. Partisans of both priests came to blows and the future saint, all but forgetting his tonsure, gave his brother's rival a sound drubbing. He was forced to flee to Pamplona but then, to escape the clutches of the police, remembered his tonsure and pointed out his status as an ecclesiastic. A complicated dispute arose over the competency of the civil courts and the Church courts to try the case, and, eventually, the whole matter was shelved.

During the capture of Najera, the cavalier of Loyola distinguished himself, generously refusing any part of the spoils of the conquered city. The Viceroy of Navarra charged him with the pacification of the province of Guipuzcoa and, in discharging this task, the young officer displayed outstanding qualities both as a politician and as a diplomat. But his most glorious undertaking remains the defense of Pamplona, during which he was the very soul of resistance. The French recognized his valor in battle and, after he had been picked up unconscious, with a fractured leg, they had him carried by litter to his native castle in the mountains of Guipuzcoa. His leg mended poorly and the surgeon was compelled to rebreak the bone in an effort to set it properly. Inigo bore the painful operation with great stoicism. Then, overcome by a terrible fever, for forty days he hovered so close to death that extreme unction was administered to him.

During his long convalescence, he asked for reading matter to distract himself. He would have preferred tales of knight errantry or love poetry, but, there being nothing better at hand, he began to peruse *The Life of Christ* by the Carthusian Ludolph of Saxony and *The Flower of the Lives of the Saints*. The reading of these books, undertaken rather against his will, ended by firing him with religious fervor, and he decided to lay down his arms and place himself at the service of Christ. It was no easy thing for him to overcome his habits, ambitions and worldly propensities, and it was precisely during his inner struggle with himself, that he conceived of and experimented on himself with the spiritual exercises that were to become and remain to this day the fundamental basis on which the Society of Jesus rests.

The remainder of Inigo's life, after he had donned the humble frock of the penitent, was equally adventurous and eventful. Having conceived a harebrained scheme to liberate the Holy Land and convert the Moslems, and after a series of peregrinations that took him to Barcelona, Rome, and Venice, he eventually succeeded in reaching Jerusalem. The Franciscan father who was Protector of the Holy Land was dumbstruck by the missionary zeal of the Spanish pilgrim and, lest complications should arise with the Arabs, with whom he had reached a truce, he ordered Inigo to leave the country at once, on pain of excommunication. After further wandering, the former army captain returned to Barcelona and, realizing that his theological and cultural training left room for improvement, for two years attended the grammar school of a professor named Ardebalo, living on handouts from well-wishers. He combined proselytism with his studies.

It was during this period that a curious episode occurred during which the future founder of the Jesuits was narrowly to escape with his skin. There happened to be in Barcelona at the time a convent of nuns of rather dubious virtue, to say the least. Inigo, with inspired and fervent sermons, led the lost sheep back to observance of their vows, including the vow of chastity. Thereupon a group of youths, who had had close relations with the sisters, waylaid him and beat him to within an inch of his life. He recovered, in fact, only after lying bedridden for some fifty-three days. He then proceeded to the celebrated University of Alcalá, where he distinguished himself in his studies and, with but four disciples, formed his first embryo association.

Inigo's eccentric and revolutionary ideas, however, aroused the suspicions of his professors. In 1526, they forbade him to wear the religious habit, which set him apart from the other students, and in March 1527, he was haled before the Inquisition, imprisoned in April, and released in June. He was forced to agree to dress like everyone else and forbidden to teach the mysteries of the faith for at least three years. Fleeing with his four followers from Alcalá to Salamanca, he was once again arrested and tried. After twenty-two days he was acquitted, but he was forbidden to explain, during the teaching of the Catechism, the difference between a mortal and a venial sin. He found this prohibition a hard pill to swallow and was wont to say, "Either what I teach is not true, and so condemn it; or it is true, so let me teach it."

To escape the oppressive atmosphere of Spain, he moved to Paris, and it was there that he started having himself be called Ignatius. At the renowned city university he came to realize that what he had thought he had learned from Ardebalo and at the Universities of Alcalá and Salamanca amounted to but very little and that he would have to start all over again from scratch. From 1528 onward, he studied with such application and profit that six years later he was awarded the cap of "master in arts," the equivalent of a professorship. It was during his Paris period that he became a friend of Francesco Saverio, Pietro Fabbro, Giacomo Láinez, Alfonso Salmerone, Nicolò Alfonso (dubbed Bodabilla) and Simone Rodriguez, who were to become pillars of the Society of Jesus. These seven students at the University of Paris constituted something of a private association whose aim was the conversion of the Moslems of the Holy Land.

They would meet together, talking and helping one another in their studies, and following particular rules of life laid down by Ignatius; they considered themselves in duty bound annually to renew their vow to make their spiritual crusade to the Holy Land. Ignatius journeyed to Spain to recover from a stomach ailment in the healthful climate of his native mountains and to attend to various business affairs of his companions. Then, after numerous adventures, traveling through Italy which was then in the throes of war between Francis I and Charles V, all seven met again in Venice, ready to set sail for Palestine. The expedition was postponed a number of times as various difficulties cropped up. In the end, it was given up entirely because of the war which had broken out between Suleiman II and the Venetian Republic.

The actual founding of the Society of Jesus took place in Rome and was solemnly recognized in a bull of September 27, 1540. The characteristic trait of the Society was that, beside the three vows of poverty, obedience, and chastity, common to other religious orders, a fourth was added—that of absolute obedience to the Pope. Ignatius' idea was to form a select corps on which the Pontiff could draw for the riskiest and most delicate undertakings, with the certainty that the men summoned would carry out their duties without the slightest hesitation or hedging. The meaning of the special vow was clearly set forth in a formula incorporated into and approved by the papal bull. It reads, "Although we have been trained by the Gospel, and through our orthodox faith we know and firmly confess that all faithful Christians bear allegiance to the Pontiff as their leader and as the Vicar of Jesus Christ, still, with a view to our Society's achieving greater humility and perfect mortification for each member, as well as the abnegation of our wills, we judge it to be most profitable that, beside the aforementioned common bond, each of us should be bound by a special vow so that whatever thing the present Pontiff and future Pontiffs may in their day command, relating to the ministering to souls and the propagation of the faith, and regardless of whatever province to which they may wish to send us, without any evasion or excuse, instantly, insofar as we can, we are bound to obey, whether they send us amongst Turks, whether amongst other infidels, even in parts which are called the Indies, whether they be heretics or schismatics, or amongst believers."

Thus, the tasks of the Society of Jesus, which were then put into action, were succinctly set forth at the very outset: propagation and strengthening of the faith among Catholics, missions to convert the infidels in distant lands, the struggle against Protestantism.

Ignatius of Loyola, thrasher of parish priests at twenty-four, crippled by a cannon ball at thirty, tried as a heretic at thirty-six, university professor and eminent theologian at forty-three, founder of a new order at forty-nine, was elected General of the Society of Jesus at fifty, and died in Rome on July 31, 1556, at the age of sixty-five, having created the most combative, the most efficient and the most widely discussed instrument the Catholic Church had ever had. At the time of his death, the Society numbered a thousand members, with a hundred colleges and homes, including one for the rehabilitation of prostitutes set up in Rome in 1544, and one for the protection of "imperiled girls." His followers were scattered throughout the world, from India (the battleground of St. Francis Xavier, who, by virtue of his moral stature, is the man who most closely resembles St. Ignatius) to Spain, Germany, Portugal, Belgium, Poland, Morocco, China, Japan, the Western Hemisphere, and to all of the Spanish and Portuguese colonies. In Europe, the first Jesuits founded homes, schools, seminaries, universities. They installed themselves in royal courts as the confessors and spiritual counselors of sovereigns, they played a decisive role in the Council of Trent and in the Counter Reformation—all told, they were a sudden and spectacular flowering that has few comparisons in history and can be measured only against such successes—which were no less explosive, extraordinary and unexpected—as those of Genghis Khan's Mongols, of the followers of Mohammed, of Alexander the Great's phalanx, and, in more recent times, of the followers of Karl Marx.

What strikes one as almost incredible is that, among Ignatius' collaborators, it is virtually impossible to find anyone of mediocre quality. All of them were men of the first rank, who succeeded in doing remarkable things in the fields entrusted to them. This phenomenon is explained, it seems to me, by their "spiritual exercises"; which is to say by the instrument which St. Ignatius devised for his own spiritual formation and for that of his followers. Taking a modern example, it is as though the coach of a football team were to invent a system of physical culture, of training, of field tactics which made his team the very best in the world. The former Spanish army captain discovered something of the same sort in the field of the spirit, that is to say, he found a way to turn out gladiators, veritable champions, of the faith by a particular method of training.

St. Ignatius' spiritual exercises are contained in a little booklet, one of the slenderest produced by asceticism in modern times and one which, on a first reading, leaves one just a little disappointed. Its style is dry, swift, without literary pretensions, rather soldierly. But its ideas are clear, its instructions precise. And that it is meant as a training manual is stressed by St. Ignatius. He writes that "just as strolling, walking, and running are bodily exercises, similarly the ways of preparing and disposing the mind, so as to divest it of all extravagant affections and, once the mind is divested of them, to try and find the Divine will as it relates to the management of one's life for the salvation of the soul, are called spiritual exercises."

The booklet deals, in short, with a course that lasts approximately four weeks and is carried out in stages of from six to eight days, so as to reach an over-all total of a month. In the first exercise, the candidate asks himself: "Why am I in the world? What is the aim of man and what is his role in creation?" The reply given by St. Ignatius is, "Man was created to praise our Lord God, to revere Him and serve Him, and by so doing to save his soul; and the other things on the face of the earth were created for man's benefit and to help him to achieve the end for which he was created." From this it follows that the Jesuit must remain indifferent in the face of worldly things in themselves, in the face of health or disease, glory or obscurity, a long life or a short one; rather, he must choose those things that most easily lead him to the ultimate aim, that is, to God.

Ignatius then proceeds to meditate on sin, considering it in other creatures, first among the angels (the revolt of Satan) and then among human beings. From the gravity of the punishments (eternal damnation), he deduces the willfulness of the sin and measures the evil against infinite good, which is God. He then compares others' sins with his own, endeavoring to discover mitigating circumstances for the others and aggravating circumstances for himself.

The next exercise is a thoroughgoing trial of himself, a re-evocation of all the sins he has committed since the age of reason, analyzing them, dissecting them, finding in them—even though they may not be recognized as crimes or violations of law—the lowest and most abject reasons for their origin. The exercise concludes with expressions of stupefaction or horror and a plea for mercy.

There then follows an exercise in which the apprentice thinks intensely on the punishments of Hell, trying to conjure up the torments with all his senses—touch, sight, hearing, smell—in the most realistic manner possible. In the next exercise, the execration of guilt is again proved, the fear of the punishments, and resolutions for a new life are made, trusting in Divine mercy.

So ends the first week and Ignatius' follower is ready for general confession and Communion, which give him heart and prepare him for what lies ahead in the second week. The Jesuit meditates on Christ's mission, trying to visualize the countryside, the cities, and the villages of Palestine which Jesus visited; he tries to imagine the Saviour alive before his eyes and to follow Him through all His vicissitudes, as though himself a participant in them. He then imagines a great battle between Satan and Christ. The devil is seated on a throne of fire and smoke, coaxing men toward perdition in an eager, persuasive voice, holding out to them the delights of wealth, power and sensual love. Christ, seated among his followers, urges on them salvation of their imperiled souls. He specifically teaches poverty, both spiritual and if necessary material, humility, disdain for one's personality, as constituting the bases of perfection. The Jesuit must feel himself to be personally chosen by Christ to wage the fight against Satan. These two weeks, in St. Ignatius' view, are the most important of all the spiritual exercises.

In the third stage, the Jesuit exercises in contemplating the Passion and death of Christ, identifying himself with His suffering and reaffirming his intention to undergo trials just as arduous and painful. The fourth and last stage consists in the contemplation of the Resurrection of Christ, of His Ascension into Heaven, and of the eternal joy of Paradise. Spiritual love and bliss are transformed into joyous emulation of the Master.

The spiritual exercises—these difficult gymnastics of the soul—are carried out under the guidance of a director, who follows the apprentice day by day, giving him direction, counsel and comfort in moments of weakness and doubt. Ignatius himself saw to it that the actual exercises were preceded by a set of notes or directions, and over the years others, tested by practice, have been added. They were all assembled by Father Acquaviva, a general of the order, in a separate book entitled *Direttorio*. Among these directions, some worthy of mention are: Before going to sleep, the apprentice must ponder intensely on the meditation which he will have during the night or the following morning (an intuition which antedates the idea of the subconscious) and which he will begin to have the moment he awakens; before commencing prayers, he must adore Him, kneeling or standing or in whatever position he finds most convenient; he must not let himself be distracted by extraneous thoughts, but must concentrate solely on the day's meditation. To help concentration, he must avoid laughing, talking inanely, letting his gaze wander; darkness or semidarkness in his room will help him in this. To continual spiritual application he must add material penitence such as going without food and sleep and mortifying his flesh, in accordance with his strength.

In order of time, the spiritual exercises are followed by a general examination. All who wish to become members of the Society of

Jesus must undergo a searching interrogation by their superiors. During this examination, which is divided into eight parts, the candidate's moral and intellectual qualities are tested, as well as the fervency of his faith, his steadfastness. At the same time it is explained to him in no uncertain terms what sacrifices he will be asked to make, including an annual repetition of the spiritual exercises, and the iron discipline to which he will have to submit, which will make him "like a corpse" in his superiors' hands. There are various grades in the Society of Jesus—the highest is that of professed, for which supplementary examinations and trials are required; then there is that of student, or of spiritual coadjutor (assistants of the professed') or temporal coadjutor (attendants, cooks, ushers, bookkeepers, etc.).

It is not true, as is commonly said, that to become a full-fledged Jesuit—that is, a professed—it is necessary to be at least thirty-three years old. In practice, however, the procedure is so long and arduous that only rarely does a member of the Society of Jesus attain the grade of professed before thirty or so. As a rule, becoming a model Jesuit takes seventeen years. First, there are the years of normal studies, next a period, which varies from three to eight years, of experience and work in various branches of the order, then another three years of theological studies, at the end of which the candidate is ordained.

The history of the Society of Jesus is extremely complicated, for it is closely bound up with relations and intrigues of the Vatican and of the various royal courts of large and small European countries where the Jesuits have occupied such key positions as confessors or counselors of sovereigns, theologians, professors, and the like.

Generally speaking, the history may be divided into a number of periods—a period of "youth and growth," dating from 1556, that is from the death of St. Ignatius, to 1580; "consolidation and prosperity," dating from 1581 to 1615; and a period of struggle, when, coincident with continued success and expansion, there began to appear strong hostility and opposition in countries where the Jesuits were operating, not to mention jealousies and intrigues against them within the Church proper and in the very Vatican itself. This period runs from 1615 to 1758. Figuring in the opposition, we find Blaise Pascal's immortal *Provincial Letters,* published in book form in 1657, which is the most determined and effective attack on the Society in all history. Raging in Pascal's day was the polemic over Jansenism, and Pascal entered the lists against the Jesuits on the side of the Jansenites. Chiefly, however, he launched his attack against the Jesuit ethic as it was developing in the works of the casuists.

Among casuist authors, the most famous were Fathers Molina, Escobar, Sanchez, Suarez, Vasquez, Lessio, Hurtado, and Enquirez, who, with a view to being able to operate more freely in the world and to attracting about them and influencing with their counsel as many people as possible, had, with subtle sophism and distortions of logic, created an extremely tolerant ethic by which it was possible to justify an infinity of sins and actual crimes, which included dueling, the killing of the offender of one's honor or of one who attempted robbery, the practice of usury, the corruption of magistrates, and so on. Here follow a few examples of casuists' writings excerpted from Pascal, "If a gentleman," Hurtado de Mendoza wrote, "who, challenged to a duel, is known not to be a churchgoer, and the sins which he is seen continually and unscrupulously to be committing lead one easily to think that, if he refuses to fight, it is not out of fear of God, but out of fear, that it may be said of him that he is a chicken and not a man (*gallina et non vir*), he may, to safeguard his honor, go to the designated place, not with the deliberate intention to fight a duel but only with that of defending himself if the challenger should attack him unjustly. And his action in itself will be entirely indifferent; indeed, what harm is there in going to a field and walking about, expecting a man, and in defending oneself if one is attacked? Thus, one in no way sins, because this is not accepting a duel, since one's intentions are addressed otherwise. Indeed, accepting a duel consists in the deliberate intention to fight, which, in this instance, is not the case."

Here is Father Escobar on the same subject, "One may kill a man who has given one a slap, even though he may flee, provided that one avoids killing in hatred or revenge and provided that it does not lead to bloodshed which is excessive and harmful to the State. And the reason is that one may pursue one's honor just as one may pursue stolen goods: because, even though your honor is not in the hands of your enemy, as stolen property would be, still one may recover it in the same way by giving signs of greatness and authority and thereby procuring the esteem of men. Indeed, is it not true that one who has received a slap is judged as being without honor until he has killed his enemy?"

To justify usury, it is enough simply not to mean to practice it. Says Father Escobar, "Usury is the taking of interest from persons to whom one has made a loan, if it is exacted as due by justice; but if it is exacted as due out of gratitude, it is not usury at all." Or one can apply the so-called *mohatra* contract. "The *mohatra*" [according to a compendium of theories of famous casuists] "occurs when a man who needs twenty Pistoian lire makes a purchase from a merchant amounting to thirty Pistoian lire, payable within a year, and then promptly sells his goods for twenty Pistoians, cash." Father Lessio, quoted by Escobar, claimed that "Property which a woman acquires by adultery comes by her in an illegitimate manner, but possessing it is legitimate."

Today, the Jesuit ethic is certainly not the same as that described by Pascal, who, for his part, often misrepresented casuist thought by overemphasizing its Machiavellian and sophist character. Many of the Fathers quoted by Pascal have been disowned by the Society, such as—to give two examples—Enriquez, defined as "subtle but false" by Father Enrico Risa in his book *The Jesuits from their Origins to Our Times*, and Vasquez, called by the same author, "undeserving because of his crafty character."

The fact remains that the works of the casuists, and even more the vast influence the Jesuits acquired in various courts, unleashed against them a wave of persecutions which reached flood tide between 1758 and 1773. The Society was banned successively in Portugal, Spain, France (where Madame Pompadour was one of its bitterest enemies), the Kingdom of Naples, in Malta, Parma, and Piacenza. Its colleges were disbanded, its property confiscated, and the Jesuits themselves were tried, imprisoned, killed or deported *en masse*. Crowded like livestock onto cargo ships, they were secretly unloaded along the coast of Latium—a contemptuous way of returning to the Pope his most faithful and combative, but also most intrusive, soldiers. Clement XIII (1758-1769) refused to allow a number of cargo ships loaded with Spanish Jesuits to dock at Civitavecchia because he considered the act an offense to his prestige, and at every port they approached thereafter they were rejected as though plague-ridden. Eventually, they were put ashore on the coast of Corsica; but since the island was not long afterward ceded to France, they were again expelled and finally, out of pity, accepted by the Vatican State.

Clement XIII's successor, Lorenzo Ganganelli, a Franciscan who assumed the name Clement XIV (1769-1774) and who, though once a great friend of the Society of Jesus, had become one of its most bitter adversaries, officially dissolved the order on July 21, 1773. The last General of the Society, Lorenzo Ricci submitted to the will of the Pope; the Pope, however, did not spare him from prison. Ricci was asked to give a rendering of the Society's holdings, universally believed to be enormous. When the Pope learned that it was not what it was thought to be, he had Ricci thrown into the Castel Sant' Angelo, where he died two years later.

Although officially suppressed and disowned by Rome, the Society, toward which Catherine the Great was particularly sympathetic, continued to get along in Russia and Poland. The Vatican, which had every intention of remaining in the graces of the mighty Russian empire, shut an eye to Jesuit activities, and St. Ignatius' followers kept up operations there, supported by the Czarist régime and ignored by Rome.

The French Revolution and the meteoric rise of Napoleon shook the old world to its foundations—a world which was aristocratic, feudal, monarchic, confessional, and narrow-minded. The Congress of Vienna did what it could to re-establish the old Jesuit order, and Pius VII (1800-1823), escaping the talons of the Corsican eagle by a hairbreadth and returning to Rome from imprisonment in Fontaine-bleau, was carried, quite naturally, on the wave of a return to the past, to see that Ignatius' Society rose again, for the order had shown itself in past centuries to be a worthy instrument in the hands of the Sovereign Pontiff.

Members of the Society of Jesus who had survived the persecution, trials, deportations, and above all the implacable scythe of Father Time numbered but a few hundred; the youngest were over seventy, the oldest ninety, and, in the words of Cardinal Pacca, who had pleaded with the Pope and got him to revive the order, "the greater part was deaf, crippled, apoplectic, who could scarcely stand with a cane even in the presence of the Pope; a sight which, had not the sad memories it kindled in the mind made it tender and touching, might have provoked laughter."

The reconstitution of the Society by the old survivors, under the foresighted guidance of Father Luigi Fortis, came about more quickly than circumstances would have warranted one to predict. Their troubles, however, were not yet over. In 1878-1879, Spain again banned the Jesuits, as did Guatemala. In Italy, after 1870, all the Jesuit homes were shut down except that of the General Superior and his procurator. In Germany, Bismarck initiated a violent struggle against the Society. General Ludovico Martin (1892-1906) had to witness further persecutions, including the banning of the Society in France and the confiscation of its property. Even so, during his tenure, the Jesuits rose from 13,292 to 15,661 members. Martin was succeeded by General Francesco Saverio Wernz, a German (1906-1914), and then came the long tenure in office of the Polish General Vladimir Ledochowski (1915-1942). The Second World War made any meeting of the General Congregation impossible, and it was necessary to wait until 1946 for the election of Father Ledochowski's successor, Father Jean-Baptiste Janssens from Belgium, who is still General. A symptom of the importance attributed in the Vatican to this order is to be found in the fact that its General is currently nicknamed "The Black Pope," a reference to the color of the Jesuits' robes.

In recent years, there has been an extraordinary increase in men wishing to become Jesuits, so that in 1957 the Society numbered 17,292 professed priests, 10,658 students, and 5,782 coadjutors and lay brothers, for an over-all total of 33,732 members, and it is continuing to increase at the rate of about 500 annually. The United States leads the roll, with 7,932 Jesuits, followed by Spain, with 6,159, whereas Italy accounts for only 2,405.

The Society is divided territorially into fifty provinces, twenty-three vice-provinces, and thirty-two missions. The provinces and vice-provinces are grouped into assistances, which include the assistance for Italy, Germany (including the Netherlands, Lithuania, and Switzerland), France, Asia, Spain, Great Britain (including Belgium and Australia), North America, the Slavic countries, and Latin America.

Today missions, schools, and publishing make up the principal activities of the Jesuits. Jesuit missionaries number more than 4,000 and are at work in every quarter of the world, but especially in Africa, China, and Latin America. In the school field, their work is overwhelming. They have more than 400 advanced and secondary schools and fifteen universities. In the United States alone, approximately 150,000 students attend Jesuit schools and of this number 109,000 attend their universities and university colleges. Equally impressive is their work in the field of periodical literature, which may be summed up as follows: 26 publications of general interest, 152 scientific publications, 77 missionary papers, 596 religious papers, and 261 periodicals issued by schools. Altogether, they have 1,112 publications issued in 50 different languages with a yearly printing of 150 million copies and 14 million subscribers. The Jesuits also engage in outstanding work in the field of science and have, scattered throughout the world, a score of well-equipped astronomical and meteorological observatories.

11

The Holy Office

THE HOLY OFFICE is the oldest—it was set up by Paul III in 1542—and the most important of the Vatican Congregations and the one around which it is easiest to weave a cloak-and-dagger atmosphere.

There still clings to the Holy Office—this heir of the terrible Inquisition Tribunals, even today surrounded by an impenetrable barrier of secrecy—the memory of the tortures and of the autos-da-fé. The truth is however that it has now become a body with ordinary administrative functions and that the implacable verdicts it once delivered have been replaced by opinions of a theoretical nature, admonishments, cautions, moral punishments and, in very rare cases, economic penalties.

But while the Holy Office today no longer inspires fear, its importance continues to be great. Of the eleven Congregations that deal with the affairs of the Church, only three—the Holy Office, the Consistorial and the Eastern Church—have as their Prefect the Pope himself. In addition, the Holy Office is the only Congregation that enjoys the title of "Supreme."

However, though the statement was made that the Supreme Sacred Congregation of the Holy Office is the heir of the Inquisition Tribunals, this is not wholly accurate, either from the historical point of view or as regards its powers and functions.

The Holy Office was founded in 1542 by Pope Paul III (1534-1549) expressly to combat the Calvinist and Lutheran revolts. The new office was given the title of Holy Roman and Universal Inquisition, a name it retained until 1908. At the time of Paul III, however, the Inquisition tribunals had already been in existence for centuries while the Spanish Inquisition likewise existed, and both continued to function independently even after the foundation of the new body which had far wider and more important aims than the simple hunting down of heretics and witches. From 1600 onward, when the Church began a policy marked by ever-increasing moderation, the two sister-institutions started gradually to decay and eventually disappeared entirely. The Holy Office alone survived. It can thus, in a way, be regarded as the heir, in a moral if not exactly a technical sense, of its two forerunners.

The Holy Office is directed by a commission of nine Cardinals, all Italians: Secretary of State Tardini, Rizzardo Giuseppe, secretary and their Eminences Cardinal Ottaviani, who acts as Secretary, and Cardinals Mimmi, Micara, Canali, Fumasoni Biondi, Ciriaci and Agagianian. This commission meets every Wednesday, in a room of the palace where the Holy Office has its headquarters, to deal with the most important business of the Congregation. There are about twenty consultors who, as in all the Congregations, form the backbone of the organization since they have to examine, investigate and prepare all the cases submitted to the Holy Office. Among the consultors are men of worth such as Monsignori Dell'Acqua, Samorè and Grano of the State Secretariat, Father Agostino Bea, who was the confessor of Pius XII, and Monsignori Traglia and Hudal.

Just what is the business of the Holy Office? It could perhaps best be defined as the "watchdog" of the Church. This is the Congregation which has to defend the faith, Catholic morals and the unity of the Church against heresies, schisms, apostasies, contacts with Freemasonry and other sects, profanation of the Host (sometimes practiced in black masses), antireligious publications, and the occasional immorality of priests and members of religious orders. Its field of competence has no limits, either territorial or in regard to persons. The sole exception is in the case of Cardinals, who were removed from the jurisdiction of this office by Sixtus V.

As regards doctrine, the Holy Office has the services of ten "qualificators," chosen personally by the Pope from the most erudite men of the Church. The best-known personalities among these are the Jesuit Father Alberto Vaccari, Mgri. Compagnoni and Garofalo, and Father Gabriele Roschini of the Servants of Mary, who is said to have undertaken the preparatory work connected with the proclamation of the dogma of the bodily Assumption of Mary into Heaven.

Among the most recent decrees of the Holy Office concerning faith and morals, as examples, are the prohibition against ecclesiastics belonging to the Rotary Club,[1] which, in general, the faithful are advised not to join; the prohibition—again affecting ecclesiastics, against indulging in financial speculation and games of chance including football pools; the warning to the faithful not to believe too readily in miraculous apparitions, of which there was a veritable spate in the 1950's. In the late 50's the Holy Office was studying the miracles attributed to the "Weeping Madonna of Syracuse," but no definite reply has yet been given. The examination of the "cures" attributed to the Madonna of the Three Fountains in Rome has also been proceeding for many years without any decision having been announced so far.

Other important prerogatives of the Holy Office include decisions on questions regarding the Pauline privilege, mixed marriages (between a Catholic and a non-Catholic), fasting before Holy Communion, the validity of the Sacraments and the authority to absolve persons from the excommunications reserved to the Holy See, except in special cases.

One of its essential functions was that of examining, and in some cases proscribing, books contrary to faith and morals. This task was once reserved to the special Congregation of the Index, founded in 1571. The Index concerned itself not only with the removal from circulation and burning of books, but also with the infliction of very severe punishments on their readers. Pius X took away from the Congregation of the Index this power, which was transferred to the normal tribunals in 1908, and in 1917 the Congregation was absorbed by the Holy Office.

At the present time, in view of the enormous number of books published throughout the world, the Holy Office no longer succeeds in keeping an eye on all of them. It now works more particularly at examining publications that deal with religious doctrine, especially books written by ecclesiastics. There is often talk of a revision of the Index (a title coming from the Latin *Index Librorum Prohibitorum*) which, especially as regards the past, contains striking incongruities and strange gaps. Indeed, it is enough to recall that some of the works of the Fathers of the Church themselves were placed on the Index soon after their publication and are still there. Darwin's studies on the evolution of species is not included, but the minor works of

[1] At first the Holy Office had advised the faithful not to belong to the Rotary, which was suspected of links with Freemasonry, but later it took up a more favorable attitude toward this organization.

many of his followers are on the list. In condemning books, the Holy Office can act either on its own initiative or as the result of a denunciation made by the faithful. Among the most recent denunciations there were several against Guareschi's *Don Camillo,* considered by particularly bigoted persons as too liberal from the point of view of religious faith and as too favorable toward the character of the Communist mayor, Don Peppone. But the Holy Office has not taken them too seriously.

At a certain point there were rumors in the Vatican that the works of three very well-known English Catholic writers—Graham Greene, Evelyn Waugh and Bruce Marshall—were going to be placed on the Index. As a matter of fact their novels were examined by the Holy Office and found to contain theological errors. But in the end the opinion prevailed that since they were all three fiction writers and not theologians, and as they had been written in good faith, nothing should be done about it. The same happened with a book on the Devil, written by the well-known Italian Catholic writer, Giovanni Papini. He had put forward the theory that, as the mercy of God is infinite, on the day of the Last Judgment, He would forgive all sinners and that Hell would remain empty. He also suggested that the Devil himself would in the end be redeemed and that good Catholics should pray for his salvation. Papini too was a very sincere Catholic and the Holy Office didn't like the idea of placing his book on the Index. Finally, the problem was solved with a short and caustic article in the *Osservatore Romano* which said that Papini's book was full of so many and such blatant errors that it wasn't worth even the trouble of placing it on the Index.[1]

The Holy Office is also empowered to grant permission for the reading of prohibited books. The great Italian poet Leopardi (1798-1837) himself applied to the Congregation of the Index to be allowed to read any work whatsoever, justifying his request, somewhat Jesuitically, by the statement that antireligious poisons cannot be combated properly except by those who know them well. Applications must be addressed to the Holy Office through one's own parish priest. At present requests of this kind reaching the Holy Office come mainly from students of the Catholic universities.

Not long after John XXIII's accession the Vatican considered not

[1] From 1948 to 1959 the Holy Office has placed on the Index only twenty-five authors including Jean-Paul Sartre, the existentialist philosopher, and his wife Simone De Beauvoir, Curzio Malaparte, Alberto Moravia, André Gide, Unamuno and Boleslaw Piasecki, the leader of the pseudo-Catholic movement "Pax" backed by the Polish Communists. But you will not find Marx, Engels, Lenin nor Stalin. Freud is also absent despite his declared atheism.

only a revision of the Index but also withdrawing it from the jurisdiction of the Holy Office and entrusting it to a special committee. This committee, to keep up with the times, should examine and condemn, besides books, also plays, films, newspaper and magazine articles and radio and television broadcasts. The whole problem is being examined by the State Secretariat.

But the Holy Office functions also as a regular court when it has to judge priests and religious accused of heresy, of belonging to non-Catholic sects, of libidinous acts contrary to nature or against persons below the age of puberty, and of the offense of "soliciting" during confession.

In criminal suits the head of the investigation section is the Father Commissioner of the Dominican Order, Paul Philippe, who has the help of two assistants, Father Raimondo Verardo and Father Feliciano Gargiulo, two other Dominicans, who bear the titles of First and Second Companions, respectively. The Commissioner of the Holy Office corresponds roughly to the Attorney General of the United States in that he initiates and prepares cases for trial.

During the trial proper the part of the Public Prosecutor is taken by the Promoter of Justice, at present Mgr. Giuseppe Graneris, who up to 1920 was called the Fiscal Advocate. This name derives from the fact that at the time of the Inquisition tribunal, when a heretic was sentenced, his possessions were nearly always confiscated.

One of the crimes with which the Holy Office has to deal pretty frequently is that of soliciting. Interpretation of the crime of soliciting is a rather complicated matter, but in practice the Holy Office interprets it in a strict and severe way. It is the duty of all the faithful to report to the local ordinaries and to the Holy Office all cases of soliciting that come to their knowledge.

These reports are fairly frequent (so much so that the Holy Office has prepared a special answer form to be filled in by those wishing to make reports) and very often they are groundless. Usually, therefore, a third denunciation is awaited before a trial is actually begun. In very serious cases the crime is punished with the unfrocking of the confessor; in serious cases, with the loss of benefices, offices and honors, and in ordinary cases, by suspension from celebrating Mass or from hearing confessions.

The officials of all Congregations are pledged to secrecy, but in the case of those of the Holy Office the pledge is especially rigorous. Those divulging official secrets would *ipso facto* be subject, without the need for any additional declaration to this effect, to major excommunication, from which only the Pope can absolve them. This is based on an ordinance issued by Pius X in 1903 which established that even the indirect revelation of such a secret leads to excommunication. One odd result of this fact is that the Holy Office is forbidden to use blotting paper, since revealing traces might be left on it. Accordingly the ink on freshly written documents is dried with fine sand, as it was centuries ago.

12

Vatican Finances

EVERY YEAR on a certain day, in all the Catholic churches of the world they collect Peter's Pence. Generally the day is June 29, the Saint's day, but in some dioceses it is done on another day more suitable for the faithful and likely to bring in more cash. This is a custom which originated in England in the eighth century and which had lapsed after the Reformation. In its present form the custom was revived in Paris in 1859 by Count de Montalambert. He formed a committee *"pour le denier de St. Pierre,"* which branched out first to Turin, then to Vienna and gradually spread to the whole of Europe, North and South America and to the mission lands. The initiative reached its climax after 1870 when, as is generally known, Rome was occupied by Piedmontese troops and the Pope, having lost his temporal power, locked himself in the Vatican in sign of protest.

In many European countries, and particularly in Germany and Ireland, the parish priests would distribute to the faithful picture-cards depicting the Pope lying on a bed of straw in a dark dungeon to corroborate the legend that he was a prisoner of the wicked Italians and reduced to extreme poverty. The people were moved and pennies, shillings, ducats, thalers, pengoes and dollars poured in, forming the main revenue of the Holy See.

With the years the importance of this type of income, the most evident and direct, gradually grew less. Today, Peter's Pence is handed over to the bishops to take to Rome in the course of their customary visit *ad limina* and present to the Pope personally in the form of a check. Peter's Pence has been valued at about $1,500,000 a year. However, it represents just a trickle when one considers the enormous tasks and the huge expenses that the Catholic Church has to face.

The Vatican is one of the greatest financial powers in the world today. Vatican finances are so complicated and surrounded by such a thick wall of secrecy that it is absolutely impossible to produce a completely exact and documented appraisal. However, on the basis of information gathered confidentially both in the Vatican and in Italian banking quarters, I shall attempt to trace an approximate picture of the Pope's financial empire.

First of all attention must be directed to the Special Administration founded by Pius XI on June 7, 1929, shortly after he had concluded a Concordat with Italy. In execution of the Concordat the Fascist Government had given to the Holy See 1,500,000,000 lire (worth about $83,000,000 at the time) as compensation for the loss of temporal power. And Pius XI, finding himself with such a vast sum at his disposal decided to create a separate financial administration. From its foundation until a few years ago the Special Administration was run by Signor Bernardino Nogara, an engineer, brother of the Director of the Vatican Museums. The Special Administration has been continuously growing in importance and has gradually taken over as well the control of the Vatican's funds abroad.

Shortly after the election of Eugenio Pacelli, strange rumors started circulating in the Vatican about the Special Administration, and it was even said that very little was left of the huge sum paid by the Italian Government. Pius XII had an administrative check carried out and was able to learn that, on the contrary, the wise and timely investments made by Signor Nogara had considerably increased the initial capital. From that moment, under Pacelli, the Special Administration was left to function practically without any form of control and it did so with great independence and efficiency. Nogara's position was the envy of all financiers. He didn't have to account to anybody except to the Pope, who understood very little about finance and who gave him a free hand. He didn't have to pay taxes, could operate in any part of the world, didn't have to show an immediate profit, could use the diplomatic privileges of the Vatican and had at his disposal a network of informants (the nuncios, the apostolic delegates, the Cardinals, the bishops, and good Catholics placed in key positions in foreign governments and big industries throughout the world) such as no other banker ever had or is ever likely to have. The late Signor Nogara, who left his post of his own free will for reasons of health, was a tall, strong, taciturn man, deeply religious, who proved to be completely dedicated to his work and absolutely scrupulous in its execution.

Under his skillful guidance the Special Administration carried on big financial deals on a world-wide scale. In his hands the initial capital handed over by Mussolini multiplied itself several times over. As no balance sheets are ever published and as the whole operation is surrounded by secrecy, it is impossible to indicate, even approximately, the value of the sums handled by the Special Administration at the present time. In Roman banking quarters the figure of $500,-000,000 has been tentatively mentioned.

Not a single cent of this capital is in the Vatican. It is distributed in Italy and abroad, primarily in the United States, Switzerland and England. The banks with which the Vatican has especially close ties are the Crédit Suisse of Geneva, Hambro's Bank in London and the J. P. Morgan and Company Bank in New York. Relations with the Crédit Suisse are so intimate that a former director of this bank, the Marquis Henri de Maillardoz, has moved to the Vatican and acts there as secretary to the Special Administration. As this organization deals only with very large and also with very few operations, it requires only a small staff. Ten executives and four accountants carry on all the work in a tiny apartment, to which entry is strictly prohibited, and which is quite close to the Pope's private apartment.

In America the actual if not official representative of the Special Administration is Cardinal Spellman, who was a very close friend of Pius XII and who has considerable influence in Wall Street quarters. There is even a rumor to the effect that the Special Administration quite exceptionally is allowed to keep a considerable gold reserve tucked away in Fort Knox. But, however many may believe that, it is, of course, erroneous. The Director of the U.S. Mint makes clear, that Fort Knox has all the gold the United States owns, and it does not have the possession of the gold of any other state, city or nation.

All the money the Special Administration had in England was at one time invested in Empire bonds. This goes back to an episode in 1948 when the Catholic Relief Organization in Germany received several shiploads of wheat which the Vatican had bought in the Argentine. The wheat was paid for by Nogara with pounds which he had in England. The British, who were still under a regime of austerity, currency restrictions and so on, quite naturally got annoyed. There were negotiations between the British Exchequer and the Holy

See and Nogara agreed to invest the money that he had in English bonds. Whether this is still the case today, I have been unable to find out.

After Nogara withdrew, he continued for several years to give his disinterested advice to the Special Administration in a private capacity. He died in 1958. Since the election of John XXIII the Special Administration has been run by Cardinal Di Jorio, whose name will turn up again in this survey of Vatican finances.

Another important financial organization of the Vatican is the Administration of the Holy See Property.

If, for the Special Administration, one has to go back to the 1929 Concordat with Italy, one must now retrace one's steps to 1870. With the Pope's loss of temporal power the Holy See was no longer able to exact taxes from its subjects and all its finances were thrown into a state of confusion. Some eight years later, on August 9, 1878, Pope Leo XIII appointed his State Secretary, Cardinal Nina, administrator of all the property that was left to the Holy See. Later, that is, in 1880 and in 1883, he appointed a committee of Cardinals to supervise the administration of Peter's Pence and of the Holy See property. Finally, in 1891, the Pope gave the Cardinals more ample power to administer the property directly and to embark on financial operations connected with it. He also ruled that the aforesaid committee could continue functioning even while the papal throne was vacant. In 1926 Pius XI further increased the power of the committee by turning over to it the administration of the apostolic palaces and the administrative sections of the various Congregations and offices.

Here once again it is impossible to estimate, even approximately, the value of the property concerned. Apart from the fact that no balance sheet is ever issued, how can one set a price tag on Michelangelo's dome, or on Raphael's frescoes, or on the thousands of masterpieces in the Vatican Museums, or on the magnificent extraterritorial palaces spread all over Rome? One should also remember that the Holy See possesses properties in various parts of the world separate from those of the religious orders, dioceses, institutes and other Catholic organizations.

Under Pacelli his nephew Prince Carlo, in his capacity as legal adviser to this Administration, was the real power behind the scenes. Under Roncalli, although Prince Pacelli has retained his position of legal adviser, the man who has the final say is the State Secretary, Cardinal Tardini.

The Administration of the Holy See Property, which had always operated with great discretion and absolute exactitude, in 1948 found itself mixed up in a huge scandal linked to the name of Mgr. Edoardo Prettner Cippico. This brilliant, young prelate, who was employed by the Vatican Archives, got himself into a tangle of financial deals which ended in disaster. In those days there were a great many currency restrictions and many Italian industrialists and businessmen were eager to transfer money abroad either for investment, or to purchase goods for import. Mgr. Cippico, who moved in high society and used to come in contact with persons of great wealth, undertook to transfer their money through the Administration of the Holy See Property, which was exempted from all Italian currency regulations.

For a certain time everything went smoothly and the young Monsignore was very popular among his friends. But, besides doing favors for them, Cippico also started embarking on financial transactions of his own. For example, he squandered a fortune to finance a film on St. Francis which never saw the light of day. To stop a gap on one side he opened a bigger one on the other. Finally he went down with a crash. People who had entrusted him with large sums to be transferred abroad, when they saw that this was not being done, claimed their money back from the Vatican. An inquiry was held, Mgr. Cippico was defrocked, arrested in his office by the Gendarmery and locked inside the Vatican prison, the Tower of the Four Winds.

This prison is nearly always empty and accordingly is not frightfully efficient. After a couple of days Cippico managed to break out of prison and went into hiding in the apartment of a widow of a former Fascist militia general in Rome. The Italian police caught him a few days later and put him in the Rome jail, *Regina Coeli* (The Queen of Heaven). An Italian court tried him and sentenced him for swindling. The Court of Appeals, however, found him not guilty and set him free. The Church has still not reinstated him. However, as it was ascertained that he never had any intention of swindling his friends, and had got himself into the mess out of inexperience, irresponsibility and megalomania, and as his repentance seemed sincere, he was allowed to go on living in an apartment belonging to the Vatican, and the Vatican even gives him some work to do as a translator.

But the Cippico scandal proved a terrible blow to the then secretary of the Administration of the Holy See Property, Mgr. Guido Guidetti, an old man of absolute integrity. Although Mgr. Guidetti was able to prove that he himself had never made the slightest profit out of Cippico's deals, it was found that he had acted with incredible carelessness in helping the young and mundane Monsignore to carry out the money transfers. He was dismissed from his job, retired to a monastery and died after two years of brooding and penances.

Another financial organization is the Institute for Religious Works which, although the name might be misleading, is just a bank. It was founded by Pius XII in June 1942 and has taken over the Administration of Religious Works set up by Leo XIII in 1887. The Pontifical Year Book explains that "the scope of the Institute is to take into custody and administer capitals destined to religious work." In practice it functions the way any other bank does. It has its counters, its cashiers (in priestly robes), it accepts deposits, opens current accounts, cashes checks, transfers money and so on. The big difference between it and other banks is that its clients are a very selected group. The only people who can open an account with the Institute are the residents of the Vatican City State, the diplomats accredited to the Holy See, some high Vatican officials who, although they reside in Rome, work in the Vatican, the members of the Roman Curia, the religious who administer schools, orders, hospitals, etc., and a very few Italian citizens to whom this privilege has been granted because of their business relations with the Vatican or because of the good work they have done in the interest of the Church. The advantages of banking with the Vatican—apart from the prestige —are that one is completely free from Italian State controls (here, too, banking secrecy exists but governments and laws might change and you never know), and that one can transfer one's money easily to any country in the world. The entrance to the bank is in the Holy Office courtyard. During Pacelli's pontificate Mgr. Alberto Di Jorio, since made a Cardinal by John XXIII, was the secretary of the Institute and in practice ran the whole show.

The fourth of the big financial organizations of the Catholic Church is the Administration of the Vatican City State. Although it is a very small State indeed it is organized more or less on the lines of any other State, with various offices that look after finances, personnel, transport, health, food, justice, the police and armed forces, public works, etc. To this must be added the administration of the Vatican Museums, the radio, the Papal summer residence at Castel Gandolfo and the astronomical observatory.

The citizens of the Vatican City State and the diplomats accredited to the Holy See are entitled to buy cigarettes, liquor, cars, gasoline and practically anything they might need without paying the ordinary Italian custom duties. They do so fairly lavishly and this too entails money changing hands and the administrative work connected with it. Adding it all up, the movements of capital controlled by this administration are quite considerable.

Under Pacelli his old friend Count Enrico Galeazzi practically ran the Vatican City State. He held the jobs of Special Delegate, Director General of Technical Services and Director General of Economic Services. (Other Vatican positions held by Galeazzi were that of technical adviser for the building of new churches in Rome, architect of St. Peter's basilica, member of the Pontifical Committee for the Cinema, Radio and Television, member of the committee for the protection of Holy See monuments and finally official representative in Rome, with the title of Procurator, of the powerful and flourishing American Knights of Columbus.)

To recapitulate the administration of Vatican finances, then, it is to be noted that under Pius XII three laymen—Nogara, Gałeazzi and Carlo Pacelli—had established a kind of monopoly with the backing of two Cardinals, Pizzardo and Canali, always present in all the committees that dealt with large sums of money.

Since Roncalli was elected Pope there have been radical changes, if not on the surface at least in substance. Nogara is dead and both Pacelli and Galeazzi, while still officially holding their jobs, have lost most of their influence and hardly ever meet the Pope. Also the Cardinals Pizzardo and Canali, while still members of the various committees, no longer hold the power they formerly had.

At present three Cardinals are actually in charge of the Vatican financial empire. One is the State Secretary Tardini, who controls the Administration of the Holy See Property, the other is Cardinal Amleto Cicognani, former Apostolic Delegate to the United States, in charge of the Vatican City State and the third is Cardinal Alberto Di Jorio, boss of both the Special Administration and of the Institute for Religious Works.

These changes were favorably received in the Vatican. The exceptional situation enjoyed by the late Pope's nephew Prince Carlo Pacelli and by his friend Count Galeazzi, although they are both men of absolute integrity and great capacity, smacked a bit of nepotism. John XXIII has gone back to normality. He has given the State Secretary the financial powers he is entitled to by tradition and he has appointed two more Cardinals, Cicognani and Di Jorio, both comparatively young and very able, to three of the four key posts in the central administration of the Church's financial affairs.

In this somewhat sketchy report on Vatican finances what has been mainly dealt with has been the central administrative offices of the

Holy See and their connections with the United States, Great Britain, Switzerland and other countries. But the real fief of the Vatican as regards investments remains Italy. The Vatican owns the shares, often the controlling shares, in several of the largest Italian banks. Among these are the Banca Commerciale, the Banca di Roma and the Banco di Santo Spirito (the Bank of the Holy Ghost). The Vatican also owns the controlling shares of most public utility companies, of the real estate companies, of the big hotels, of the insurance companies and of several companies in other fields of economic activity. To give an idea of how close the ties are between Italian and Vatican finances, it may be repeated that Count Galeazzi, for example, is a member of the boards of directors of the following companies: the Generale Immobiliare (which is the biggest Italian real estate company, of which he is vice-president) the Riunione Adriatica di Sicurtà (a very powerful insurance company), the financial company Invest, the Centrale Group (electric power plants), the Società Romana di Elettricità (electricity for home consumption), the Società Imprese Centro Italia (railways), the Società Acqua Pia (water for domestic consumption), the Istituto per l'Edilizia Economica (building) and the Italian tourist company CIT. Prince Carlo Pacelli follows him very closely, holding almost as many and almost as important positions. The other two nephews of the late Pope, the Princes Giulio and Marcantonio, are also in business—but to a minor degree.

In the opinion of many foreign observers and even of some Vatican officials this is not a good state of affairs. The concentration of Vatican investments in Italy no doubt offers some advantages such as geographical position, the possibility of influencing the economic policy of the Italian government through the strong Christian Democratic Party, which has been in power since the end of the war, and the Italian nationality of the men the Vatican has placed in key posts of the Italian economy. But it also has some very serious drawbacks. First of all the Vatican has put most of its eggs in one basket, which is not one of the wisest things to do. Then there is the psychological factor. The Italian man in the street, who every month pays his gas, light, telephone and water bills, who has to take trolleys and buses to go to work, who pays his insurance premiums, who stays at hotels, who buys a railway ticket from the tourist office, who happens to have to pay interest on an overdraft with the Bank of the Holy Ghost, and who knows that each of these actions results in a profit for the Vatican, is bound to feel a bit sore and to accumulate a fund of anticlericalism.

The lavishness of the ceremonies in St. Peter and in other churches in Rome, the fact that so many high dignitaries of the Church, living in luxurious apartments and driving around in big automobiles, are concentrated in Rome, all tend to give the Italians the impression that the Church is rolling in money. The big, black, shiny limousines of the Cardinals, of the Vatican diplomats and other big shots have a number plate with the initials S.C.V. (Vatican City State). Whereupon the cynical Romans declare that these initials stand for "Se Cristo vedesse" (If Christ only saw this!).

On the other hand only very rarely is the same man in the street reminded of the really imposing work of relief, of social assistance, of education that the Church is carrying on both in Italy and in other countries. Nor is he reminded of the fact that he owes some gratitude to the Church for preserving countless monuments and works of art, for encouraging artistic production, for keeping ancient archives, even for financing scientific studies.

However, if Vatican investments were not so concentrated in Italy but were spread more widely over several other countries, the Italians wouldn't be so impressed by the wealth of the Church and their hostility toward this side of the picture wouldn't be so great nor their criticism so sharp.

The four big financial organizations here described all belong to the central organization of the Church. But who is it that deals with the smaller, everyday financial problems of each diocese, with the innumerable expenses the Church has to sustain from Ireland to New Zealand, from Korea to Cambodia, from Tunisia to Colorado, in other words wherever in the world there are Catholics? This kind of current administration is under the control of the Congregation of the Council. The Congregation gives instructions on the use and administration of ecclesiastical properties, on the execution of wills in favor of religious works, on the acceptance of legacies and trusts, on the sale or mortgage of real estate properties and so on. It also fixes the fees to be collected for Masses and other church ceremonies and the sums which the bishops can draw from the estates of the respective dioceses.

It is the task of this Congregation to study all the projects which require considerable sums of money and to examine, on the basis of a sound economy, the possibilities of borrowing money. When some local initiative looks promising but cannot be accomplished for lack of funds, the Financial Office of the Congregation steps in with its own contribution. It also finances the reconstruction of churches, schools, parish buildings destroyed by war, earthquakes, floods or other disasters; it supervises the use to which ecclesiastical properties are put and gives financial assistance to particularly poor priests or to those dioceses that most need help. Also the building of hospitals, in especially urgent cases, is financed by this office.

The importance and the technical character of business dealt with by this Congregation require a specialized staff. In 1919 Benedict XV attached to the financial office a school for the training of officials, a school attended by young priests who take a three-year course.

Finally it is to be noted that the various Congregations have their own separate administrations. The biggest is that of *Propaganda Fide* which must look after the financial needs of missionaries scattered over the most faraway countries. Since this Congregation was founded by Gregory XV (1621-1623) the principle has been established and maintained never to ask any financial help of the natives so that they should clearly understand that the missionary is moved solely by the desire of saving their souls. It's a sound and attractive idea but the result is that this particular Congregation very often finds itself in the red and has to rely for help on the over all budget of the Church.

To conclude, the administration of Vatican finances, as a whole, is efficient, honest and exact, flexible and carried out with a minimum of employees and not too much red tape. The Church knows how to exploit to the maximum the resources at her disposal, she is a master in the art of economizing, she has far-reaching vision and constitutes an organization from which many governments could learn a great deal.

It is only in certain sectors of the central administration that the Church has become a big capitalist and financier. As a whole she has remained what she was from the beginning—an institution which draws money from charity and spends money for charity.

In this respect the Catholics of the United States are right up in front. More deeply religious than Catholics in the Latin countries and in Europe in general, well organized, led by a numerous and dynamic clergy, much richer than their fellow-believers in other countries, the Catholics of the United States give to the Church regularly and generously. After local needs have been covered, the sums collected are sent to Rome and from here they flow out again in a thousand streams to meet the necessities of the Church the world over.

13

The *Sacra Rota* and Marriage Annulment

THE ORIGINS of the *Sacra Romana Rota,* or Sacred Roman Rota, chief judiciary organ of the Holy See, are very remote. Its descent is to be traced from the Apostolic Chancery. It was to these chaplains that the Pontiffs, at first at odd intervals and then regularly, entrusted preliminary proceedings in law suits. In that capacity they were known as *auditores causarum curiae domini papae.* Then, in view of the fact that the number of suits continued to increase, Innocent III (1198-1216) gave them the additional power to pass sentences. And since Gregory X (1272-1276), the Pope's chaplains have constituted a permanent tribunal.

The origin of the name Rota (wheel) is questionable and often questioned. According to some, it derives from the fact that the auditors sat in a circle when passing judgment on suits; others hold that it comes from the custom of considering cases by turns—that is, in rotation; still others trace the origin back to a porphyry wheel once embedded in the center of the floor where the cases were heard; lastly, there are those who attribute it to a revolving wooden stand or set of shelves where the law codes were kept.

Election of the auditors was always a prerogative of the Pope, although some nations were permitted to name a certain number of them—Spain, two, Germany, one, and France, one, whereas the dioceses of Bologna, Milan, Venice, Ferrara, and Perugia were given the privilege of appointing one auditor each. They had to be chosen from among the most celebrated doctors of law and had, moreover, to be renowned for their prudence and personal rectitude.

In 1870, the Rota's work came virtually to a complete halt and did not resume regular hearings until the ascension of Pius X, who re-formed it. At present, it passes judgment *videntibus omnibus*, that is, in the presence of all the auditors. The Rota is the regular tribunal of the Vatican City State as well as, since 1834, the appeals court for all ecclesiastical suits falling within the jurisdiction of the Roman Curia. However, it also passes judgment on suits of the first instance within the jurisdiction of the Holy See and on those submitted by the Pope with the rescript of the Apostolic Signature.

The prelate-auditors are seventeen in number, of whom half are Italians. They are presided over by the Dean, the American Mgr. Francis O'Bremen from Shenandoah, Pennsylvania. Attached to the tribunal, whose seat is located in the beautiful Chancery Palace in Rome, there is also a school for lawyers wishing to try cases before the *Sacra Rota*. The course lasts three years and instruction is given by five professors. Pius XII's three nephews, Princes Carlo, Giulio, and Marcantonio, as has been noted, are all attorneys of the *Sacra Rota*.

The bulk of this court's work, which, in the eyes of the public is also its most fascinating aspect, involves marriage annulments. Auditors of the *Sacra Rota* throw up their hands in horror at any mention of "divorce." And, for that matter, they do not even recognize the term "annulment," preferring, rather, to define their sentences as "declarations of nullity." The distinction is considerable. The Church not only does not grant divorces, it does not annul marriages. The *Sacra Rota* confines itself exclusively to noting that some marriages have never been valid and, therefore, it is as though they had never been contracted. In the words of Monsignor Giuseppe Trezzi, Defender of the Marriage Tie, a post which is similar to that of Public Prosecutor, "Something that has never existed cannot be annulled."

The reasons which make a marriage invalid are substantially the same as those given by Don Abbondio in Manzoni's *The Betrothed* to which reference has already been made. And they are, in Don Abbondio's Latin: *"Error, conditio, votum, cognatio, crimen, cultus disparitas, vis, ordo, ligamen, honestas, si sis affinis."* They correspond to the following conditions:

1) If there is a case of mistaken identity. Rather rare, this occurs when a person believed he or she was marrying one person and instead married another (*Error*).

2) If, before marriage, stipulation of some particular physical state of either party had been made and was not respected. To give a pedestrian example, let's say that a woman married a man thinking he was completely sound in body and that, after the wedding, she discovers he has a glass eye or a wooden leg (*Conditio*).

3) If before marriage either of the two parties had taken a religious vow not to marry (*Votum*).

4) If husband or wife is godfather or godmother, as the case may be, of the other (*Cognatio*).

5) If the marriage has been preceded by a crime resulting in the marriage itself (*Crimen*).

6) If the two parties are of different religions (*Cultus disparitas*).

7) If the will of one of the two parties has been bent by physical or moral violence. This is one of the most usual cases, in that brides, fairly frequently, are forced into ceremonies by their fathers or mothers, and men, who may have seduced the girl, go to the altar because they are afraid that the offended family may take revenge on them (*Vis*).

8) Membership in a religious order (*Ordo*).

9) If there has already been a previous marriage (*Ligamen*).

10) If the bride turns out not to be a virgin when there are good reasons to believe that the groom thought her to be one (*Honestas*).

11) The fact of being blood relations up to second cousin (*Si sis affinis*).

Then, too, there are regularly contracted but unconsummated marriages. In such cases, the Rota cannot pronounce a marriage null. However, the Pope himself can intervene and free the couple, after first hearing the opinion of the Congregation of the Sacraments.

Here are some concrete examples to show the way the *Sacra Rota* works. Many years ago, Marina Volpi, daughter of the late Count Volpi, former Finance Minister under Mussolini and in his day probably the richest man in Italy, married Prince Puccio Ruspoli. Some years later, however, the *Sacra Rota* declared their marriage null because it was shown that young Marina, though she had not actually been threatened, still had felt herself so under the influence of her highly placed father, who favored the marriage, that she pronounced the fateful "I do" really against her will.

Much more complicated was the case of General Attilio Teruzzi, former Chief of Staff of the Fascist Militia and Minister for the Italian possessions in Africa, who requested that his marriage with one Miss Wymann, an American heiress, be annulled. The General claimed that he had set as a condition of marriage that Miss Wymann should be a virgin, whereas he was later to learn that she was not one. However, he was unable to prove this or even that he had set such a condition, and his request for an annulment was thrown out of court. Having lost the first case, Teruzzi initiated a second, this time claiming that when they were married Miss Wymann did not believe in the indissolubility of the marriage tie and, therefore, that she had contracted the marriage in bad faith. The first ruling in the second case went against Teruzzi, whereas findings in the two succeeding ones were in his favor and the marriage was at last declared null.

I have mentioned two successive judgments because all sentences of the Rota have to be confirmed. Teruzzi's lawyer in the case was Prince Carlo Pacelli. A curious aspect of the matter is that Miss Wymann, charged with not believing in the indissolubility of the marriage tie, was the one opposed to the annulment of the marriage.

Compared with the Teruzzi case, the annulment of the marriage of Guglielmo Marconi, inventor of the radio, was child's play. The experts in Canon Law discovered that he was a member of a parish in Ravenna, his wife of one in Bologna, and that they were married in Milan without notifying either the Bologna or Ravenna parish of the event. The marriage was declared null on grounds of a procedural error.

As one auditor pointed out to me, in questions of matrimony, the *Sacra Rota* functions only as a higher court and can pass decisions only on such cases as have already been heard by the lower courts; that is, by one of the fifteen regional ecclesiastical tribunals in Italy or by one of the diocesan tribunals in other countries. The number of suits tried by the *Rota* is continually increasing.

The most recent figures which I have pertain to the judiciary year 1957. In that period, the Rota handed down 236 sentences, of which ninety-two cost the applicants nothing. This last figure is of particular interest in that it refutes the fairly widespread public notion that only the very rich are able to get annulments from the Vatican court. Of the 236 cases, 233 involved marriage. Of these only 108 received affirmative sentences, dissolving the tie; the remaining 125 marriages were found to be binding. As regards the reasons put forth for annulments, seventy-four cited violence and compulsion in obtaining consent; seventy, denial of the right to have offspring; and twenty-nine, impotence. That same year, there was also an extraordinarily high enrollment of students in the courses of the Rota school—124 in all, representing thirty nationalities, including even one student from Tahiti.

In view of the growing movement in Italy for the introduction of divorce and the imposing growth in the number of legal separations, the question has arisen whether there is any possibility that the Catholic Church may review its position as regards the indissolubility of matrimony. In this connection, an auditor of the Rota told me that such a possibility has not even been considered. Said he, "The Church has weathered many other storms in the past. Rome preferred to lose all England rather than yield to the request of Henry VIII, who asked that his marriage be annulled."

The Church's inflexibility on this point can at times result in almost comic effects. As happened, for example, in the case of Admiral Stone, former head of the Allied High Commission in Italy. Admiral Stone was allowed to marry the Baroness Renata Arborio Mella of Sant'Elia, niece of the Vatican's Master of Ceremonies, even though he had been married twice before in the United States. His third marriage, celebrated with great pomp in St. Peter's, even received the papal blessing.

It may be asked, if the Catholic Church does not recognize divorce, how is it that Admiral Stone was able to marry for a third time with the most high approbation of the Pope? An expert in Canon Law explained it to me: "Admiral Stone married the first time in America, and though the wedding was a Protestant one, it was perfectly valid. Then he got a divorce and married a second time. But since we do not recognize divorce, in the eyes of the Catholic Church his second marriage never existed and we found him still married to his first wife. Thus, when his first wife died, Admiral Stone became a widower and was therefore perfectly entitled to remarry."

However, to get back to the question of the amount of money necessary to obtain an annulment from the *Sacra Rota*, it must first be noted that the ratio between cases handled free in 1957 (that is, 92) and those for fees (141) does not at all reflect the proportions as between the various social classes. To put it another way, if 141 well-off people applied to the Rota for annulments, those of the poorer classes ought to have been not 92, but a thousand or some tens of thousands. The 92 cases accepted without any costs being charged were unique, cases which were very clear or hardship cases.

However, it must not be assumed that one has only to pay out enough money and an annulment is certain. Auditors of the *Sacra Rota* are all prelates of uncommon honorability and rectitude and they certainly cannot be bribed. They move with leaden feet, passing judgment with great scrupulousness. And what is more, their sentences, as has been noted, must always be confirmed by the three judges of the subsequent session. The cost of an annulment, which ranges from between five to six hundred thousand lire and several millions, is determined by the length of the procedure, which can often drag on for years, due to the fact that all the documents have to be translated into Latin (a requirement which, in my opinion, could easily be dispensed with). Last but not least there is the matter of fees to the lawyers of the Rota. These lawyers are all outstanding men in their field and it is only natural that they should demand high fees for their specialized services.

Moreover, it must be borne in mind that, before an application for annulment is approved and the marriage is dissolved, agreement between the couple concerned is virtually always a prerequisite. In the words of one eminent lawyer of the Rota, "It is easier to get an annulment with both spouses agreeing to it, even though the reason put forth may not exist—a reason, naturally, among those recognized by Canon Law—than if there *is* a reason but one of the spouses is against annulment."

The public at large tends to be disturbed by sentences of the *Sacra Rota*. It cannot, for instance, understand how Marconi was able to get an annulment with comparative ease on a simple and rather trivial technicality, whereas some poor unlucky veteran, after four years away at war, who returns home to find himself saddled with two or three illegitimate children cannot dissolve a tie which he now finds odious, and has to resign himself to a legal separation which does not permit him to form a new family.

It is here necessary to repeat and to remember that, for the Church, marriage is an indissoluble sacrament. It pronounces null only such marriages as may have appeared valid but which actually were not valid. It is necessary always to return to the fateful "I do"; that is to say, to the time when the couple gave its consent before a priest. If at that moment there was something amiss, if the "I do" was pronounced against the will of either of the parties or with serious mental reservations, such as not wanting to have children (and having children is one of the principal ends of a Catholic marriage), if there were impediments of which the priest was not aware, then the marriage can be declared null. What happens after the "I do" is of no importance, except in cases of ratified but unconsummated marriages, and these, as already pointed out, fall not within the jurisdiction of the *Sacra Rota*, but within that of the Pope himself.

From the point of view of Italian law, the competency of the *Sacra Rota* is guaranteed by the Concordat which, at the same time, compels Italian lawmakers not to allow divorce and to recognize, wherever it may arise, the provisions of Canon Law. The Italian legal code enters in, and has juridical power, only insofar as it concerns civil or penal aspects of torts or as it concerns disputes between married couples either in their personal affairs or affairs relating to their rights and obligations in society. Nonetheless, Italian courts are authorized to declare null or annullable marriages contracted under circumstances which Italian law regards as criminal (this occurs most often where there is lack of consent). In practice, however, Italian courts are less lenient than the *Sacra Rota*. Jews, Protestants, Moslems, atheists, and Catholics who have backslid, marrying with only a civil ceremony, have less of a chance to annul their marriages before an Italian court than have those who apply to the *Sacra Rota*, a situation which has been paradoxically summed up in the statement that "only Catholics can be divorced in Italy."

Pope John XXIII being borne in procession into the Basilica of St. John in Lateran—*Attualità Giordani.*

Richard Cardinal Cushing of Boston kissing the ring of the Pope—
Attualità Giordani

Newly appointed American Cardinal, Aloisius J. Muench, a native of Milwaukee, Wis., formerly Papal Nuncio to the West German government—*Wide World*

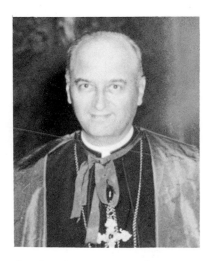

Another American of Milwaukee recently elevated to Cardinal, Monsignor Albert G. Meyer, head of the archdiocese of Chicago—*Wide World*

Cardinal Montini embraces Cardinal Mimmi—*Attualità Giordani*

Domenico Cardinal Tardini, Vatican Secretary of State, greeting Japanese Prime Minister Nobusuke Kishi—*Attualità Giordani*

Pope John XXIII talking to Francis Cardinal Spellman of New York. In the center is Cardinal Cicognani.

The makeup row in the linotype room of the Vatican City daily, *L'Osservatore Romano—Wide World*

Pope John XXIII in a private audience with Prince Rainier and Princess Grace of Monaco—*Wide World*

The geniality of Pope John XXIII demonstrated at the audience between the Pontiff and President Eisenhower in December, 1959—the second audience of an American president with a Pope. (The first was that of President Woodrow Wilson with Pope Benedict XV.) The others in the photograph are Lt. Col. Vernon Walters, the President's interpreter, and Mrs. John Eisenhower, his daughter-in-law—*Wide World*

Artist's reconstruction of the shrine over St. Peter's tomb

RECONSTRUCTION OF SHRINE OVER ST. PETER'S TOMB

THE SHRINE IS STANDING AGAINST A WALL OF RED BRICKS

HOLE IN THE RED WALL WHERE THEY FOUND A TINY MARBLE BOX CONTAINING FRAGMENTS OF BONES

ARCH AT THE BOTTOM OF THE RED WALL. REMAINS OF A SKELETON WITHOUT THE HEAD WERE FOUND HERE

Human bones found buried under the Red Wall near St. Peter's tomb

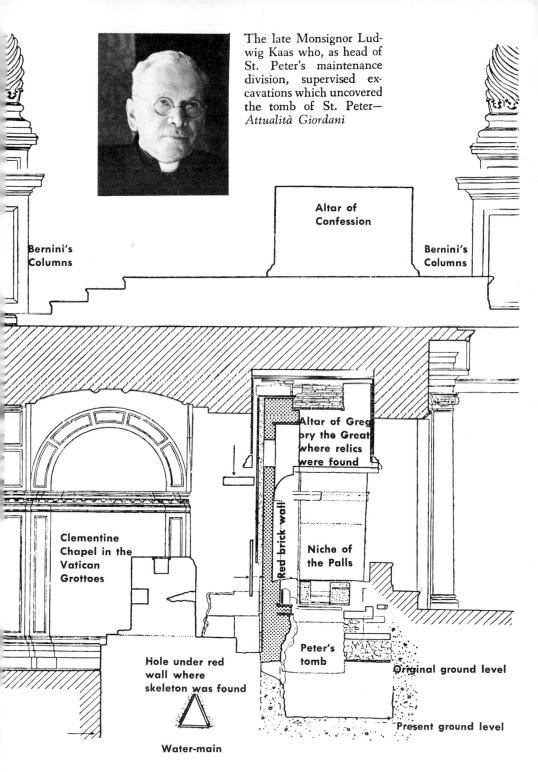

The late Monsignor Ludwig Kaas who, as head of St. Peter's maintenance division, supervised excavations which uncovered the tomb of St. Peter—*Attualità Giordani*

Altar of Confession

Bernini's Columns

Bernini's Columns

Altar of Gregory the Great where relics were found

Clementine Chapel in the Vatican Grottoes

Red brick wall

Niche of the Palls

Hole under red wall where skeleton was found

Peter's tomb

Original ground level

Present ground level

Water-main

The various ground levels under the Basilica of St. Peter's

The Bernini columns and canopy over the papal altar in St. Peter's—
Attualità Giordani

14

Steps to Sainthood

PIUS XII, in the nineteen years of his reign, proclaimed thirty-three new saints and about as many blessed. His predecessor, Pius XI, had to his credit one saint less. But the record still belongs to Pius IX, the Pope who reigned longest, with fifty-two saints.

Although the number of beatifications and canonizations has increased considerably in modern times, it's still not so easy to become a saint. Several important characters have been trying for centuries but are still in the waiting room.

Among them are to be noted Christopher Columbus, a very pious man who donated a whole continent to Christianity, Dante Alighieri, who visited and described Paradise while he was still alive, the fiery Florentine preacher and reformer Girolamo Savonarola and Alessandro Manzoni who, in his novel *The Betrothed*, produced probably the most effective Catholic propaganda ever written.

The movement in favor of granting a halo to Columbus is growing continuously. The Holy See has already received nearly two thousand pleas, many of them from America, asking that the beatification cause, promoted since 1844 by the French writer Count Roselly de Lorgues, and favorably received by Leo XIII, be taken up again and successfully completed. Leo himself expressed his pleasure at this initiative in an encyclical full of praise for the great navigator.

Columbus was not only a practicing and fervent Catholic. He was also moved by an intense missionary spirit and was determined to bring to India, which he was aiming for, the religion of Christ. (Before sailing he wrote that he intended to go "toward certain parts of the Ocean to achieve very useful things in the service of God. . . .") To all this one can add the special worship of the Immaculate Conception by Columbus himself and by his crew during their momentous voyage.

The beatification of Columbus, however, finds a very serious obstacle in a matter concerning his private life—the illegitimate relation he had, after the death of his wife, with Beatrix Erignes de Haraña, with whom, in 1488, he had a son, Fernando, the future humanist and geographer. Columbus' life is still, for many of its periods, wrapped in mystery and the reasons are not known that prevented him from contracting a regular marriage with Beatrix. At any rate, this is the insidious rock against which the ship of Columbus' beatification has so far been shipwrecked.

As for Dante, in his case the difficulties are even greater and the voices interceding in his favor have been getting always fewer and fainter. Dante himself, a very sincere man, often confessed his own faults. For one thing he was much too fond of women to be considered a saint. Further, according to the more strict theologians, he exalted beyond recognized limits the power of reason, which he considered capable of satisfying completely his thirst for knowledge. Dante however was a Christian in the full sense of the word. He observed fasting very strictly, he went to confession often, he took the Holy Communion, he hated blasphemy and he was devoted to the Madonna and to St. Francis.

With Manzoni too there are difficulties in his case, connected with both his private life and his philosophical outlook. He was married twice, while he should have known that St. Paul advised widowers to remain widowers. As for his philosophy he has never been quite cleared of a suspicion that he shared the heresy of Cornelius Jansen, the Dutch theologian. (It's all about some subtle points relating to the vexed question of the freedom of the will. It was the Jansenist viewpoint that the great French mathematician and philosopher Pascal defended against the Jesuits in his masterly *Provincial Letters*.)

Finally, to block Savonarola's inclusion in the list of saints, there are his intolerance with and his revolt against the authority of Rome. The fact that his candidature was seconded by no less than St. Filippo de Neri, (1515-1595) didn't help him much.

However, the Church is continuously evolving, though slowly, even in her historical and critical appraisal of the great figures of the past. The last word, therefore, has not yet been said. This pertains particularly to Columbus, whose chances are far greater than those of the others just mentioned and whose beatification cause may well come to a happy conclusion during the reign of John XXIII.

Joan of Arc, as an instance, had to wait several centuries; she succeeded in becoming a saint only a few decades ago. Considering that she had been burned at the stake as a heretic, it really didn't take too long for her to get official admittance into Heaven.

But the real gate-crasher, the holder of the speed record, is a 14-year-old girl, St. Maria Goretti, born in Nettuno, south of Rome, who died a saintly death after having forgiven the man who had first tried to rape her and then stabbed her to death. She died on the 6th of July, 1902, was beatified on the 27th of April, 1947 and canonized on the 24th of June, 1950. It was the first time in history that the mother of a saint was able to take part in the canonization ceremony in St. Peter's. Her murderer, Alessandro Serenelli, who received a life sentence, was freed by amnesty after thirty years in jail. He had found work as a gardener in a monastery and listened on the radio to the canonization of Maria with tears streaming down his wrinkled and weatherbeaten face.

As for John XXIII he seems to have toward the saint-making process the same direct and commonsense approach that he shows in other matters. On several occasions he has shown impatience with the overcautious, slow and legalist attitude of the officials of the Congregation of Rites who deal with such matters. He has told them that, if they were convinced of the saintliness of a certain person, they should go ahead and bring to a favorable conclusion the causes of beatification and canonization. One can therefore safely predict that the rate of new saints will rise during his pontificate.

Incidentally, John XXIII was the first Pope to proclaim an American-born saint from the United States, Mother Elisabeth Seton, founder of a religious order. The other American, Mother Cabrini, who was made a saint by Pius XII, had been born in Italy and had acquired her American citizenship only at a mature age.

And now let's see how one becomes a saint. It is a difficult, long and costly procedure. First of all one must behave rather well during one's lifetime, at least during the latter part of it; then one must die "in odor of sanctity" and one must, possibly but not necessarily, perform some miracles while alive. This done, however, one has only just begun.

What really counts is what one does after death. And this is logical, since being a saint is a quite supernatural thing. What you have to prove is that you are sitting next to Almighty God and that you have some influence on Him. For, according to the Catholic doctrine, only God can perform miracles. The saint or the blessed enters into it merely as a go-between, inasmuch as he or she receives the pleas addressed to him or her by the faithful and passes them on to God, thus interceding in man's favor.

Accordingly, in order to become a saint, it is necessary to have to one's credit at least four miracles—two before beatification and another two before canonization.

The Holy See as such never takes the initiative of proclaiming a new saint. It's up to private persons or to a religious order to ask the bishop of the diocese to which the candidate belonged to start an investigation. The bishop then appoints a committee which begins nosing into the life and miracles of the prospective saint with meticulous care. All his actions are examined and weighed, his writings are carefully scanned, hundreds of witnesses are questioned, either contemporaries of the saint who happen still to be alive, or people who witnessed his miracles. Usually it takes tens of years before the committee concludes its researches.

If the findings are favorable the case is then referred to Rome, that is, to the Sacred Congregation of Rites. The Congregation studies the report and if they think there is something in it, they appoint a *Consultore,* or consultant. The consultant starts the inquiry all over again, checks all the conclusions and personally questions all the witnesses who in the meantime happen not to have died off and who remember what it was all about. This is known as the apostolic trial.

If the consultant has found everything to be in order, the Congregation next reports to the Pope. If the Pope too is convinced of the soundness of the case, he then issues a decree to proclaim the "heroic virtues" of the candidate for a halo. From that moment on one has become a "venerable." It's a step forward, although he is not yet ready to be the object of public worship.

After this the candidate must perform at least two miracles confirmed by precise and exhaustive testimony. And now the cause enters its third stage, which is perhaps the most difficult, certainly the longest. All the written material assembled goes back from the Pope to the Congregation for even more meticulous study. At this point an extraordinary character appears on the scene. He is the Promoter of the Faith, a kind of public prosecutor, also known confidentially as the "Devil's Advocate." The man to whom such a sinister name applies is usually an elderly, learned, suave prelate with a heart of gold who has the unpleasant duty of finding the basest motives in all the most noble actions of the purported saint, of casting all sorts of doubts upon his moral integrity and of shaking the authenticity of his miracles. The evidence produced in favor of the candidate must be really overpowering to silence this representative of Satan.

In connection with the way the Devil's Advocate proceeds I was once told a rather curious episode by an official of the Congregation of Rites. The Congregation was examining the beatification cause of a Polish monk, a famous seventeenth century preacher, and everything seemed to be proceeding smoothly. Then the Devil's Advocate announced that he had discovered in some old archives a description of the monk by a contemporary. This reported that the monk in question was very dirty, was covered with fleas and lice and that he actually had a bad smell. The supporter of the monk's candidature, known as the Postulator of the Cause, replied that this might well have been true, but that it just confirmed the ascetic life led by the Polish preacher and his desire to mortify the flesh. The Devil's Advocate was not convinced. He retorted that when the monk entered a church to preach, most of the populace instead of gathering around him fled and that this was not too good for religion. The cause of this monk's beatification has never made any progress since.

Now, let's follow a hypothetical cause to its favorable conclusion. When the two miracles have been confirmed the whole dossier goes once again to the Pope who by a special decree certifies the authenticity of the miracles. But, believe it or not, the Congregation is still not satisfied. Can one be absolutely certain that no mistake has been made, that nothing has been overlooked? Again the officials of the Congregation meet to re-examine everything from the beginning and finally, if no more doubts have cropped up, they issue the so-called *tuto* decree (from the Latin which means *surely, safely*). After that the Pope can, with a clear conscience, authorize the beatification.

The beatification takes place in St. Peter's in the morning, in the course of a very solemn ceremony. At the beatification the Pope is not present but in the afternoon he descends into the basilica and venerates the new blessed.

If the blessed goes on performing miracles (there must be at least two after he has been beatified) then one can start considering whether this is a case of promoting him to saint. A new cause is started, the two miracles are checked, the Devil's Advocate reappears to cast his nasty doubts, the Postulator does his best to dispel them, the Pope intervenes again to authenticate the two miracles and the Congregation issues another *tuto* decree. The candidate has finally reached the threshold of officially recognized sainthood.

And here, to put things straight, I must explain that it's neither the Church nor the Pope that "makes" a saint. According to Catholic doctrine every single person who has been admitted to Heaven is automatically a saint. The meaning of the whole complicated procedure, which reaches its climax in the canonization ceremony, is that the Church has come to the conclusion, on the strength of the evidence produced by the candidate (that is, the miracles he has performed after death), that this particular person is actually sitting in the presence of God.

Miracles nowadays are not what they used to be. No longer are there rose petals raining down from a clear sky, nor an abyss opening up in the ground to save the pious damsel from the infidels hot on her trail, nor ships lolling peacefully on a smooth patch of water while the mighty ocean roars and rages around them, nor mysterious characters wrapped in clouds who support the roof of some collapsing edifice.

Modern miracles are all of a medical nature. They are less picturesque, but equally difficult to explain from a scientific point of view. The 132 miracles attributed to the thirty-three saints proclaimed by Pius XII were all healings and so are all the miracles the Congregation of Rites is at present examining. Let's take one completely at random just as an example. This was performed by the Portuguese saint, Father Joa de Britto, who died in 1685 as a martyr in India. Two hundred and fifty-three years later, that is in 1938, the mother of a ten-year-old Portuguese boy, Antonio Marques de Silva, who was suffering from a tubercular infection of the bone of his right foot, applied an image of the martyr to the diseased part. After a long, deep sleep the boy woke up completely cured. Three well-known doctors authenticated the healing and declared that medical science could not explain it. In 1947 Father Joa de Britto was proclaimed a saint.

But if modern miracles might appear a bit dull, the same can certainly not be said of the canonization ceremony which is the most brilliant, the most colorful and solemn of the Catholic Church. It's a moving, unforgettable spectacle in a unique setting, with a display of pageantry preserved and perfected through the centuries.

St. Peter's is lavishly decorated for the great occasion with gold draperies, silver and golden candelabra and gold-decorated scarlet tapestries. Huge paintings depicting the miracles of the new saint are hung inside the enormous church.

The Pope opens this ceremony, usually at half-past eight in the morning, by kneeling in Michelangelo's Sistine Chapel to intone the solemn "Ave Maria." Then, garbed in flowing white robes reaching down to his silken slippers, wearing a gold miter and holding a huge candle in his left hand, the Pope enters St. Peter's on his gestatorial chair, the state chair in which the Pope is carried shoulder high on special occasions.

Surrounded by the Swiss and the Palatine Guards and flanked by the Noble Guards with sabers drawn, the Pope follows a long procession formed by members of the Congregation of Rites, Cardinals, other high prelates and members of the papal court, led by banners depicting the miracles performed by the new saint. A blast of silver trumpets announces the Pope's arrival in the basilica. Moving down the center aisle the procession stops in front of the high Altar of the Confession where the Pope takes his seat on a golden throne.

The Procurator of the canonization cause, usually a Cardinal, approaches the Pope carrying a lighted candle in his right hand, then kneels in front of him and recites in Latin a plea "to enter in the catalogue of the saints of Jesus Christ" the new saint.

The Pope replies in Latin, through his Secretary of Briefs, that he must first invoke the aid of the Holy Virgin, of the Apostles Peter and Paul and of the celestial cohorts. The plea is then voiced a second time and the Pope prays for the aid of the Holy Ghost. After the plea has been pronounced a third time the Pope stands up and, as head of the Universal Church, proclaims the new saint and assigns to him a date in the calendar.

The Postulator then pronounces a short speech to thank the Pope. While the Pope intones the *"Te Deum,"* from the height of the dome silver bugles sound in rejoicing and the huge bronze bells of St. Peter's toll the announcement that the Church of Rome has one more saint.

The Postulator of the saint's cause then presents his gifts to the Pope—two huge candles weighing sixty pounds each and painted with scenes of the miracles, two loaves of newly baked bread, a small barrel of wine and one of water, and three gold and silver cages containing doves and pigeons which represent the Eucharistic sacrifice and the purity of the new saint.

The Pope then sings the *"Pax Domini,"* recites the *"Agnus Dei,"* kisses the altar and imparts his apostolic blessing on all present. To close the ceremony the Archpriest of St. Peter's presents the Pope with a velvet purse containing fifteen *giuli,* an ancient silver coin, as symbolic compensation for the high mass he has recited.

As regards money, I stated at the beginning that the process of becoming a saint is difficult, long and costly. I think I have given you a sufficiently clear idea of the difficulties, the length of time required and the complications of procedure. Now comes the matter of cost. Vatican experts have reckoned for me that a beatification costs somewhere between $32,000 and $40,000. This somewhat staggering figure includes many items: the fees for the postulator or postulators of the cause (it takes so long that very often the initial postulator dies before his job is completed and he has to be replaced by another), the printing of books and pamphlets about the candidate's life and miracles, the medical evidence, the translation into Latin of all the documents produced, the fees for the painter or painters of the pictures and banners depicting the blessed's miracles, the decorating of St. Peter's, the lighting, the music and the choir.

The canonization usually costs a bit less—between $16,000 and $24,000—because most of the spade work (publications, translations, fees for the postulators, etc.) has already been done. Usually the cost is borne by the religious order of which the candidate was the founder or a member. Sometimes the fund is raised through public subscriptions by the faithful in whose diocese the saint lived, or more exceptionally, when the candidate is a really outstanding personality and has no financial backing, by the Holy See itself.

The most amazing candidate for a halo, and one who has quite a good chance of success, is Don Juan, the great seducer. The news of this startling development has reached me from Seville, our hero's home town, and has been confirmed, although with some reservations, by the Vatican.

But, you may ask, did Don Juan actually exist? Historians and literary critics mention three real-life characters who, they say, have by the example of their lives started the legend of the ardent hero no woman could resist. One is Don Juan Tenorio, member of a wealthy and powerful Spanish family, the second Don Juan Ulloa, belonging to an equally well-known family, and the third is Don Miguel de Mañara.

Don Juan Tenorio is no doubt the best known of the trio, but historically he hasn't got a leg to stand on. Some researchers have even suggested that he was a Portuguese and not a Spaniard as is commonly believed, which makes the blood of all good Spaniards boil! Even less is known about Don Juan Ulloa.

By contrast there is a wealth of information about Señor Mañara, including the dates and places of his birth and death, his family background, the name of his wife, a portrait of him and even a last will and testament written by his own hand. The people of Seville, according to an oral tradition still very much alive, are absolutely convinced that de Mañara is the one and only real Don Juan. Many famous writers have shared this opinion. Among them, Prosper Mérimée (*"Les Ames du Purgatoire"*), Alexandre Dumas père (who, getting a bit mixed up as usual called him de Maraña instead of

Mañara), Edmond Haraucourt (*"Don Juan de Mañara"*), Latour (*"Don Miguel de Mañara"*), O. V. de Milosz (*"Miguel Mañara," Mystère en six tableaux"*) and the twentieth century Spanish playwright Manuel Machado (*"Don Miguel de Mañara"*). And it is this character, Don Miguel de Mañara, who is now a candidate for a halo.

What do the people of Seville have to say about their dear saintly sinner? According to them Don Miguel de Mañara Vincentelo de Leca was born in the Calle Lievès on March 3, 1627 of an aristocratic and very wealthy family descending from the Emperors of Byzantium and related to the princely Colonna family of Rome. According to tradition, from his early youth the handsome, dashing, violent Don Miguel, who to his drinking and fencing companions was known as Don Juan, led a life of debauchery. He seduced one woman after another, fought many duels, killing or badly wounding his opponents, until one day he committed a crime so horrible that not even the power and wealth of his family could cover it up.

He induced a young girl of the Seville aristocracy to visit him one night in a garden pavilion by the Guadalquivir river and at the same time informed the girl's brother about this secret rendezvous. When the brother arrived Don Juan was already locked inside the pavilion with the girl and the helpless brother could do nothing but listen to what was going on behind the door. Then Don Juan left the pavilion with the girl, fought a sword duel with the brother and killed him.

The legend adds that Don Juan then drew a cigar from his pocket, only to find that he had no fire to light it. In a loud, challenging voice he asked the Devil to give him a light. A furry hand is said to have emerged from the darkness and a flame sprang up from one of the Devil's fingers. Don Juan coolly lit his cigar and went his way. As is to be seen, the idea of a pact with the Devil, later developed by Goethe in his *Faust,* was already connected with the Seville seducer.

At all events, Devil or no Devil, his last crime caused such an uproar that Don Juan, alias Don Miguel de Mañara, was compelled to flee from Spain. He enlisted in the Spanish army under an assumed name and fought with great bravery in Holland. His military exploits won him a royal pardon and he was able to return to Seville.

He came back just as arrogant and full of lust as before. To defy his fellow-citizens he published a list of all the women he had seduced and of all the men he had cuckolded, from plain citizen to Emperor. At this point one of his companions in debauchery pointed out that there was a name he would never be able to add to his list.

"And which is that one?" asked Don Juan.

"That of God," replied the friend.

"You are wrong," Don Juan retorted. "I'll get him on my list too."

To accomplish such a sacrilegious project Don Juan decided to seduce a nun, that is, a spouse of Christ. With a touch of sadism he chose as his victim the very girl whose brother he had killed and who after the tragedy had entered a convent.

The day before the night when he was supposed to climb over the convent wall, in one of Seville's narrow, cobbled streets he came upon a funeral. He inquired of one of the mourners who it was that had died and was told, "Don Juan." Frightened, he ran home and was put to bed with a high temperature. He experienced terrible hallucinations and almost died. All the beautiful women he was chasing in his dreams turned into skeletons as soon as he took them in his arms. When he finally recovered Don Juan, the seducer, was gone and Don Miguel, the future saint, had taken his place.

He married an eighteen-year-old girl, Gerónima, the only daughter of Don Diego Carrillo de Mendoza, Señor de Guelago y Fonelas and of Doña Ana de Castrillo. He adored his young and beautiful wife and became a model husband. But she died soon after and Don Miguel, according to the Seville oral tradition, after having planted a rosebush on her tomb, spent six whole months in the cemetery dressed in sackcloth as a penance.

Then he called on Don Diego Mirafuentes, head of the Holy Charity Brothers, a small fraternity that looked after the sick and organized the funerals of the poor, and asked to become a member. The good Brothers, quite understandably, were far from enthusiastic and told him to wait a little longer and think it over. Don Miguel continued to have visions and one day, as he was kneeling by the rosebush in the cemetery, he saw God chasing the Devil away. That same evening he was accepted in the fraternity of the Charity Brothers. (By the way, in the Seville cemetery they still show you the rosebush "planted by Don Juan" and they tell you that in the spring its roses smell sweeter than any other flower.)

Our hero now plunged into monastic life with the same ardor and recklessness that he had displayed in chasing women. He submitted himself to the most painful penances and fasts, he donated his entire wealth to the needy and founded a hospital for the poor which is still to be seen in Seville. Only a year after he had entered the fraternity he was elected head of the Charity Brothers. Among his gifts to the fraternity there is a famous and terrifying painting by Valdes Real. It shows two open coffins with a body in each. The face of one of the bodies, in a state of advanced decay, is that of Don Miguel de Mañara.

He died in a cell of the Monastery of Our Lady of the Snow, near Seville, on May 9, 1679, at the age of fifty-two. After his death the two characters, Don Juan the seducer and Don Miguel the Charity Brother, who had in turn occupied the same body, went their separate ways. The legend of Don Juan grew and grew and plays, poems, novels, operas, even psychoanalytic essays were written about him. Here are just a few of the better-known writers and composers who treated the Don Juan theme: Tirso da Molina, José Zorrilla, Antonio de Zamora, Manuel Machado, Unamuno, Corneille junior, Blaze de Bury, Balzac, De Villiers, Baudelaire, Molière, De Musset, Haraucourt, Prosper Mérimée, Alexandre Dumas, Byron, Goldoni, De Ponte, Heyse, Chekhov, Alexander Tolstoi, Pushkin, Rank, Kirkegaard, Bernard Shaw, Gluck, Purcell, Hoffmann, Richard Strauss, Dargomyzskij . . . and I was almost forgetting Mozart!

As time went on, Don Juan became ever more expert in the use of his deadly sword, more subtle in his art of seduction and his famous list of conquered women reached a truly imposing figure. To sing it with Leporello (libretto by Da Ponte, music by Mozart),

In Italia seicento e quaranta	640
In Germania duecento e trentuna	231
Cento in Francia	100
In Turchia novantuna	91
Ma in Ispagna son già mille tre.	1,003
(Total)	2,065

But though all the authors agreed that Don Juan had a way with women and that he was a bit of a rascal, they disagreed on how to bring his career to an end. Da Ponte had him, unrepenting and shouting his defiance, dragged to Hell by a gang of demons; Paul von Heyse drove him to the brink of despair and of Vesuvius and made him commit suicide by jumping into the crater; José Zorrilla y Moral and Blaze de Bury, anticipating historical developments, had him repenting and going to Paradise. Otto Rank, the disciple of Freud, was content with settling him comfortably on a couch and psychoanalyzing him.

In a less sensational but equally sure way, the fame of Don Miguel, the Charity Brother, has been growing through the centuries. Only two months after his death, on July 27, 1679, the people of Seville, grateful for all the good he had done and impressed by his penances and saintly death, sent a petition to the Vatican asking that Don Miguel de Mañara be made a saint.

Causes of canonization, as I have shown, are always very long drawn-out affairs. In this particular case the Vatican was, quite naturally, extracautious. A whole century had to go by before Pope Pius VI, in 1778, authorized the "introduction" of the cause. This meant that the Holy See had recognized that there was enough evidence of Don Miguel's saintliness to justify the opening of a formal procedure. It also meant that Don Miguel had become a "venerable," which entitles him, if not to the full glory of the altar, at least to a limited form of cult.

Not much has happened since 1778, but now at last things seem to have got moving again. The Brothers of Charity and the management of the Seville hospital founded by Don Miguel are urging the Vatican to get on with the cause. In this connection my Seville informant related a rather moving detail: The Charity Brothers, he told me, own a small olive grove which produces about 3,500 litres of oil a year. The money they get from the sale of the oil is put aside to finance the cause. The Charity Brothers have also reprinted a book on Don Miguel first written in 1680 by the Jesuit Father Juan de Cárdenas.

I inquired how the cause was progressing of the Postulator, Father Nicolás, an elderly, learned Spanish monk who has been following it in Rome on behalf of the Charity Brothers. Father Nicolás told me:

"We are up against a technical hitch. As you know, before one can be proclaimed a saint or even a blessed, it has to be proved that the person in question has exercised the Christian virtues to a heroic degree. One year after the death of Don Miguel about fifteen witnesses were questioned and they testified beyond doubt about his heroic virtues. But unfortunately the questioning was not carried out according to the Canon Law. The substance of these testimonies was correct, but the form was wrong. To overcome the difficulty we shall have to ask the Holy Father to dispense us from the normal procedure and to proclaim the heroic virtues of the Venerable Don Miguel de Mañara on the strength of the already existing documents."

The next move, therefore, will be an appeal to the Pope and if the outcome is favorable, as is expected in Vatican quarters, then the case will go on and will be carried through the various stages of beatification and canonization. The process is made easier by the fact that the Vatican doesn't officially recognize that Don Miguel had been a bit of a Don Juan, nor that he it is who inspired the saga of the seducer.

"It's all a legend," Father Nicolás assured me. "Don Miguel really was quite a good man. And even if it hadn't been so," he added relenting a bit, "it wouldn't really matter."

"Look at St. Francis," I prompted him, "who in his youth wasn't exactly an angel."

"Yes," said Father Nicolás, "and what about St. Augustine . . . and lots more. Beside, as far as Vatican legal procedure is concerned, it's only the last ten years of one's life that count. This has been firmly established by Pope Benedict XIV (1740-1758) who dictated very precise rules for the beatification and canonization causes."

But was Don Miguel, in the early part of his life, really such a good man as his Postulator would like to make him out? And is there really nothing in the Seville oral tradition? On this I have my doubts and I call as a witness Don Miguel de Mañara himself. In his will, whose authenticity is recognized also by the Vatican, Don Miguel thus described his life before he was struck by Divine light:

I, Don Miguel Mañara, ash and dust, miserable sinner, have offended for the majority of my unfortunate days the Supreme Majesty of God whose vile creature and slave I confess myself. I have served Babylon and its Prince the Devil with a thousand abominations, pride, adulteries, oaths, scandals and robberies. My sins and bad actions are innumerable and only the great wisdom of God can count them, his infinite patience bear them and his infinite mercy forgive them.

With the exception of murder, all the crimes attributed by the legend to Don Juan are there. No wonder, then, that in his will the repenting Don Miguel, the saintly Brother of Charity, instructed that on his tomb there should be no name, but only the following words, which are still to be seen today:

Here lie the bones and dust of the worst man there ever was in the world. Pray God for him.

15

The Pope's Army

WHAT OF THE PHYSICAL POWER on which the Supreme
Pontiff can rely?

In his memoirs Sir Winston Churchill relates how he once intervened with Stalin on behalf of religious freedom in the Soviet Union.
He pointed out to the Soviet dictator the great political importance
of the Vatican and the utility of having the Catholic Church as an
ally in the war against Germany. Stalin's reply was in the form of
an ironical question, "How many divisions has Pius XII?" When the
episode was related to the Pope he is said to have remarked, "Signor
Stalin will meet my legions in the other world."

But apart from these celestial cohorts, the Pope has his troops in
flesh and blood also, and their scanty numbers and poor armament
are compensated for by the splendor of their uniforms and the
nobility of their traditions. Before turning to the Swiss Guard, which
is the most picturesque and the best known of the papal forces,
mention must be made of the Vatican's three other armed bodies—
the Noble Guard, the Palatine Guard and the Gendarmery. The
task has been made much easier by Lieut. Gastone Imbrighi, of the
Palatine Guard, who has written a noteworthy volume on the Pontiff's armed forces.

The Noble Guard, as its name indicates, is a corps chosen from
among the aristocracy. Its regulations stipulate that candidates who

wish to join it must possess "a gallant nobility of at least a century" and "an income sufficient to live decently in Rome." Before 1929 only the nobles of Latium, Umbria, the Marche and Romagna, that is, of the regions which composed the former Pontifical State, could be admitted to the corps. After that year recruits for the Noble Guard were permitted from the aristocracy of the whole of Italy. The commander, who has the rank of lieutenant general, is chosen personally by the Pope from the princely and ducal families of Rome. At present the post is held by Prince Mario Del Drago. The standard bearer of the Noble Guard is Marquis Patrizio Patrizi.

There are no private soldiers or corporals in the Noble Guard; its members are all officers. After the commander come two "lieutenants," whose rank corresponds to that of a normal brigadier general. Next come eleven *esenti* with the rank of colonel, among whom are the two nephews of the late Pius XII, Don Giulio and Don Marcantonio Pacelli. Then there are ten "cadets" with the rank of lieutenant colonel, nine "guards" with the rank of captain, eighteen with that of lieutenant and fifteen with that of second lieutenant. Among the members of the Noble Guard are some of the finest names of the Italian aristocracy—Barberini, Odescalchi, Del Drago, Theodoli, Patrizi, Serlupi, Nasalli Rocca, etc.

This select corps, which has precedence over the others and never appears on parade unless the Pope is present, has its origin in the *Guardia dei Cavalleggeri* (Light Horse Guard) and the *Guardia delle Lance Spezzate* (Broken Lances Guard), a company of nobles who rode alongside the papal carriage during processions and journeys. The two corps were disbanded in 1798 when the French occupied Rome. In 1801 Pius VII formed the Noble Guard, which retained the character of a bodyguard and honorary escort of the Pope. For some decades now the Noble Guard has no longer been mounted, although it still wears spurs. Its standard is white with the coat-of-arms of the reigning Pontiff.

The members of the Noble Guard are on duty for one week every month and receive a grant of about 40,000 lire a month. They are not allowed to marry without permission of the commander, who in turn informs the State Secretariat, which looks after the administration of the corps. At the present time the task of the Noble Guard is limited to duty in the pontifical antechamber and escorting the Pope, and serving as an honor guard for him during ceremonies and audiences.

The Palatine Guard represents the main body of the Vatican forces and might be described as the palace guard. Its remote predecessors were those men of the Roman populace who voluntarily hurried to defend the Pope during the frequent disturbances of the Middle Ages. Several salient features have come down to the Palatine Guard from this distant origin. They are all volunteers, they ask no payment for their services and they must be Romans by origin. Strictly speaking the Palatine Guard originated in the amalgamation of the *Guardia Civica Scelta* (Chosen Civic Guard) and the *Milizia Urbana* (Urban Militia) decided upon in 1850, by Pius IX who also granted the new corps the honor of possessing its own flag.

There is no snobbery about the Palatine Guard. In its ranks are found university professors alongside butchers, barbers shoulder to shoulder with lawyers, then peasants, workmen, railroadmen, students, doctors, civil servants, streetcar conductors and so on. Altogether, including the young cadets, the Palatine Guard numbers over 500 men, many more, that is, than the other Vatican armed bodies put together. In 1943 during World War II a large number of auxiliary cadets were taken on to guard the extraterritorial buildings of the Vatican and the papal villa at Castel Gandolfo. There was also the further aim of saving many young men from the German round-ups of Italian manpower.

The Palatine Guard is under the command of Count Francesco Cantuti di Castelvetri, who has the rank of colonel and during processions occupies a place in front of the left pole of the gestatorial chair. The Palatine Guard is composed of a headquarters staff of twelve officers, two battalions of three companies each, a band (the only one in the Vatican) and a drum section. To quote the Pontifical Year Book, the Palatine Guards "spontaneously give their services for the care and dignity of the person of the Supreme Pontiff and his residence, in the antechamber, at pontifical ceremonies and in the papal chapels." The minimum height for the guards is 5 feet 5 inches. Once a week they meet in their barracks for recreation, to watch films and listen to music and debates.

As to the Pontifical Gendarmery, this is a regular police force. Its duties are to maintain public order, to see that the laws of the Vatican City State are not broken, to carry out investigations, to make arrests, to control traffic and so on.

The gendarmes are the successors of preceding police forces and received their present title and organization from Pius IX in 1849. The minimum height for a gendarme is 5 feet 9 inches, but most of them are much taller. If you should ever chance to meet a gendarme of really impressive stature who is getting on in years, it is almost certain that he is a former king's cuirassier. In fact a number of these finely built men, after completing their term of service at the Quirinal Palace, have passed through the Bronze Door and donned the Napoleonic uniform. The rest of the recruits usually come from the carabinieri or have seen service in the police force somewhere in Italy.

The Pontifical Gendarmes, numbering 100 in all, serve under a Commanding Officer, Francesco Saverio Bernardo, and seven officers. In addition to board and lodging they receive pay starting at a minimum of about 30,000 lire a month. Like the Noble Guard they, too, must obtain permission to marry. Marriage does not exempt them completely from the obligation to stay the night in the Vatican. In fact, one third of the married N.C.O.'s have to take turns each night in spending the night in barracks. A peculiarity of their regulations is that they must have their children baptized within eight days of birth and then hand the relevant certificate to the commanding officer.

The most picturesque unit of the pontifical armed forces is, however, the Swiss Guard, whose origins go back quite far in history. As early as the fourteenth century a certain number of Swiss mercenaries entered the service of the Holy See, though enlistments were always made individually. Attempts by Sixtus IV (1471-1484) to enlist compact groups of Swiss mercenaries were also made, by agreements between Rome and the Federal States, but only a few of these agreements came to anything and among them can be mentioned the one concluded on January 21, 1480.

But the idea of creating a stable and disciplined corps, composed entirely of Swiss, goes back to Julius II (1503-1513) in whose reign two hundred Swiss were enlisted under the command of Peter von Hertenstein. Only one hundred and fifty reached Rome in their triumphal entry into the city from the Piazza del Popolo and were afterward blessed in St. Peter's Square by the Pope, who appeared on the loggia of Paul II.

Subsequently the Swiss Guard was several times disbanded and re-formed as the fortunes of the Holy See rose or fell. In the Sack of Rome of 1527 the Swiss fought with great gallantry; 147 were killed in the attempt to prevent the enemy from entering the Vatican and only forty-two saved their lives by taking refuge in Castel Sant'Angelo together with Pope Clement VII (1523-1534).

The latest reorganization of the Swiss Guard was carried out by John XXIII in 1959. The Swiss Guard has four officers, including the commander, thirty N.C.O.'s, seventy halberdiers (guards) and a chaplain. The effectives are rarely at full strength since there exist noteworthy difficulties in the way of recruitment. Besides, many of its members enlist for only short periods with the object of getting to know Rome and learning Italian, and when their term of service is up they do not extend it.

The Swiss Guards are chosen from all the Swiss cantons except the Ticino Canton, because the latter was part of Italy until 1803 and the rules have not been altered to include it. The last thirty-three recruits took the oath on May 6, 1958, bringing the number of the guards to eighty.

The Swiss Guard's flag consists of a white cross standing out in full, at the center of which is the coat-of-arms, enwreathed with laurels, of the commanding officer. Two quarters of the field of four quarters contain the coat-of-arms of the reigning Pontiff and that of Julius II (1503-1513), on a red background; the other two quarters are filled with five horizontal bands with the blue, gold and red colors of the principal Swiss cantons with which the Holy See reached recruiting agreements.

The main task of the Swiss Guard is to guard the Pope. It serves in his antechamber and escorts him during religious and public ceremonies. Another of its tasks is to protect the Apostolic Palaces and it mounts guard at the main entrances to the Vatican—the Bronze Door, the *Arco delle Campane* and St. Anne's Gate as well as the *Portico di Costantino* and the great door of the Mint.

After the Conciliation between Church and State in 1929 and the signature of the Lateran Pacts, new regulations were made concerning the position of the Swiss Guard in the Vatican City State. In the law of June 7, 1929 under which the Vatican City State was established, it was confirmed that the Swiss Guard was under the direct control of the Pope. But it was also established that the governor of the Vatican City State may ask the Swiss Guard to carry out, whenever necessary, security and police tasks that are normally performed by the Gendarmery.

The Swiss Guard has a drum and fife section. On great ceremonial occasions the guards wear the medieval cuirass over their yellow, orange and dark-blue striped uniform. And this brings up the oft-debated question of who designed the latter. Some say Michelangelo, others Raphael. It would seem, however, that when the Swiss arrived in Rome for the first time they were already wearing a uniform very similar to their present one. As time went on the uniform was gradually modified to such an extent that when Pius X reorganized the corps in 1914, it was decided to return to the old design. The uniform of a Swiss Guard painted by Raphael in a room of the Vatican was then taken as a model.

For over twenty years and up to quite recently the Swiss Guard was under the command of Baron Enrico de Pfyffer d'Altishofen.

The Commander is now Colonel Robert Nünlist, a brilliant officer of the Swiss Army General Staff who was an instructor at the War School and a teacher of philosophy. The choice of a new commander from outside the Corps created some discontent among the Swiss Guard's officers who for more than twenty years had been awaiting promotion and would have been able to rise at least one step. It is a fact, however, that during the last years of Baron de Pfyffer's command his poor health led to a great deterioration in discipline and the Pope therefore preferred to choose an officer of proved worth and experience who did not already belong to the Corps.

The pay of the Swiss Guard is certainly not very attractive and this is undoubtedly one of the reasons for the difficulty in recruitment. It is about 40,000 lire a month, from which a mess charge is deducted. In Switzerland, on the contrary, a recruit receives 500 francs a month, that is, about 75,000 lire. The only reasons why Swiss young men enlist are the fascination of Rome, the chance of being near to the Pope, and religious sentiment. That is why men with money of their own who come from fairly high up in the social scale are often to be found in the Corps. The Guard is proud of having had in its ranks well-known writers, painters, musicians, priests and monks.

Another difficulty arises from the fact that recruiting must be carried out if not exactly secretly at least on the quiet. Swiss law, in fact, lays down the ruling that anyone who serves in a foreign army thereby loses his Swiss citizenship. An exception is made only in the case of the Vatican, on condition, however, that recruiting is not done publicly. So the job of recruiting is left to the halberdier who has gone home for a holiday and who talks to his friends about joining, as well as to an association of former guards. When Baron de Pfyffer was still in command of the Corps, a well-known publicity firm in the United States sent him a detailed program for a recruiting campaign, which included even radio and television interviews. The old Baron became quite desperate and told some of his friends, "They'll end up by suggesting that I send posters to Switzerland showing some fine-looking Roman girl in the foreground with the dome of St. Peter's at the back."

Members of the Swiss Guard must be at least 5 feet 9 inches tall and must, of course, all be Roman Catholics. The other inhabitants of the Vatican City State consider them rather thick-headed, sticking far more closely to the letter than to the spirit of the regulations. A story is told of something that happened about twenty years ago. After the theft of a large cauldron in the Vatican, an inquiry was held and the Swiss Guards on duty at the exits were questioned to try to get a description of the thief. One of the Swiss replied: "I can't say what the thief's face was like because the cauldron covered up half of him."

Far more ingenious, on the other hand, was a sergeant of the Guard whom Pius IX had asked what time his nephew, well known to be leading a gay and idle life, had returned home. Replied the sergeant, "I can't say exactly, your Holiness. But I know I never say good night to the young count. It's always good morning."

16

The Search
for Peter's Tomb

THE TOMB of one of Emperor Nero's slaves, discovered by chance in the Vatican, might well be the archeological "missing link" to prove that St. Peter was buried right under the main altar of the basilica of St. Peter's. This has implications reaching far beyond archeology and history. For many Protestant scholars are still disputing not only that the first of the Apostles was buried under St. Peter's, but that he ever came to Rome at all. On the other hand, the claim of the Roman Catholic Church to be the only true one is based partly on the assumption that Peter did come to Rome, was crucified there and was the first Roman Pontiff from whom all the others descended in an uninterrupted line.

But before dealing with the significance and importance of this tomb, which was colorfully described to me by a Vatican archeologist as *"la vendetta di San Pietro"* (St. Peter's revenge), I should like first to give an account of one of the most exciting archeological adventures of all time—the search for St. Peter's tomb. This includes the patient sleuthing into the past, the technically arduous and sometimes even dangerous probing under St. Peter's foundations that led the

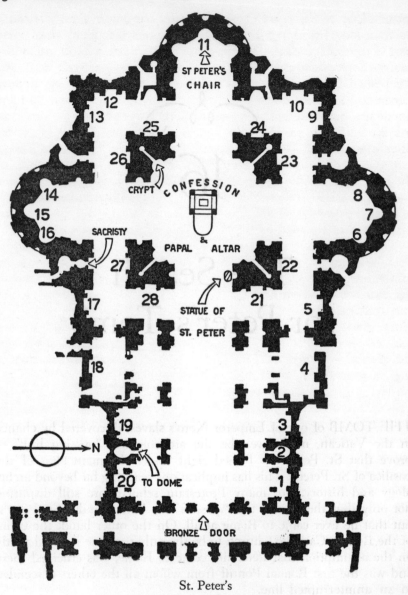

St. Peter's

Vatican archeologists and Pius XII himself to form the conviction that the tomb of the Prince of the Apostles has indeed been found.

The main credit for the find must go to Pius XII and to his courageous, enlightened approach to the problem. For a kind of taboo —unwritten but no less powerful—had been hanging over this type of research. Back in 1594 a group of workers, while reinforcing the foundations of St. Peter's directly under the main altar, noticed a patch of loose bricks in a wall. They were replacing these bricks when part of the wall caved in, revealing on the other side a dark, forbidding cavity. Pope Clement VIII (1592-1605) was immediately told. Accompanied by members of the papal court carrying flaming torches, Clement VIII went down to inspect the mysterious opening. In the uncertain, flickering light he saw a golden cross glowing at him from the back of the cave. Awed and frightened, he returned to his private apartment. There he found a messenger waiting to inform him that one of his closest friends had just died. The coincidence of the vision and of the death of his friend was interpreted as a divine warning by the mystically-minded Clement, who ordered that the hole in the wall be closed immediately and that no more probing be carried out in that area.

The taboo was broken some 350 years later by Pius XII on the 28th of June, 1949 when, during a visit to the Vatican Grottoes, the underground church, he instructed the late Mgr. Carlo Respighi, Secretary of the Pontifical Committee for Sacred Archeology, to try and find St. Peter's tomb. A few weeks later the *sampietrini* (the name given to the corps of St. Peter's maintenance workers) lifted part of the floor of the Vatican Grottoes and started probing into the ground. The first find was rather ironical and somewhat disturbing. A statue of Bacchus, the god of wine and sensuous pleasures, was lying near the place where St. Peter's tomb was supposed to be. Pius XII, who had disregarded Clement's taboo, was not shocked by Bacchus' vine leaves. Not only did he encourage the archeologists to go on but when they ran out of money he financed the excavations out of his personal funds.

Little by little the bowels of the earth yielded their secret. The excavators found a road flanked by two rows of pagan tombs belonging to upper middle-class Roman families of the second century. These tombs were extremely well-preserved, almost intact. The explanation is this: When Emperor Constantine decided to build the first basilica of St. Peter, the ground of the Vatican Hill had to be raised on one side to make a level foundation. Constantine's architects did not bother to demolish the pagan tombs that stood there, but just made a hole in the roof of each of them, filled them with earth and debris and did their building on top of them. The tombs were thus sealed away for sixteen centuries.

Excavating these tombs from the earth and from the surrounding debris proved much more difficult than was at first expected. For Bernini's main altar, with its four gigantic, corkscrew, bronze columns and the baroque, ornate canopy, was resting with its enormous weight squarely over the pagan cemetery. It was a work that could never have been completed without a skillful and daring application of the most modern techniques of steel and reinforced concrete construction. Even so, the risk of having the main altar sink into the ground was very real and probably the excavations would not have gone on had not the Pope assumed full responsibility for the consequences. Another danger that threatened the archeologists was a subterranean river, whose waters are believed to come from the distant Bracciano lake. Every time the *sampietrini* dug a hole it filled with water and the engineers had to identify the course of the underground stream and build waterproof barriers before they could proceed with the excavations. Also, a water diviner was called in to help in locating the stream.

But in the end the efforts of the engineers, the archeologists and the *sampietrini* were well rewarded. For what they found was an early Christian shrine, a tomb, and even some bones that quite possibly belonged to St. Peter.

The fact that St. Peter's basilica was built over the tomb of the first bishop of Rome is one of the oldest traditions of the Catholic Church. The earliest historical evidence of the existence of this tomb is to be found in a theological dispute between the Roman presbyter, Gaius, and the Middle Eastern sect of the Cataphrygians, back in the second century. The Cataphrygians claimed to be the only true interpreters of Christ's teaching and, to back this up, they boasted the possession of the bones of the Apostle Philip. To this, Gaius retorted that if the Cataphrygians came to Rome he would show them the tombs of Peter and Paul lying on the Vatican Hill and on the road to Ostia, respectively, where St. Paul's basilica still stands today. Gaius actually used the Greek word *Tropaion*, which means a trophy or a memorial. But as it was the habit of the early Christians to build memorials over the tombs of their martyrs and as the controversy with the Cataphrygians concerned the relics of the Apostles, there is little doubt that the Roman presbyter meant that the body of Peter was on the Vatican Hill and that of Paul on the Ostia road.

According to later documents the shrine over St. Peter's tomb was built around 160 A.D. and in 313, when Emperor Constantine started building the first basilica of St. Peter, it was encased into a larger monument of precious marble.

The Vatican archeologists, led by Professor Enrico Josi, a layman, and by the Jesuit Fathers Engelbert Kirschbaum, a German, and Antonio Ferrua, an Italian, found some of the marble slabs that belonged to Constantine's monument. Two of these slabs, one of porphyry and the other of *paonazzetto* (a red marble) can be seen at the back of the Clementine Chapel in the Vatican Grottoes. Probing deeper under the main altar they found, completely embedded in the brick foundations, substantial remains of the little shrine first mentioned by Gaius. They consist of two marble columns, part of a travertine slab on which they were resting, part of another slab supported by the two columns which protected St. Peter's tomb from the rain, and two niches in a wall of red bricks, one above the other. These remains have allowed the archeologists to reconstruct the shrine with a fair degree of accuracy.

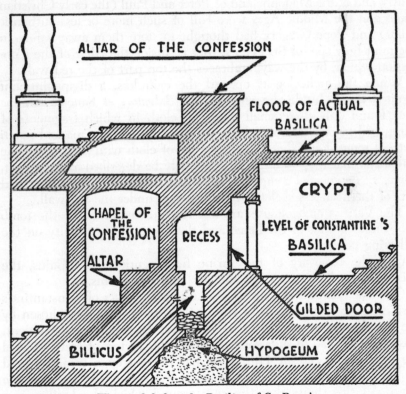

The tomb below the Basilica of St. Peter's

Under the shrine there was a hole in the ground, as there would have been if St. Peter had been buried there. In those days poor men's graves were just narrow trenches dug in the ground and covered by bricks upon which loose earth was piled. At the bottom of this hole the foundations of the red brick wall formed an arch, and tucked under this there were remains of a skeleton minus a head. It is believed that the workers laying the foundations of the red brick wall found these bones and rather than remove them from the spot, built an arch and placed the bones under it.

Another find, this one unexpected, was that of a tiny marble box inside the north wall of the shrine, containing minute fragments of bones and dust. This marble box contained two small silver cylinders bearing in red paint the following inscriptions: *Salvatori et Sanctae Mariae* and *sancti Petri et sancti Pauli.* The style of the handwriting dates these two cylinders between 650 and 750 A.D. but under the red paint the archeologists discovered the same words written in capital letters of a still earlier period. They were obviously "relics" of Christ and of the Madonna and of Peter and Paul (the early Christian times and the Middle Ages were full of such more or less authentic relics) and Pope Gregory had thought to store them away safely in the most holy spot of St. Peter's, that is, inside the Altar of the Confession which, by the way, embraces the top part of the red wall.

When the archeologists opened the cylinders, a disappointment awaited them. Inside the one marked *Salvatori et Sanctae Mariae* they found only three small pieces of cloth in which fragments of bones had presumably once been wrapped. In the one marked *sancti Petri et sancti Pauli* there were two bits of cloth with such tiny bone fragments that they could more accurately be described as bone dust. There was no way of comparing these relics with the more substantial part of the head-less skeleton found tucked under the red wall.

The Vatican archeologists are absolutely convinced that the tomb they found is that of St. Peter and they base their certainty on the following points:

(1) The discovery of the shrine first mentioned by Gaius, the existence of which was confirmed by later documents.

(2) The fact that this shrine is in the exact center of Constantine's basilica, as the foundations of the basilica prove. The spot chosen by the first Christian Emperor could not have been more inconvenient. His architects had to shift some 40,000 cubic meters of earth to level the very steep Vatican Hill, they had to destroy a cemetery and probably to divert the Triumphalis highway that ran close to the tomb. All this shows that the spot around which the basilica was built must have had a very special significance for Christianity and was closely connected with St. Peter. And what could have been more significant than St. Peter's tomb?

(3) Scattered around the tomb the archeologists found about 1,500 coins ranging from the second century to the Middle Ages, proving that the spot was a place of worship for hundreds of years.* It was

* Many of these coins come from distant countries, including England, France, Spain, Germany, Hungary and the Near East.

the habit of pilgrims to toss coins on to the tombs of the martyrs as contributions to the Church. Even today contributions to the Catholic Church are called *"l'obolo di San Pietro"* (St. Peter's coin) or "Peter's Pence." Furthermore hundreds of inscriptions scratched or chalked on the walls near the shrine and dating back to the end of the first century indicate that the tomb was regularly visited by early Christians who wanted to record their presence there.

(4) According to tradition St. Peter was crucified in Nero's circus, and ruins of this circus were found near St. Peter's. It is therefore quite logical that he should have been buried in the vicinity.

The first mention made by Pius XII that the burial place of St. Peter had been identified, was in a radio broadcast on the 13th of May, 1942, on the 25th anniversary of his consecration as a bishop. His words, however, were drowned out by the rumble of war. The day he made his announcement the Germans were in the midst of a big offensive to capture the Kerch peninsula in the Crimea and claimed to have taken 40,000 Russian prisoners. The Japanese boasted they had sunk two United States aircraft carriers, one United States and one English battleship, while Mussolini claimed the sinking of three British destroyers between Sollum and Crete. The largest Italian paper *Il Corriere della Sera,* gave a few lines to the Pope's broadcast but not a word to the part dealing with St. Peter's tomb.

It was not until the end of the Holy Year in 1950 that the Pope again spoke on the subject. This time, in his Christmas radio message, he solemnly announced the finding of the tomb, although he was more cautious as far as the bones were concerned. Pius XII said:

"The excavations under the Altar of the Confession, at least as regards the tomb of the Apostle (a search on which we set our heart since the first days of our pontificate), and their scientific study have been happily concluded during this Holy Year. Within the shortest of time a documented publication will make known the result of these very thorough explorations.

"The result has been of the highest value and importance. But here is the essential question: Has St. Peter's tomb really been found? To such question the final conclusion of the work and the studies answers with a very clear 'Yes. The tomb of the Prince of the Apostles has been found.'

"A second question [the Pope went on] subordinate to the first one, regards the relics of the Saint. Have they been found? On the edge of the sepulcher have been found remains of human bones which, however, cannot be proved with certainty to belong to the body of the Apostle. This however leaves unchanged the historic reality of the tomb. The gigantic dome arches over the sepulcher of the first bishop of Rome, of the first Pope; it was originally a very humble tomb over which the veneration of later centuries, with a wonderful succession of constructions, has erected the greatest temple of Christianity."

And here, in a rough, incomplete outline, is the "succession of constructions" the Pope referred to:

64 or 67 A.D.	Peter is crucified in Nero's circus and is buried by his fellow-believers, probably at nighttime and in great secrecy, in the nearby pagan cemetery on the Vatican Hill. The tomb is just a hole in the ground covered by bricks *"a cappuccina,"* that is, in a tent-like fashion, which was the customary burial in those days for humble slaves, criminals and outcasts.
160 approx.	The early Christians build a little shrine over St. Peter's tomb to protect it from the rain. This is the shrine referred to by the presbyter Gaius, the remains of which have been found by the Vatican archeologists.
313 to 349	The first Christian Emperor, Constantine, and then his son Constans, build a large basilica with its center exactly over the tomb. For further protection the little shrine is encased in a monument of precious marble. According to tradition the tomb with Peter's body was surrounded by bronze slabs. On the top slab that closed the tomb Constantine was reported to have placed a golden cross with his own name and that of his mother Elena. This is probably why Pope Clement VIII thought he saw a golden cross glowing at him from the cavity accidentally discovered in 1594. No traces of the bronze slabs or the golden cross have been found by the Vatican archeologists.
6th century.	Gregory of Tours reports that the tomb of the first Apostle is right under the altar of the basilica. Pilgrims cannot go near it, but, by putting their head through a small window, they can look down at it. Gregory also reports that the pilgrims used to tie a piece of cloth to a string and let it down so that it touched St. Peter's tomb. They thus obtained a

precious relic which they took back to their countries and cherished.

600 approx.	Pope Gregory the Great has the main altar moved directly over the tomb of the Apostle. To do this he had to raise the level of the presbytery.
846	The basilica is looted and badly damaged by the Saracens during a daring raid on Rome. The main altar is also ravaged.
1198-1216	During the reign of Pope Innocent III a new altar was built on the top of the Gregorian one.
1506-1612	It was in 1506 that Pope Julius II laid the first stone for the new church and that Bramante started pulling down the walls of Constantine's basilica, which were on the point of collapsing. The task of building St. Peter's, as it now appears, took over a century and Bramante's original plan was changed, enlarged, and added to by Raphael, Michelangelo, Maderno, Sangallo, to mention only some of the many artists who contributed to the construction of the largest church in the world.
1633	Bernini builds a new main altar and places a huge bronze and marble canopy over it.

The question arises—can one visit St. Peter's tomb? Well, the answer is yes and no. The general public is not permitted inside the maze of narrow passages, of steep, slippery steps dug by the *sampietrini* under the Vatican Grottoes and the Altar of the Confession. In some spots the passages are so narrow that a number of Cardinals with their large waistlines simply could not get through. Pius XII, who was lean and agile for his age, had no difficulty in completing the visit. John XXIII, on the contrary, is so plump that he hasn't ever tried. But to let the hundreds of thousands of pilgrims and tourists who daily visit St. Peter's into the bowels of the church would be asking for trouble. And so only a few people—VIPs, archeologists, scholars, journalists—are from time to time accompanied "down below" by one of the Vatican archeologists.

Probably it is just as well that the general public is not let in as, for a non-expert like me, the visit proved a bit of a disappointment. I expected, and so probably would you, to be shown a hole in the ground and to be told: "Here is where the Apostle was buried." But that isn't so at all. The "succession of constructions" that has been described has completely altered the original ground level and has encased the tomb, the shrine and Constantine's monument inside brick foundations, so that approaching them from different sides, you can see only parts of the remains. Starting from down below, that is, from the pagan cemetery that lies under the Vatican Grottoes, you can, if you are thin enough, climb up a kind of air-vent and take a look at the base of one of the two small columns of the early shrine. The other column you can see after a long zigzag detour through the pagan cemetery and another climb up steep steps dug in the foundations. Back in the Vatican Grottoes you can walk around the Altar of the Confession from below, that is, skirting its foundations, and you then find yourself inside the Clementine Chapel. There, at the back of the chapel, are two slabs of marble which belonged to the monument built by Constantine to protect the early shrine.

The tomb itself can be reached from St. Peter's basilica proper. In front of Bernini's main altar there is a semicircular balustrade and on the other side of the balustrade there are steps leading down to the kneeling statue of Pope Pius VI. In front of the kneeling Pope there is a square recess closed in by a bronze grille. Inside this recess there are silver urns containing the palls, that is ecclesiastical vestments worn over the shoulders on solemn occasions only by the Pope and some Metropolitans and Archbishops as a sign of distinction. When the Pope grants the pall to an Archbishop the grille is opened, the pall is taken out of the urn and put over the shoulders of the recipient by the Pope's own hands. These vestments are made out of the wool of very special lambs. Every year, on the 21st of January, in the ancient Basilica of St. Agnes on the Via Nomentana, two snow-white lambs are blessed, placed in a basket adorned with ribbons and flowers and taken to the Vatican where they are presented to the Pope. The Pope in turn hands them over to the nuns of the Santa Cecilia convent near the Tiber, who keep them till Easter. Shortly before Easter they are shorn and out of this wool the nuns weave the palls which are then taken to St. Peter's and placed under the main altar. Immediately after they have been shorn, the lambs, I'm sorry to say, lose their sacred character and end up as *abbacchio arrosto*, that is, ordinary roast lamb.

Inside the recess where the palls are kept there is a hole and at the bottom of it, about twelve feet under the main altar, is St. Peter's tomb and the spot where large portions of a human skeleton were found. The smaller fragments of bones and the dust enclosed in the tiny marble box were found inside the altar built by Gregory the Great over Gaius' shrine.

I shall return to the mystery of the skeleton and of the bone fragments, the most controversial point of the finds and a puzzle worthy
of the imagination of an outstanding writer of detective fiction. But
before that it must be remembered that not all archeologists are convinced by the evidence here outlined that it was really St. Peter's
tomb that was found. Their main objections are the two rows of
pagan tombs already mentioned, lying under Bernini's main altar.
The disbelievers argue, "The tombs belong to rather wealthy, respectable Roman citizens, while Peter, by Roman standards, was considered
an outcast, a foreigner and a criminal. He would hardly have been
buried in such respectable company. Also, what is more important,
the tombs date from the second to the third century, which shows
that, at the time Peter died, the Vatican Hill was not yet used as a
cemetery at all. How could he possibly have been buried there?"

Up to a short while ago the Vatican archeologists had no cut-and-
dried answer to these serious objections. But now they think they
have one and here is where the tomb of Nero's slave comes in and
why it has been described as *la vendetta di San Pietro.*"

Like any other respectable capital, the tiny Vatican City too has
its traffic and parking problems. The Vatican itself owns about 200
automobiles, buses and trucks (the automobiles are for the use of
the Pope, the Cardinals and high officials; the buses and trucks belong
to the Pontifical Relief Committee) while there are a number of cars
privately owned by Vatican employees and those of visitors from
outside, mostly diplomats. To relieve the congestion it was decided
to build an underground garage below the already existing parking
space near the premises of the Vatican newspaper *Osservatore
Romano.*

In December 1957, while digging for the new underground garage,
a gang of workers came upon a Roman cemetery. The supervision of
the excavations was taken over by Professor Filippo Magi, Director
of the Vatican Museums, who threw a cloak of secrecy over the work.
The veil was lifted at the end of June 1958 when the Director of
the Vatican Museums presented a full report to the Pontifical Roman
Academy of Archeology. Even then the audience who heard it was
a quite specialized and restricted one and the significance of the finds
did not reach the general public.

A whole pagan cemetery came to light under the pickaxes and
shovels of the workers digging for the underground garage. They
unearthed two parallel rows of small, square funerary memorials, surrounded by more humble graves, that is, what appeared to be a
middle-class cemetery and a poor man's cemetery thrown together.
More isolated tombs discovered outside the Vatican City, some be-

neath St. Peter's Square near the central obelisk, others near the
Rome municipal Food Office, provide sufficient evidence that not
only the southern slopes and the Triumphalis road, on which St.
Peter's is built, but also the Cornelia road going up the Vatican Hill
on the other side were used as a cemetery in Roman days. The fact
that in the area there are graves of slaves, workers and anonymous
bodies strengthens the theory that such an outcast as Peter might
have been buried there.

One important objection, that of the age of the cemetery, however
remained and this was overcome by the finding of Nero's slave tomb,
which Vatican archeologists consider as the "missing link," already
referred to, that confirms that the tomb under St. Peter's main altar
is really that of the first Apostle. For this tomb bears an inscription
that allows it to be dated fairly accurately. The Latin inscription runs
as follows, *"Nunnius, Neronis Claudi Cesaris saltuarius, sibi et Ma
uxori suae et Crescenti filio suo benemerentibus."* That is, in a free
translation, "Nunnius, gamekeeper of Nero Claudius Caesar, built
this tomb for himself, for his wife Ma and for his son Crescentius
who deserved it." The Latin word *saltuarius* can mean either a gamekeeper, an overseer of woods or an administrator of a rural estate. In
this case, as Nero had made a beautiful garden on the Vatican Hill
for himself, Nunnius was probably the chief gardener.

And now, my dear Watson, as Sherlock Holmes would say, Nero
was such a bad man and he left behind him such a legacy of hatred
that it is hardly likely that such an inscription would have been
written on the memorial after his death. In other words, our gamekeeper or chief gardener Nunnius must have had this tomb built
for himself and his family before 69 A.D., that is before the time
when Nero, deposed by a palace revolution and tracked by his enemies, committed suicide by throwing himself on to a sword. The
Vatican Hill accordingly was already a cemetery before 69 A.D.; this
coincides perfectly with the year of St. Peter's death, which some
historians place in 64 and others in 67 A.D.

To strengthen the evidence that the Vatican Hill was used as a
cemetery at the time Peter died, other clues were found by the Vatican
archeologists in addition to the fundamental one of Emperor Nero's
slave. Inside some of the poor men's graves were found skeletons
with coins between their teeth. It was the custom of the age to put
a coin in the mouth of the dead. The coin was called the *"obolus"*
and the dead were supposed to pay it to Charon, the son of Erebus,
whose duty it was to ferry the souls of the dead over the waters of
the Styx and Acheron to the infernal regions. A great many of the

coins found inside the skulls of the underground garage skeletons belong to the first part of the first century.

Another strange find in this site, which has nothing to do with St. Peter's tomb, but which may be worth mentioning, is the grave of a Roman writer. In this tomb were found a cylindrical copper inkpot, of beautiful design, pens, quills, waxed tablets and other paraphernalia that were the ballpoint pens and typewriters of the Romans. The inkpot still had some ink at the bottom, dried up, of course. This ink powder has been treated chemically by Vatican experts so that one can write with it again. It has been used for comparisons with the ink on certain ancient manuscripts in the Vatican Library that are suspected of being forgeries or later copies. These tests are reported to have proved very helpful.

But to go back to the mystery of the bones. Some of the Vatican archeologists are absolutely convinced that the bones found under the main altar are those of St. Peter. They were quite disappointed when the Pope spoke about them in doubtful fashion, saying that "they cannot be proved with certainty as belonging to the body of the Apostle."

These bones, as has been stated, were found at the beginning of 1942 but nothing was said about them officially until the papal Christmas broadcast at the end of 1950. There were, of course, all sorts of rumors going around about them, but nothing definite or authoritative since all those connected with the find were, and still are, pledged to secrecy.

Why was the Pope so cautious about the bones, when he had been so outspoken and categorical about the tomb? And why, if he was sure that the tomb was that of Peter, should the bones found near it not be Peter's? The official answer to these questions is not known, but here are some of the arguments that might have induced Pius XII to soft-pedal this part of the finds.

First of all, remember that according to a theory adduced at the end of the last century by the French archeologist Mgr. Duchesne, the bodies of Peter and Paul were at a certain time removed from the Vatican Hill and from the Ostia road, respectively, and buried again in the catacombs of St. Sebastian on the ancient Appian Way. This is supposed to have occurred in 258 A.D., during the persecution of the Christians by Emperor Valerian. The Emperor, among other things, ordered the confiscation of all Christian cemeteries and the Christians, to prevent the bodies of Peter and Paul from falling into the hands of the pagans, transferred them to the catacombs on the Appian Way. The catacombs were likewise a cemetery but they offered the advantage of being in the private grounds of a Roman citizen who protected the Christians, and therefore they could not be confiscated.

Now, if the body of St. Peter was taken to the catacombs of St. Sebastian, how is it possible for it to have turned up in 1942 in its original tomb, that is under the main altar of St. Peter's? According to Mgr. Giulio Belvederi, Secretary of the Pontifical Institute of Christian Archeology, when Constantine accepted Christianity as the official State religion, the bodies of the two martyrs were taken back to their original places of burial where the Emperor had built two huge basilicas. This, which seems fairly logical, is however contradicted by an inscription that Pope Damasus I (366-384) is reported to have placed in the St. Sebastian catacombs to record that the bodies of the two Apostles were buried there. The inscription can no longer be seen today but historians have no doubt that it was once there. As Pope Damasus's pontificate was long after Constantine's basilica had been completed, the theory that St. Peter's body had been taken back to the Vatican Hill by Constantine does not hold water. Additional proof that the bodies of the two Apostles were buried in the St. Sebastian catacombs is provided by inscriptions on the walls of the underground cemetery by Christians later than the fourth century. There is also evidence that a special religious service, which was called *"refrigerium"* and which was performed over tombs only, used to take place in these catacombs in honor of Peter and Paul after Constantine had built his two basilicas.

A much more ingenious explanation of the mystery was offered to me by Dr. Alessandro Carletti, another Vatican archeologist, who suggests that at the time of Valerian's persecution in 258, the Christians transferred to the catacombs for safety not the whole body of Peter but only his head. This would be in accordance with the principle of Roman law stated by the famous second century jurist Paulus, according to whom *"ubi caput ibi corpus,"* that is, "where the head is, there is the body," which was applied when there was a question of deciding the legal burial place in doubtful cases. The early Christians, pressed by their persecutors, probably smuggled the heads of Peter and Paul from their graves to the catacombs, a feat that could have been more easily performed than carrying the whole bodies all across Rome.

This theory can explain several things:

(1) Why the skeleton found under St. Peter's main altar was without a head.

(2) The inscription of Pope Damasus I in the catacombs would no longer be contradictory, as the heads could have been in the cata-

combs while the rest of the skeletons would have remained on the Vatican Hill and on the Ostia road.

(3) It could explain the existence of two famous relics of uncertain origin, the heads of St. Peter and of St. Paul, kept in the basilica of St. John in Lateran. These two skulls were placed inside silver busts of the two Apostles and they are exposed on the main altar of St. John's during solemn ceremonies.

Although fascinating, this theory leaves several questions unanswered. Why didn't Emperor Constantine transfer the head of Peter from the catacombs back to the basilica? How and when were the two heads taken from the catacombs to St. John in Lateran? And what is the meaning of the little marble box with tiny bone fragments found inside the red brick wall?

With all these question marks, and a good many more, hanging in the air, it can easily be understood why the Pope should have been rather cautious in speaking about the bones. That, however, was in 1950. Since then a lot of water has flowed under the bridges of the Tiber and a lot of scientific tests, researches and studies have been carried out on these bones.

All those who have taken part in this research are pledged to secrecy by a solemn oath and they would incur papal excommunication should they violate it. This is why not even the fact that such an examination was being carried out has reached the public ear. It is only through a fortunate coincidence that I stumbled across authentic inside information and that I am now able to lift a corner of the veil. But please don't ask me to reveal the source or sources of my information. [I must also hasten to add that none of the people mentioned in the course of this chapter have been guilty of betraying their oath of secrecy.]

To begin with, I can report that there is not one but that there are two secret committees dealing with the problem of the bones. The first is a restricted committee made up of a pathologist, an osteopath, a chemist, a physicist, and other experts.

The restricted committee has been making a direct examination of the bones and submitting its conclusions to a wider committee. The second and wider committee comprises a number of Cardinals, including Giuseppe Pizzardo and Gaetano Cicognani, and by theologians, historians, archeologists and other scholars. (Cardinal Cicognani is the Prefect of the Congregation of Rites which deals, among other things, with holy relics, and Cardinal Pizzardo is head of the Pontifical Institute of Christian Archeology). Their task is to check and evaluate the strictly technical findings of the restricted committee and to see to what degree they fit in or clash with theological principles, the Catholic Church tradition, and data supplied by history, archeology, epigraphy and other branches of knowledge. The final task of the wider committee will be to decide whether the bones are those of Peter or not, and what form the announcement, when it is made, shall take. It could be either a kind of White Paper published by the committee itself or a solemn proclamation made by the Pope *ex cathedra*, in which case all Catholics will be bound to believe whatever will be said by reason of the dogma of the Pope's infallibility. According to my information, both the restricted and the wider committee are still quite undecided.

As soon as the bones were found, which was, as has been said, at the beginning of 1942, they were whisked away by the late Mgr. Ludwig Kaas, former leader of the German Catholic Party, who supervised with an iron hand all the work going on in St. Peter's. Father Kirschbaum, one of the archeologists who found them, wanted to photograph them to record exactly the position in which they were lying, but he was given only enough time to take a few, not very successful, snapshots. Mgr. Kaas, as has been noted, was a very close friend of the late Pope, probably the only real friend Pius XII ever had, and this gave him an authority that went far beyond his official position. The former German politician was a man of great intelligence and integrity, whose sharp tongue and almost brutal frankness made him feared by everyone in the Vatican. Mgr. Kaas placed the bones in a box and locked them in a cupboard in his own private office.

There they remained for some time until Professor Galeazzi Lisi was asked by the Pope to take a first look at them. The Professor sorted them out, classified them and proceeded carefully to reconstruct the skeleton, which was then varnished and placed in a special, airtight coffin, easily accessible for further inspections. Rumor had it this coffin was kept in the Pope's private apartment on the third floor of the Vatican Palace, directly under the altar of the small chapel where Pius XII used to say Mass every morning, and where John XXIII says it now. The idea of the reigning Pope celebrating Mass over the bones of the first Pope was evidently both evocative and appealing. But contrary to this rumor the bones are actually kept in one of the many halls of the Vatican, which has been entirely reserved for this purpose, and to which only the experts of the restricted committees have access.

The first thing Galeazzi Lisi and his collaborators were able to ascertain was that the bones belonged to a medium-height, heavily-built man who died at an advanced age; data that coincides with the little that is known about Peter. The head, as has been said, was missing, and a natural thing to do was to compare the skeleton with the relic of St. Peter's head kept in St. John in Lateran. Strangely enough this was not done until 1956, fourteen years after the finding of the bones. But in a way the reluctance of the Vatican to compare the two relics was quite understandable. Supposing the check showed that the skull and the skeleton belonged to different persons? Evidently the Church would have had to disclaim one of the two relics. But which one? The skull in the silver bust is a very famous, officially accepted relic, although there is practically nothing, except tradition, to prove its authenticity. The bones, on the contrary, although not accepted for certain by the Pope as being those of Peter, were found in such a place and in such circumstances that it is possible that they are those of the first Apostle. It would have been extremely embarrassing to have to choose between the two relics.

However, as far as my information goes, everything went well with the check. The skull was taken out of its silver container, measured, photographed and tiny samples of it were chemically analyzed and submitted to other tests. The conclusion was that it, too, belonged to an elderly man and that, because of its size, it could fit the bones now lying in a hall of the Vatican. Again this made it more probable that the skull and bones were those of Peter; however it constituted no decisive proof.

It has been suggested that the two relics be submitted to the carbon C 14 test for radioactivity. All living matter—plants, animals and, of course, man—contains an isotope of carbon called C 14, which is radioactive. After death, C 14, like all other radioactive elements, starts losing its radioactivity at a regular, calculable rate. The loss of radioactivity thus allows the nuclear physicist to calculate how long ago the organic matter being examined ceased to live. The idea was to submit to such test the bones and the skull to see how many centuries ago their owner or owners had died.

The test, however, has not been carried out and for very good reasons. I discussed the question with Dr. Francesco Bella, a young scientist of the Institute of Physics of the Rome University, who is in charge of this type of research. He explained to me that the apparatus at his disposal, the only one in Italy, requires a standard amount of eight grams of pure radioactive carbon. As only very small amounts of C 14 are contained in the human body, the bones would have to be completely destroyed to obtain enough radioactive carbon to make them "confess" their age. As for the skull, it would certainly not contain enough C 14.

Moreover, the radioactivity test is not absolutely accurate but gives only an approximation of about 5 per cent, which in our case, over a period of nearly 2,000 years, would be a century. Dr. Bella told me, "To check the margin of approximation, we have tested the wood of the Roman ships found in the lake of Nemi. We chose these ships because, through historical records, we know exactly the year in which they were built. The test was only 70 years off the real date, which means a margin of error of less than 5 per cent. . . . We have also been asked to test the Holy Sindon, and to settle a dispute between two monasteries of Benedictine monks who both claim the possession of St. Benedict's bones." The Sindon, or Christ's shroud, is one of the most controversial relics of the Catholic Church, and it is kept in the Turin cathedral. It is a large linen sheet, measuring 14.3 feet by 3.6 feet, in which, it is said, Jesus was wrapped when He was taken down from the Cross. It bears stains of blood and sweat that show in what parts of His body Christ was wounded. It also bears a kind of imprint of Christ's face. The forehead, the nose, the cheek-bones, the mouth and the bearded chin, soaked in blood, have left stains on the cloth, while other parts of the face have not, giving a startling effect of a photographic negative.

This relic made its first appearance in history as late as 1353, when Geoffroy de Charny donated it to the church of Lirey, near Troyes in France. There is no record of where it came from or of how it happened to be in possession of the de Charny family. Two years later the bishop of Troyes declared it a forgery and forbade its cult. But the faithful went on venerating it all the same and a few centuries later the Church admitted it could be a copy of the original shroud and that therefore it had a certain holy character. It was not until 1898 that the Sindon acquired the importance it has today. It was in that year that it was photographed for the first time and the sensational discovery made that the negative showed very clearly the features of a man who died in agony—the only contemporary portrait of Christ, should the relic be authentic. If one could prove by a radioactivity test that the linen it is made of is 2,000 or more years old, this would no doubt become the most important relic of Christianity.

"We had to turn the requests down," Dr. Bella explained, "because, as I told you, to carry out these tests we should have to destroy the relics. In the future, however, we shall have a much more modern, delicate apparatus, which works on gases, and which can establish the ages also of very small pieces of organic matter. Then we shall see. Anyhow, I can tell you that as far as the bones found in St. Peter's and the skull in St. John's are concerned, we have never been asked by the Vatican to test them."

Faced with the impossibility of carrying out the carbon C_{14} test, the wider committee dealing with the bones had to content itself with the findings of Galeazzi Lisi and his team of experts. The tomb of Nero's slave and also, I understand, some inscriptions newly discovered by Professor Margherita Guarducci[1] in the pagan cemetery under the main altar have been taken as supporting the theory that the bones are those of Peter.

The death of Pius XII, however, postponed all decisions. First of all, the fact that Galeazzi Lisi had to relinquish all his Vatican posts has left the restricted committee without a chairman. Moreover, a strange rumor is going around in the Vatican to the effect that Galeazzi Lisi made a mistake when he reconstructed the skeleton and that the bones belong not to one but to two men. Finally, nobody yet knows how John XXIII feels about this issue and about the problem of relics in general.

What can be stated with certainty is that in the old days the Catholic Church, confronted with the finding of the tomb and of some bones near it, would have jumped to conclusions and declared that they belonged to Peter. Today, however, the Church has become far more cautious, she has a much less emotional approach to such questions and lets herself be guided by science. It is therefore likely that the mysterious bones, which for so many years had remained locked up in the drawer of the despotic Mgr. Kaas, will not be officially declared as being those of St. Peter, unless, of course, some new discovery or some new method of scientific research should throw more light on this fascinating riddle.

[1] *The Tomb of St. Peter: the New Discoveries in the Sacred Grottoes of the Vatican,* by Margherita Guarducci, New York, Hawthorn Books, Inc., 1960.

17

The Future
of the Church

WE HAVE been wandering together, a little at random, through the Vatican labyrinth, taking a peep through half-closed doors and also sometimes unashamedly bending down to look through the key holes of closed ones. Now that I have come to the end of this book I am perturbed by the number of things I have left out, which may exceed the ones I have managed to put in. But still I feel that some ground has been covered and that this little journey behind the Bronze Door has not been entirely fruitless.

I have tried to show what kind of a man Pius XII was and what he did for the Church. I have also indicated what kind of a man the present Pope is, what he had already done and what he is likely to do. I described what went on in the Sistine Chapel when the Cardinals locked themselves in to elect John XXIII. The organization of the Church has been dealt with, trying to explain in simple, lay terms the actual functions of the various Congregations, offices and tribunals with their strange Latin or medieval names, which form the central administration of the Church. I have probed into the vast financial empire of the Vatican. I have associated with monks, friars and nuns and the men and women who go around in civilian clothes looking more or less like you and me but who have taken the vows of chastity, poverty and obedience. I have presented an outline of the dramatic struggle between the Vatican and the Kremlin as well as a quick survey of the many problems the Catholic Church is facing in the world. The complicated business of how saints are recognized and how marriages are annulled has been discussed. I have reviewed the Pope's tiny but colorful army and we have descended together under the foundations of the great basilica in search of Peter's tomb and bones.

In the course of this excursion a number of rather unusual characters have crossed our path: ascetic, dignified, indefatigable Pius XII; his devoted housekeeper, Mother Pasqualina, his three nephews, his two unorthodox doctors, Galeazzi Lisi and Niehans; the witty, benevolent John XXIII; Vatican bankers and archeologists; the nun with the permanent wave and fur coat; the Devil's Advocate; Don Juan, the saintly sinner; the "secret monks" of Opus Dei who control the political, intellectual and economic life of Spain; and the Cardinals Spellman, Tisserant, Mindszenty, Wyszynski, Tardini and Montini, just to list a few of the many people who have appeared in this narrative. Some of them you may have liked, others disliked, but I hope you have found it worth your while to have met them.

And now, before we part, a final question: What is the conclusion to be drawn from all this? In other words, what is the future of the Catholic Church?

To good Catholics the question is unnecessary. They believe that the Church is of Divine origin and that it will last to the day of Universal Judgment. They believe in the words on the inside of St. Peter's dome, "Thou art Peter and upon this rock I will build my Church, and the gates of hell shall never prevail against it, and to thee I shall give the keys of the Kingdom of Heaven." They recognize that the Church of Rome has been many times on the point of being wiped out, but that she has always recovered in an incredible, almost miraculous way. They admit that the Church moves slowly and seems to be constantly lagging behind the times, but they also boast that in the end she always manages to "get there" somehow. They firmly believe that even the worst of Popes cannot err because, in matters where the faith is concerned, he receives Divine inspiration. Their belief in the future of the Church is unshakable because it is based on supernatural motives.

But, for an outsider like myself, the answer is not so simple or so categorical. Despite her half-billion believers, her wealth, tradition, prestige and powerful organization, the Catholic Church—like all other religious denominations of our times—seems to be threatened by an enemy even more dangerous than communism, that is, indifference. Communism could end or rather—which seems more likely to be the case—change from within and come to terms with religion. The liberalization process started by Khrushchev is under way and nobody can tell where it will end. Signs of a religious revival have been reported even from Russia. As has often happened before, the persecution the Church has been submitted to in Poland, Hungary and the other Iron Curtain countries seems to have strengthened the faith of the people instead of shattering it.

Indifference, on the other hand, is something else, something more difficult to fight because of its evasive and subtle nature. In this respect I find it significant that the Church of Rome is gaining in those countries, such as the United States, Great Britain, Holland, the Scandinavian nations, etc., where she is in a minority and where she finds competition, and is losing her grip in those which are theoretically 99 per cent Catholic, such as Italy and the whole of Latin America.

John XXIII has clearly sensed the peril and has made the grave and courageous decision to call an Ecumenical Council. For an Ecumenical Council is not a routine affair. All the preceding twenty Councils (on an average, one a century) were summoned in moments of extreme danger or to patch serious rifts inside the Church. The scope of the coming Council is not only to try to bring about a reunion with the Eastern Churches, not only to streamline the organization of the Church, but above all to fight indifference, to shake the faithful and reawaken in them a deeply felt and active religious feeling. The future of the Catholic Church depends to a great extent on the success of this Council and on the decisions that will be taken by this great assembly.

APPENDIX

APPENDIX

LIST OF POPES

ST. PETER, Prince of the Apostles, who received from Jesus Christ the Supreme
Pontificate, to be transmitted to his successors. He lived first in Antioch,
then, according to the Chronograph of the year 354, for 25 years in
Rome, where he suffered martyrdom in the year 64 or 67 of the Christian
era.

ST. LINUS, of Tuscia, A.D., 67-76

ST. ANACLETUS or CLETUS, Roman, 76-88

ST. CLEMENT, Roman, 88-97

ST. EVARISTUS, Greek, 97-105

ST. ALEXANDER I, Roman, 105-115

ST. SIXTUS I, Roman, 115-125

ST. TELESPHORUS, Greek, 125-136

ST. HYGINUS, Greek, 136-140

ST. PIUS I, of Aquilea, 140-155

ST. ANICETUS, Syria, 155-166

ST. SOTER, of Campania, 166-175

ST. ELEUTHERIUS, of Nicopoli in the Epirus, 175-189

ST. VICTOR I, African, 189-199

ST. ZEPHYRINUS, Roman, 199-217

ST. CALLISTUS I, Roman, 217-222

    (ST. HIPPOLYTUS, Roman, 217-235)

ST. URBAN I, Roman, 222-230

ST. PONTIAN, Roman, 21-VII-230—28-IX-235

ST. ANTERUS, Greek, 21-XI-235—3-I-236

ST. FABIAN, Roman, 10-I-236—20-I-250

ST. CORNELIUS, Roman, ...III-251—...VI-253

    (NOVATIAN, Roman, 251)

ST. LUCIUS I, Roman, 25-VI-253—5-III-254

ST. STEPHEN I, Roman, 12-V-254—2-VIII-257

ST. SIXTUS II, Greek, 30-VIII-257—6-VIII-258

ST. DIONYSIUS, country unknown, 22-VII-259—26-XII-268

ST. FELIX I, Roman, 5-I-269—30-XII-274

ST. EUTYCHIAN, of Luni, 4-I-275—7-XII-283

ST. CAIUS, Dalmatia, 17-XII-283—22-IV-296

ST. MARCELLINUS, Roman, 30-VI-296—25-X-304

ST. MARCELLUS I, Roman, 27-V-308—16-I-309

ST. EUSEBIUS, Greek, 18-IV-309—17-VIII-310

ST. MILZIADE or MELCHIADES, African, 2-VII-311—11-I-314

ST. SILVESTER I, Roman, 31-I-314—31-XII-335

ST. MARK, Roman, 18-I-336—7-X-336

ST. JULIUS I, Roman, 6-II-337—12-IV-352

LIBERIUS, Roman, 7-V-352—24-IX-366

    (FELIX II, Roman, ...355—22-XI-365)

ST. DAMASUS I, Spanish, 1-X-366—11-XII-384

    (URSICINUS, 366-367)

ST. SIRICIUS, Roman, 15 or 22 or 29-XII-384—26-XI-399
ST. ANASTASIUS I, Roman, 27-XI-399—19-XII-401
ST. INNOCENT I, of Albano, 22-XII-401—12-III-417
ST. ZOSIMUS, Greek, 18-III-417—26-XII-418
ST. BONIFACE I, Roman, 28 or 29-XII-418—4-IX-422
    (EULALIUS, 27 or 29-XII-418—419)
ST. CELESTINE I, of Campania, 10-IX-422—27-VII-432
ST. SIXTUS III, Roman, 31-VII-432—19-VIII-440
ST. LEO THE GREAT, of Tuscia, 29-IX-440—10-XI-461
ST. HILARY, Sardinian, 19-XI-461—29-II-468
ST. SIMPLICIUS, of Tivoli, 3-III-468—10-III-483
ST. FELIX III (II), Roman, 13-III-483—1-III-492
ST. GELASIUS I, African, 1-III-492—21-XI-496
ANASTASIUS II, Roman, 24-XI-496—19-XI-498
ST. SYMMACHUS, Sardonian, 22-XI-498—19-VII-514
    (LAWRENCE, 498-501—505)
ST. HORMISDAS, of Frosinone, 20-VII-514—6-VIII-523
ST. JOHN I, of Tuscia, 13-VIII-523—18-V-526
ST. FELIX IV (III), of Sannio, 12-VII-526—22-IX-530
BONIFACE II, Roman, 22-IX-530—17-X-532
    (DIOSCORUS, of Alexandria, 22-IX-530—14-X-530)
JOHN II, Roman, 2-I-533—8-V-535
ST. AGAPITUS I, Roman, 13-V-535—22-IV-536
ST. SILVERIUS, of Campania, 1-VI-536—11-XI-537
VIGILIUS, Roman, 29-III-537—7-VI-555
PELAGIUS I, Roman, 16-IV-556—4-III-561
JOHN III, Roman, 17-VII-561—13-VII-574
BENEDICT I, Roman, 2-VI-575—30-VII-579
PELAGIUS II, Roman, 26-XI-579—7-II-590
ST. GREGORY THE GREAT, Roman, 3-IX-590—12-III-604
SABINIAN, of Biera in Tuscia, 13-IX-604—22-II-606
BONIFACE III, Roman, 19-II-607—12-XI-607
ST. BONIFACE IV, of the Marsi region, 25-VIII-608—8-V-615
ST. DEUSDEDIT or ADEODATUS I, Roman, 19-X-615—8-XI-618
BONIFACE V, of Naples, 23-XII-619—25-X-625
HONORIUS I, of Campania, 27-X-625—12-X-638
SEVERINUS, Roman, 28-V-640—2-VIII-640
JOHN IV, Dalmatia, 24-XII-640—12-X-642
THEODORE I, Greek, 24-XI-642—14-V-649
ST. MARTIN I, of Todi, . . . VII-649—16-IX-655
ST. EUGENE I, Roman, 10-VIII-654—2-VI-657
ST. VITALIAN, of Segni, 30-VII-657—27-I-672
ADEODATUS II, Roman, 11-IV-672—17-VI-676
DONUS, Roman, 2-XI-676—11-IV-678
ST. AGATHO, Sicilian, 27-VI-678—10-I-681
ST. LEO II, Sicilian, 17-VIII-682—3-VII-683
ST. BENEDICT II, Roman, 26-VI-684—8-V-685

ST. JOHN V, Syrian, 23-VII-685—2-VIII-686
CONON, country unknown, 21-X-686—21-IX-687
    (THEODORE, ...687)
    (PASCHAL, ...687)
ST. SERGIUS I, Syrian, 15-XII-687—8-IX-701
JOHN VI, Greek, 30-X-701—11-I-705
JOHN VII, Greek, 1-III-705—18-X-707
SISINNIUS, Syrian, 15-I-708—4-II-708
CONSTANTINE, Syrian, 25-III-708—9-IV-715
ST. GREGORY II, Roman, 19-V-715—11-II-731
ST. GREGORY III, Greek, 18-III-731—...XI-741
ST. ZACHARY, Greek, 10-XII-741—22-III-752
STEPHEN II, Roman, 23-III-752—25-III-752
STEPHEN III, Roman, 26-III-752—26-IV-757
ST. PAUL I, Roman, ...IV, 29-V-757—28-VI-767
    (CONSTANTINE, of Nepi, 28-VI, 5-VII-767—769)
    (PHILIP, 31-VII-768)
STEPHEN IV, Sicilian, 1, 7-VIII-768—24-I-772
ADRIAN I, Roman, 1, 9-II-772—25-XII-795
ST. LEO III, Roman, 26, 27-XII-795—12-VI-816
STEPHEN V, Roman, 22-VI-816—24-I-817
ST. PASCHAL I, Roman, 25-I-817—11-II-824
EUGENE II, Roman, ...II-V-824—...VIII-827
VALENTINE, Roman, ...VIII-827—...IX-827
GREGORY IV, Roman, ...827—...I-844
    (JOHN, ...I-844)
SERGIUS II, Roman, ...I-844—27-I-847
ST. LEO IV, Roman, ...I, 10-IV-847—17-VII-855
BENEDICT III, Roman, ...VII, 29-IX-855—17-IV-858
    (ANASTASIUS, the Librarian, ...VIII-855—...IX-855, ✝c. 880)
ST. NICHOLAS I THE GREAT, Roman, 24-IV-858—13-XI-867
ADRIAN II, Roman, 14-XII-867—14-XII-872
JOHN VIII, Roman, 14-XII-872—16-XII-882
MARINUS I, of Gallese, 16-XII-882—15-V-884
ST. ADRIAN III, Roman, 17-V-884—...IX-885
STEPHEN VI, Roman, ...IX-885—14-IX-891
FORMOSUS, Bishop of Porto, 6-X-891—4-IV-896
BONIFACE VI, Roman, ...IV-896—...IV-896
STEPHEN VII, Roman, ...V-896—...VIII-897
ROMANUS, of Gallese, ...VIII-897—...XI-897
THEODORE II, Roman, ...XII-897—...XII-897
JOHN IX, of Tivoli, ...I-898—...I-900
BENEDICT IV, Roman, ...I-II-900—...VII-903
LEO V, of Ardea, ...VII-903—...IX-903
    (CHRISTOPHER, Roman, ...VII or ...IX-903—...I-904
SERGIUS III, Roman, 29-I-904—14-IV-911
ANASTASIUS III, Roman, ...IV-911—...VI-913

LANDON, of Sabina, ...VII-913—...II-914

JOHN X, of Tossignano (Imola), ...III-914—...V-928

LEO VI, Roman, ...V-928—...XII-928

STEPHEN VIII, Roman, ...XII-928—...II-931

JOHN XI, Roman, ...11-III-931—...XII-935

LEO VII, Roman, 3-I-936—13-VII-939

STEPHEN IX, Roman, 14-VII-939—...X-942

MARINUS II, Roman, 30-X-942—...V-946

AGAPITUS II, Roman, 10-V-946—...XII-955

JOHN XII, Ottaviano, *of the counts of Tuscolo,* 16-XII-955—14-V-964

LEO VIII, Roman, 4, 6-XII-963—1-III-965

BENEDICT V, Roman, 22-V-964—4-VII-966

JOHN XIII, Roman, 1-X-965—6-IX-972

BENEDICT VI, Roman, 19-I-973—...VI-974

    (BONIFACE VII, Roman, *Francone,* ...VI—...VII-974; for the ...VIII-984—...VII-985).

BENEDICT VII, Roman, ...X-974—10-VII-983

JOHN XIV, of Pavia, *Pietro,* ...XII-983—20-VIII-984

JOHN XV, Roman, ...VIII-985—...III-996

GREGORY V, of Saxony, *Brunone of the dukes of Carinzia,* 3-V-996—18-II-999

    (JOHN XVI, of Rossano, G. Filagato, ...IV-997—...II-998).

SILVESTER II, of Auvergne, *Gerberto,* 2-IV-999—12-V-1003

JOHN XVII, Roman, *Siccone,* ...VI-1003—...XII-1003

JOHN XVIII, Roman, *Fasano,* ...I-1004—...VII-1009

SERGIUS IV, Roman, *Pietro,* 31-VII-1009—12-V-1012

BENEDICT VIII, *Teofilatto of the counts of Tuscolo,* 18-V-1012—9-IV-1024

    (GREGORY, ...1012)

JOHN XIX, Roman, *of the counts of Tuscolo,* ...IV-V-1024—...1032

BENEDICT IX, *Teofilatto of the counts of Tuscolo,* ...1032—...1044

SYLVESTER III, Roman, *Giovanni,* 20-I-1045—10-II-1045

BENEDICT IX (2nd term), 10-IV-1045—1-V-1045

GREGORY VI, Roman, *Giovanni Graziano,* 5-V-1045—20-XII-1046

CLEMENT II, of Saxony, *Suitgero of the lords of Morsleben and Hornburg,* 24, 25-XII-1046—9-X-1047

BENEDICT IX (3rd term), 8-XI-1047—17-VII-1048

DAMASUS II, of Bavaria, *Poppone,* 17-VII-1048—9-VIII-1048

ST. LEO IX, of Lorraine, *Bruno of the counts of Egisheim-Dagsburg,* 12-II-1049—19-IV-1054

VICTOR II, German, *Gebeardo of the counts of Dollnstein-Hirschberg,* 16-IV-1055—28-VII-1057

STEPHEN X, of Lorraine, *Federico of the dukes of Lorraine,* 3-VIII-1057—29-III-1058

    (BENEDICT X, Roman, *Giovanni,* 5-IV-1058—24-I-1059, ✠...?)

NICHOLAS II, of Burgundy, *Gerardo,* 24-I-1059—27-VII-1061

ALEXANDER II, *Anselmo of Baggio* (Milan), 1-X-1061—21-IV-1073

    (HONORIUS II, Veronese, *Cadalo,* 28-X-1061—...1072)

ST. GREGORY VII, of Tuscia, *Ildebrando,* 22-IV ✝, 30-VI-1073—25-V-1085
   (CLEMENT III, of Parma, *Wiberto,* 25-VI-1080—24-III-1084—8-IX-1100)
* B. VICTOR III, of Benevento, *Dauferio (Desiderio),* 24-V-1086—16-IX-1087
B. URBAN II, French, *Eudes de Lagery,* 12-III-1088—29-VII-1099
PASCHAL II, of Bieda (Ravenna district), *Raniero,* 13, 14-VIII-1099—21-I-1118
   (THEODERIC, Bishop of St. Rufina, ...1100, ✝1102)
   (ALBERT, Bishop of Sabina, ...1102)
   (SYLVESTER IV, Roman, *Maginulfo,* 18-XI-1105—...1111)
GELASIUS II, of Gaeta, *Giovanni Caetani,* 24-I, 10-III-1118—28-I-1119
   (GREGORY VIII, French, *Maurizio and Burdino,* 8-III-1118—...1121,
   ✝...?)
CALLISTUS II, *Guido di Borgogna,* 2, 9-II-1119—13-XII-1124
HONORIUS II, of Fiagnano (Imola), *Lamberto,* 15, 21-XII-1124—13-II-1130
   (CELESTINE II, Roman, *Tebaldo Buccapecus,* ...XII-1124)
INNOCENT II, Roman, *Gregorio Papareschi,* 14, 23-II-1130—24-IX-1143
   (ANACLETUS II, Roman, *Pietro Petri Leonis,* 14, 23-II-1130—25-I-1138)
   (VICTOR IV, *Gregorio,* ...III-1138—29 V—1138, ✝...?)
CELESTINE II, of Città di Castello, *Guido,* 26-IX-, 3-X-1143—8-III-1144
LUCIUS II, Bolognese, *Gerardo Caccianemici,* 12-III-1144—15-II-1145
B. EUGENE III, of Pisa, *Bernardo perhaps of the Paganelli di Monte Magno,*
   15,18 II-1145—8-VII-1153
ANASTASIUS IV, Roman, *Corrado,* 12-VII-1153—3-XII-1154
ADRIAN IV, English, *Nicholas Breakspear,* 4, 5-XII-1154 1-IX-1159
ALEXANDER III, of Siena, *Rolando Bandinelli,* 7, 20-IX-1159—30-VIII-1181
   (VICTOR IV, *Ottaviano de Monticello* (Montecelio, Tivoli), 7-IX, 4-X-
   1159—20-IV-1164)
   (PASCHAL III, *Guido da Crema,* 22, 26-IV-1164—20-IX-1168)
   (CALLISTUS III, *Giovanni,* Abbazia di Strumi (Arezzo), ...IX-1168—
   29-VIII-1178)
   (INNOCENT III, of Sezze, *Lando,* 29-IX-1179—...1180)
LUCIUS III, of Lucca district, *Ubaldo Allucingoli,* 1, 6-IX-1181—25-IX-1185
URBAN III, Milanese, *Uberto Crivelli,* 25-XI, 1-XII-1185—20-X-1187
GREGORY VIII, of Benevento, *Alberto de Morra,* 21, 25-X-1187—17-XII-1187
CLEMENT III, Roman, *Paolo Scolari,* 19, 20-XII-1187—...III-1191
CELESTINE III, Roman, *Giacinto Bobone,* 30-III, 14-IV-1191—8-I-1198
INNOCENT III, of Anagni, *Lotario of the counts of Segni,* 8-I, 22-II-1198—
   16-VII-1216
HONORIUS III, Roman, *Cencio Savelli,* 18, 24-VII-1216—18-III-1227
GREGORY IX, of Anagni, *Ugolino of the counts of Segni,* 19, 21-III-1227—
   22-VIII-1241
CELESTINE IV, Milanese, *Goffredo Castiglioni,* 25, 28-X-1241—10-XI-1241
INNOCENT IV, Genovese, *Sinibaldo Fieschi,* 25, 28-VI-1243—7-XII-1254
ALEXANDER IV, of Anagni, *Rinaldo of the counts of Segni,* 12, 20-XII-1254—
   25-V-1261
URBAN IV, of Troyas, *Giacomo Pantaléon,* 29-VIII, 4-IX-1261—2-X-1264
* B in this list is an abbreviation for *Blessed.* Ed.

CLEMENT IV, French, *Guido Fulcodi*, 5, 15-II-1265—29-XI-1268

B. GREGORY X, of Piacenza, *Tedaldo Visconti*, 1-IX-1271, 27-III-1272—10-I-1276

B. INNOCENT V, of Savoy, *Pietro di Tarantasia*, 21-I, 22-II-1276—22-VI-1276

ADRIAN V, Genovese, *Ottobono Fieschi*, 11-VII-1276—18-VIII-1276

JOHN XXI, Portuguese, *Pietro Juliani*, 8, 20-IX-1276—20-V-1277

NICHOLAS III, Roman, *Giovanni Gaetano Orsini*, 25-XI, 26-XII-1277—22-VIII-1280

MARTIN IV, French, *Simone de Brion*, 22-II, 23-III-1281—28-III-1285

HONORIUS IV, Roman, *Giacomo Savelli*, 2-IV, 20-V-1285—3-IV-1287

NICHOLAS IV, of Ascoli, *Girolamo Masci*, 22-II-1288—4-IV-1292

ST. CELESTINE V, of Isernia, *Pietro del Murrone*, 5-VII, 29-VIII-1294—13-XII-1294, 19-V-1296

BONIFACE VIII, of Anagni, *Benedetto Caetani*, 24-XII-1294, 23-I-1295—11-X-1303

B. BENEDICT XI, of Treviso, *Niccolo Boccasini*, 22, 27-X-1303—7-VIII-1304

CLEMENT V, French, *Bertrando de Got*, 5-VI, 14-XI-1305—20-IV-1314

JOHN XXII, of Cahors, *Giacomo Duèse*, 7-VIII, 5-IX-1316—4-XII-1334

(NICHOLAS V, of Covaro (Rieti), *Pietro Rainallucci*, 12, 22-V-1328—25-VIII-1330, ✠16-X-1333)

BENEDICT XII, French, *Jacques Fournier*, 20-XII-1334, 8-I-1335—25-IV-1342

CLEMENT VI, French, *Pierre de Beaufort*, 7, 19-V-1342—6-XII-1352

INNOCENT VI, French, *Stefano Aubert*, 18, 30-XII-1352—12-IX-1362

B. URBAN V, French, *Etienne de Grimoard*, 28-IX, 6-XI-1362—19-XII-1370

GREGORY XI, French, *Pierre Roger de Beaufort*, 30-XII-1370, 5-I-1371—26-III-1378

URBAN VI, of Naples, *Bartolomeo Prignano*, 8, 18-IV-1378—15-X-1389

BONIFACE IX, of Naples, *Pietro Tomacelli*, 2, 9-XI-1389—1-X-1404

INNOCENT VII, of Sulmona, *Cosma Migliorati*, 17-X, 11-XI-1404—6-XI-1406

GREGORY XII, Venetian, *Angelo Correr*, 30-XI,19-XII-1406—4-VII-1415

(CLEMENT VII, *Roberto of the counts of the Genevois*, 20-IX, 31-X-1378—16-IX-1394

(BENEDICT XIII, Aragonese, *Pietro de Luna*, 28-IX, 11-X-1394—23-V-1423)

(ALEXANDER V, of the island of Crete, *Pietro Filargo*, 26-VI, 7-VII-1409—3-V-1410)

(JOHN XXIII, of Naples, *Baldassarre Cossa*, 17, 25-V-1410—29-V-1415)

MARTIN V, Roman, *Oddone Colonna*, 11, 21-XI-1417—20-II-1431

EUGENE IV, Venetian, *Gabriele Condulmer*, 3, 11-III-1431—23-II-1447

(FELIX V, of Savoy, *Amedeo Duke of Savoy*, 5-XI-1439, 24-VII-1440—7-IV-1449)

NICHOLAS V, of Sarzana, *Tommaso Parentucelli*, 6, 19-III-1447—24-III-1455

CALLISTUS III, of Jàtiva (Valencia), *Alonso de Borja*, 8, 20-IV-1455—6-VIII-1458

PIUS II, of Siena, *Enea Silvio Piccolomini*, 19-VIII, 3-IX-1458—15-VIII-1464

PAUL II, Venetian, *Pietro Barbo*, 30-VIII-, 16-IX-1464—26-VII-1471

SIXTUS IV, of Savona, *Francesco della Rovere*, 9, 25-VIII-1471—12-VIII-1484

INNOCENT VIII, Genoese, *G. B. Cibo*, 29-VIII, 12-IX-1484—25-VII-1492

ALEXANDER VI, of Jàtiva (Valencia), *Rodrigo de Borja*, 11, 26-VIII-1492—18-VIII-1503

PIUS III, of Siena, *Francesco Todeschini-Piccolomini*, 22-IX, 1, 8-X-1503—18-X-1503

JULIUS II, of Savona, *Giuliano della Rovere*, 31-X-, 26-XI-1503—21-II-1513

LEO X, Florentine, *Giovanni de' Medici*, 9, 19-III-1513—1-XII-1521

ADRIAN VI, of Utrecht, *Adrian Florensz*, 9-I, 31-VIII-1522—14-IX-1523

CLEMENT VII, Florentine, *Giulio de'Medici*, 19, 26-XI-1523—25-IX-1534

PAUL III, Roman, *Alessandro Farnese*, 13-X, 3-XI-1534—10-XI-1549

JULIUS III, Roman, *G. M. Ciocchi del Monte*, 7, 22-II-1550—23-III-1555

MARCELLUS II, of Montepulciano, *Marcello Cervini*, 9, 10-IV-1555—1-V-1555

PAUL IV, of Naples, *Gian Pietro Carafa*, 23, 26-V-1555—18-VIII-1559

PIUS IV, Milanese, *Giovan Angelo de'Medici*, 25-XII-1559, 6-I-1560—9-XII-1565

ST. PIUS V, of Bosco (Alessandria), *Antonio (Michele) Ghislieri*, 7, 17-I-1566—1-V-1572

GREGORY XIII, Bolognese, *Ugo Boncompagni*, 13, 25-V-1572—10-IV-1585

SIXTUS V, of Grottamare (Ripatransone), *Felice Peretti*, 24-IV, 1-V-1585—27-VIII-1590

URBAN VII, Roman, *G. B. Castagna*, 15-IX-1590—27-IX-1590

GREGORY XIV, of Cremona, *Niccolò Sfondrati*, 5, 8-XII-1590—16-X-1591

INNOCENT IX, Bolognese, *G. Antonio Facchinetti*, 29-X, 3-XI-1591—30-XII-1591

CLEMENT VIII, Florentine, *Ippolito Aldobrandini*, 30-I, 9-II-1592—3-III-1605

LEO XI, Florentine, *Alessandro de' Medici*, 1, 10-IV-1605—27-IV-1605

PAUL V, Roman, *Camillo Borghese*, 16, 29-V-1605—28-I-1621

GREGORY XV, Bolognese, *Alessandro Ludovisi*, 9, 14-II-1621—8-VII-1623

URBAN VIII, Florentine, *Maffeo Barberini*, 6-VIII, 29-IX-1623—29-VII-1644

INNOCENT X, Roman, *G. B. Pamphilj*, 15-IX, 4-X-1644—7-I-1655

ALEXANDER VII, of Siena, *Fabio Chigi*, 7, 18-IV-1655—22-V-1667

CLEMENT IX, of Pistoia, *Giulio Rospigliosi*, 20, 26-VI-1667—9-XII-1669

CLEMENT X, Roman, *Emilio Altieri*, 29-IV, 11-V-1670—22-VII-1676

B. INNOCENT XI, of Como, *Benedetto Odescalchi*, 21-IX, 4-X-1676—12-VIII-1689

ALEXANDER VIII, Venetian, *Pietro Ottoboni*, 6, 16-X-1689—1-II-1691

INNOCENT XII, of Naples, *Antonio Pignatelli*, 12, 15-VII-1691—27-IX-1700

CLEMENT XI, of Urbino, *G. Francesco Albani*, 23, 30-XI, 8-XII-1700—19-III-1721

INNOCENT XIII, Roman, *Michelangelo dei Conti*, 8, 18-V-1721—7-III-1724

BENEDICT XIII, Roman, *Pietro Francesco (Vincenzo Maria) Orsini*, 29-V, 4-VI-1724—21-II-1730

CLEMENT XII, Florentine, *Lorenzo Corsini*, 12, 16-VII-1730—6-II-1740

BENEDICT XIV, Bolognese, *Prospero Lambertini*, 17, 22-VIII-1740—3-V-1758

CLEMENT XIII, Venetian, *Carlo Rezzonico*, 6, 16-VII-1758—2-II-1769

CLEMENT XIV, of St. Arcangelo (Rimini), *G. Vincenzo Antonio (Lorenzo) Ganganelli*, 19, 28-V, 4-VI-1769—22-IX-1774

PIUS VI, of Cesena, *G. Angelo Braschi*, 15, 22-II-1775—29-VIII-1799

PIUS VII, of Cesena, *Barnaba (Gregorio) Chiaramonti*, 14, 21-III-1800—20-VIII-1823

LEO XII, of Genga (Fabriano), *Annibale della Genga*, 28-IX, 5-X-1823—10-II-1829

PIUS VIII, of Cingoli, *Francesco Saverio Castiglioni*, 31-III, 5-IV-1829—30-XI-1830

GREGORY XVI, of Belluno, *Bartolomeo Alberto (Mauro) Cappellari*, 2, 6-II-1831—1-VI-1846

PIUS IX, of Senigallia, *Giovanni M. Mastai Ferretti*, 16, 21-VI-1846—7-II-1878

LEO XIII, of Carpineto (Anagni), *Gioacchino Pecci*, 20-II, 3-III-1878—20-VII-1903

ST. PIUS X, of Riese (Treviso), *Giuseppe Sarto*, 4, 9-VIII-1903—20-VIII-1914

BENEDICT XV, Genoese, *Giacomo della Chiesa*, 3, 6-IX-1914—22-I-1922

PIUS XI, of Desio (Milan), *Achille Ratti*, 6, 12-II-1922—10-II-1939

PIUS XII, Roman, *Eugenio Pacelli*, 2, 12-III-1939—9-X-1958

JOHN XXIII, of Sotto il Monte (Bergamo), *Angelo Giuseppe Roncalli*, 28-X, 4-XI-1958, now reigning

INDEX

Index

(Prepared by Warren Paul)

265